PORTFOLIO

NOBODIES TO SOMEBODIES

Peter Han is a thirty-year-old Harvard graduate who cofounded his own software company and sold it in 2002. He has written for *The New York Times*, *Boston Herald*, Associated Press, and magazines like *The Corporate Board Member* and *Marketing Management*. He now works for Microsoft and lives in Seattle with his wife, Meredith. Visit Peter Han at www.nobodiestosomebodies.com.

NOBODIES to SOMEBODIES

HOW 100 LEADERS IN BUSINESS, POLITICS, ARTS, SCIENCE, AND NONPROFITS GOT STARTED

PETER HAN

PORTFOLIO

Dedicated to my family
—PKH

PORTFOLIO
Published by the Penguin Group
Penguin Group (USA) Inc., 375 Hudson Street, New York, New York 10014, U.S.A.
Penguin Group (Canada), 90 Eglinton Avenue East, Suite 700, Toronto, Ontario, Canada
M4P 2Y3 (a division of Pearson Penguin Canada Inc.)
Penguin Books Ltd, 80 Strand, London WC2R 0RL, England
Penguin Ireland, 25 St. Stephen's Green, Dublin 2, Ireland (a division of Penguin Books Ltd)
Penguin Group (Australia), 250 Camberwell Road, Camberwell, Victoria 3124, Australia
(a division of Pearson Australia Group Pty Ltd)
Penguin Books India Pvt Ltd, 11 Community Centre, Panchsheel Park,
New Delhi – 110 017, India
Penguin Group (NZ), cnr Airborne and Rosedale Roads, Albany, Auckland 1310,
New Zealand (a division of Pearson New Zealand Ltd)
Penguin Books (South Africa) (Pty) Ltd, 24 Sturdee Avenue, Rosebank,
Johannesburg 2196, South Africa

Penguin Books Ltd, Registered Offices:
80 Strand, London WC2R 0RL, England

First published in the United States of America by Portfolio,
a member of Penguin Group (USA) Inc. 2005
Published in Penguin Books 2006

10 9 8 7 6 5 4 3 2 1

Copyright © Peter Han, 2005
All rights reserved

THE LIBRARY OF CONGRESS HAS CATALOGUED THE HARDCOVER EDITION AS FOLLOWS:
Han Peter.
    Nobodies to somebodies : How 100 great careers got their start / Peter Han.
        p.   cm.
    Includes bibliographical references and index.
    ISBN 1-59184-086-4 (hc.)
    ISBN 1-59184-130-5 (pbk.)
    1. Leadership.   2. Career development.   I. Title.
HD57.7.H356   2004
658.4'092—dc22   2004062004

Printed in the United States of America

Contents

END GAME: USING A LITTLE MAGIC

Introduction

I started the project that became this book a couple of winters ago, as the weather turned cold in Seattle and it hit me that lots of people my age were thinking about the same Big Questions. This realization came suddenly as I returned one day from lunch with a coworker, a good friend who'd been through a grueling start-up business experience with me. As we walked back to the office bundled against the chilly air, we had the kind of conversation that all of us do sometimes: looking into the future, sharing dreams, alternately joking and being serious, asking questions, trading opinions.

"So many people I know, from about college age into their thirties, are trying to figure out what to do with their lives," I started. "A lot of us are similar: well educated, well mannered, wanting to do well, but not sure how to add it up professionally. We go to good schools, we start our careers as eager beavers, we make witty conversation at dinner parties and call our parents dutifully every week or month, and yet—"

And yet, many of us, those same well-scrubbed twenty- and thirty-somethings, don't have a clear idea of how our work today relates to our goals tomorrow. When will we find the so-called meaning of life—our destiny—and the big opportunities to achieve that meaning? Which early career experiences and episodes will contribute most to the eventual story of our lives? Who are the key mentors, bosses, and peers from whom we should learn? What place does work have among other priorities like family, friends, and recreational hobbies?

Talking to my buddy, I realized that plenty of us move through our days wondering vaguely about these things. Generation X or Y, or whichever label is in vogue, consists of more than the stereotypical slackers portrayed in popular media. Sure, the affluence of modern civilization has produced greater luxuries of time and opportunity for many young people today than in the past. And yes, the increase in options, in potential life paths, can paralyze people with indecision or complacence at the start of their careers. Still, we do aspire. The innate human impulse to dream and to better ourselves remains plenty strong among twenty- and thirtysomethings. As a member of that sprawling generation myself, I can attest to it.

On one hand, I'm old enough to joke that I remember when Bono was just another rock star, the lead singer for U2 and not some globe-trotting activist trying to solve third-world debt and AIDS. On the other hand, I'm young enough to be moved by Bono's idealism and continued hustle. I remember watching him once on *Oprah*. In the delightful cadence of his Irish brogue, Bono told Oprah and her audience a great story. Back in his native Ireland, Bono said, people look up at the so-called rich folks' houses up in the big hills, and they shake their fists to curse the injustices and exploitation that enabled such wealth. By contrast, Bono said, in this country, even today, we look up at the hills—and dream of being there ourselves. "I'll get there someday," we say.

Although not all dreams are held by Americans, and not all dreams center on material possessions, Bono was right. Aspiration continues to animate us. The issue confronting young people today is not whether we have aspirations and goals, but rather how to identify the best ones, and how to achieve them in a noisy and distraction-filled world.

Different as it was from our mobile phone/beeper/e-mail-driven world, the environment in which many of our parents and grandparents grew up produced more linear life stories. Anchored by a hometown, an alma mater, and a loyal employer, they have more immediately apparent bodies of life work and webs of relationships that have been constructed strand by strand over decades. What guidance could these older people possibly have to share with the current generation of rising young people in society?

It can be tempting to dismiss the world of our parents and grandparents as less relevant than it once was. Surveying my own life and those of my contemporaries, I see more jagged pieces to the puzzle, more discontinuity, and fewer natural linkages from one step in life to the next. The end of lifetime employment with single companies, the growth of startups and small businesses relative to giant corporations, and the globalization of the economy have scrambled the very notion of career development. The concept of the "company man" or "the man in the gray flannel suit" seems as antiquated as the 1950s book that coined the terms.

However, closer examination reveals that earlier generations had plenty of their own disruptions and challenging history. The 1960s brought upheaval in political, cultural, and business norms, and those growing up in the 1950s faced the Cold War. Further back, of course, the 1940s was dominated by World War II and its aftereffects—talk about a potential wrench in something as mundane as career plans!—and the 1930s started with the Great Depression. In short, recent history has been anything but dull, and it's laughable to argue that today's young adults are uniquely challenged by historical circumstance.

As my friend and I discussed these issues, two ideas thus emerged at lunch that day in Seattle, perhaps a bit old-fashioned and counter to current conventional wisdom: Young people remain hungry for perspective on how to translate their aspirations to achievement, and older people remain capable of offering that perspective. My response to those ideas is the book you now hold in your hands. I decided to seek the wisdom of successful leaders for the benefit of young people starting their careers. I've tried also to keep the material readable and interesting, grounded in the details of stories about real people, but at the same time having enough rigor and depth to make its conclusions solid. The book's title, which I picked on that very first day, speaks to the notion of aspiration, of moving from being a Nobody to a Somebody in the world through a lifetime of intelligence, integrity, and hard work.

Three factors make this book different from other leadership studies and biographical profiles. First, rather than focusing on just one or a few individuals, I deliberately pushed for a depth of perspective by interviewing and researching the backgrounds of 100 elite achievers, leaders who've become society's Somebodies. Individually focused biographies yield more on a given person's experiences and perspectives, but I tried to capture a fuller picture of the issues young people face by talking to numerous leaders and forming a composite picture of their experiences.

Second, I aimed also for breadth. Instead of looking at just one field, like business, or science, or the arts, this book captures a range of perspectives. Specifically, the 100 leaders whom I researched come with these qualifications in the following fields:

- **Business:** CEOs of Fortune 1000–size companies, typically those with more than $1.5 billion in annual revenue
- **Government:** Congressional representatives, senators, governors, presidential Cabinet officers, and mayors of the largest American cities
- **Arts and entertainment:** Winners of recent Emmy, Grammy, Oscar, Pulitzer, or Tony awards
- **Nonprofits/organizations:** Current leaders of major institutions in society, and leaders of progressive, difference-making institutions
- **Science and academia:** Nobel Prize winners in economics, chemistry, medicine or physiology, or physics

The 100 leaders who shared their insights, and discussed their own rises from Nobodies to Somebodies, are:

FORTUNE 1000 CEOS (32)

Brad Anderson, Best Buy
Norman Axelrod, Linens 'N Things
Mark Baker, Gander Mountain
Daniel Burnham, Raytheon
Bob Catell, Keyspan
Curt Culver, MGIC
James DeGraffenreidt, Washington Gas
Daniel DiMicco, Nucor
Matt Espe, IKON Office Solutions
Paul Fireman, Reebok
Jay Gellert, Health Net
Gerald Grinstein, Delta Airlines

James Hagedorn, Scotts Company
Dennis Highby, Cabela's
Thomas Johnson, Greenpoint Financial
Bruce Karatz, KB Home
Parker Kennedy, First American
Lowry Kline, Coca-Cola Enterprises
Kathleen Ligocki, Tower Automotive
Jim Middleton, USAA Insurance
Gil Minor, Owens-Minor
Bill Mitchell, Arrow Electronics
Paul Norris, WR Grace
William Nuti, Symbol Technologies
Steve Odland, AutoZone
Robert Peiser, Imperial Sugar
Ron Sargent, Staples
Craig Sturken, Spartan Stores
Kirk Thompson, JB Hunt
Roy Vallee, Avnet
Lars Westerberg, Autoliv
Felix Zandman, Vishay Intertechnology

GOVERNMENT OFFICIALS (19)

Chris Bell, Congressman, Texas
Bill Bradley, Former U.S. Senator, Presidential Candidate
Jennifer Dunn, Congresswoman, Washington State
Dan Evans, Former Governor, Washington State
Dan Glickman, President of Motion Picture Association of
    America, Former Presidential Cabinet Officer
    (Agriculture), and U.S. Congressman
Slade Gorton, Former U.S. Senator, Washington State
Chuck Hagel, U.S. Senator, Nebraska
Jeremy Harris, Mayor, Honolulu
Mickey Kantor, Former Presidential Cabinet Officer
    (Commerce)
Greg Laughlin, Former Congressman, Texas
Linda Lingle, Governor, Hawaii
Gary Locke, Governor, Washington State

Thomas Petri, U.S. Congressman, Wisconsin

Ann Richards, Former Governor, Texas

Mike Rounds, Governor, South Dakota

Bill Ruckelshaus, Former Presidential Cabinet Officer (EPA, FBI)

Donna Shalala, Former Presidential Cabinet Officer (Health and Human Services)

James Watkins, Former Presidential Cabinet Officer (Energy)

Rick White, President of TechNet, Former U.S. Congressman

WRITERS (15)

Russell Carollo, *Dayton Daily News,* Pulitzer Prize Winner

Tom Clancy, *New York Times* Bestselling author

Bill Dietrich, *Seattle Times,* Pulitzer Prize Winner

Bruce Dold, *Chicago Tribune,* Pulitzer Prize Winner

Eric Freedman, Professor, Michigan State University, Pulitzer Prize Winner

Tom Hallman, *Oregonian,* Pulitzer Prize Winner

Maria Henson, *Austin-American Statesman,* Pulitzer Prize Winner

Blair Kamin, *Chicago Tribune* Architecture Critic, Pulitzer Prize Winner

Bill McKibben, *New York Times* Bestselling Author

Alan Miller, *Los Angeles Times,* Pulitzer Prize Winner

Paul Salopek, *Chicago Tribune,* Pulitzer Prize Winner

Lloyd Schwartz, Professor, University of Massachusetts-Boston, Pulitzer Prize Winner

David Shaw, *Los Angeles Times,* Pulitzer Prize Winner

David Shribman, *Pittsburgh Post-Gazette,* Pulitzer Prize Winner

Michael Vitez, *Philadelphia Inquirer,* Pulitzer Prize Winner

NOBEL PRIZE WINNERS (15)

Peter Agre, Johns Hopkins University (Chemistry)

Aaron Ciechanover, Technicon Haifa (Chemistry)

James Heckman, University of Chicago (Economics)

Alan Heeger, UC Santa Barbara (Chemistry)

Daniel Kahneman, Princeton University (Economics)

Harry Kroto, University of Sussex (Chemistry)

Anthony Leggett, University of Illinois Urbana-Champaign (Physics)

Paul Nurse, Cancer Research Institute—UK (Physiology or Medicine)

Douglas Osheroff, Stanford University (Physics)

Bill Phillips, National Institute of Standards and Technology (Physics)

Rich Roberts, New England Biolabs (Physiology or Medicine)

Phillip Sharp, MIT (Physiology or Medicine)

William Sharpe, Stanford University (Economics)

Michael Spence, Stanford University (Economics)

John Sulston, Sanger Institute—UK (Physiology or Medicine)

NONPROFIT/ORGANIZATIONAL LEADERS (10)

Carol Bellamy, Executive Director, UNICEF; Former Director, Peace Corps

Morris Dees, Founder, Southern Poverty Law Center

Marsha Evans, President, American Red Cross

Larry Fahn, President, Sierra Club

Millard Fuller, Founder and President, Habitat for Humanity

John Hennessy, President, Stanford University

Wendy Kopp, Founder and CEO, Teach for America

Chip Pitts, Chairman, Amnesty International USA

Nadine Strossen, President, ACLU

Shirley Tilghman, President, Princeton University

ARTISTS AND ENTERTAINERS (9)

Gordon Clapp, Actor, Emmy Award Winner

Julian Fellowes, Actor, Oscar Award Winner

David Frankel, Director, Oscar and Emmy Award Winner

John Lithgow, Actor, Emmy and Tony Award Winner

Mike Luckovich, Cartoonist, Pulitzer Prize Winner

Paula Newby-Fraser, Eight-Time Ironman Triathlon World Champion

April Saul, *Philadelphia Inquirer* Photographer, Pulitzer Prize Winner

Tia Sillers, Songwriter, Grammy Award Winner
William Snyder, *Dallas Morning News* Photographer, Pulitzer
    Prize Winner

With the varied backgrounds of the 100 leaders above, it may be difficult to keep track of each person's achievements. Rather than disrupt the book's narrative flow to introduce the Somebodies fully as they appear, I've included an appendix at the end of the book that contains capsule biographical sketches. These can be a helpful reference for anyone interested.

Third, and most important, this book differs from others before it in that it focuses primarily on leaders' early career development—who they were, what they did, and how they balanced competing interests and issues—*before* they became Somebodies, when they were still Nobodies. To do this, when I interviewed the 100 leaders, most of my questions centered on the period around their first full-time jobs after college or graduate school. In the course of free-flowing conversations, many of the leaders shared biographical tidbits from earlier in their lives— childhood experiences frequently came up—and provided narratives linking their first jobs to later positions and professional experiences. This focus on the period of early life around the first job marks a key difference between this book and others. Biographies tend to focus on the history-making Big Events and not so much on the little details that round out leaders' portraits. This book captures some of those details.

While big personalities, big ideas, and big deals ripple through this book, the first job provides the most relevant vehicle for our aims. The experiences described here, after all, occurred before these individuals had become major successes, before they had earned large sums of money, fame, power, or whatever good it is they sought. In their most elemental beginnings, today's leaders had to deal with many of the same basic challenges with which young people today grapple. Learning how they responded to those challenges, what they thought about, and how they felt as twenty-and thirtysomethings themselves, fascinated me.

Pondering the lessons of society's Somebodies was far more than an academic exercise. I consider myself squarely in the target audience for this book, and in fact started the project as a labor of love, a way to answer questions that I and my friends frequently considered. This context is worth understanding briefly before delving into the research and conclusions that follow.

I've often joked with my family and friends about being a kind of Willy Loman character, happily middlebrow in my tastes and behaviors. I grew up with two loving parents, a sister, and a dog in a basically upper-middle- or middle-class lifestyle. Our typical summer vacations involved drives to national parks like the Grand Canyon. My first car as an adult was a Honda Accord, then the best-selling vehicle in the country. My favorite beer was Budweiser, the best-selling brew. I grew up in Texas, in the same town and with the same friends for most of my childhood, and then went east for college. Though I was a very good student, the nerdy type in crowds at school, I was a decent athlete growing up, and shared a typically adolescent distaste for cultural elitism—I typically preferred blockbuster movies to art house flicks, popular journals and books to academic texts, and sporting events to high culture at the museum, symphony, or opera.

I share these details not to sound aggressively anti-intellectual, but to show that in many respects I grew up with similar experiences and attitudes as the 69.5 million other Americans born between 1966 and 1985 and who are today's twenty- and thirtysomethings.[1]

Even the thing that marks me outwardly as most different from average—my status as the child of immigrants and the resulting ambition and drive to make myself from a Nobody to a Somebody—is far from unique in America. We are a nation of immigrants, as many have noted, and the intense striving that most obviously characterizes the newly arrived is a long-standing part of the country's cultural heritage.

In any case, any broader cultural or historical implications of my research were less important to me when I started than, quite simply, finding answers to my questions about the future. I was twenty-eight years old, an enthusiastic and ambitious young person who had reached a significant crossroads in life and who was wondering about the future. After graduating from a good university, I had spent a couple of years on a well-established career track, first at a boutique strategy consulting

---

1. Source: U.S. Department of Commerce, Census Bureau

firm that helped large corporations set their business direction, and then in a marketing group at Dell Computers. Doing what young people do, though, I abruptly quit the job at Dell, in Austin, to move to Seattle for a girl (now my wife) and for a shot at start-up life. A trusted partner and I built a small Internet services firm from the ground up and got a heady taste of pursuing dreams, acting boldly and independently, and removing the yoke of conventional careerism. In the summer of 2002 we sold the technology from our start-up to a larger software company, and after a brief period of transitional consulting work for that company, I was left to ponder what came next.

In many ways, then, I finished the economic roller-coaster years, the period from approximately 1998 to 2002, in a situation roughly similar to many others around my age: well edified by the experience, glad for having had the courage to try an untested path, but not sure how the episode fit into a larger story. Media postmortems at the time characterized many who had joined Internet-based businesses as greedy, quick-buck artists, and undoubtedly some of them were, but in my view, even for those who hadn't achieved what they set out to do, there was no inherent shame in having tried to reach for a dream. Whether to build a new technology, company, or industry, many people had put in honest work for an attempt at honest return. The question was, and is, how to apply age-old lessons on career management to the new circumstances prompted by the last few years' economic tumult.

Before diving into my findings, a brief description of the research methodology: it followed two tracks. First, I solicited and conducted interviews with the respondents themselves, engaging them on a personal level to get perspectives on their first jobs. Second, I supplemented the firsthand perspectives leaders gave me by reading more documents, like company annual reports (in the case of business persons) or Nobel Prize acceptance speeches and autobiographical sketches (in the case of scientists), as well as news articles in the popular press.

The work began in the winter of 2003 and continued for approximately fifteen months, through early 2004. A research assistant and I found leaders' e-mail addresses, which despite the current tidal wave of spam were, gratifyingly, often available in the public domain after a bit of intrepid sleuthing, and sent them mail explaining a bit about my background and my interest in talking with them. In a few cases, I used personal connections to talk with individual leaders, but with the large majority of the 100 Somebodies, I had no previous relationship. They evaluated the project on its merits and chose to share anywhere from thirty to ninety minutes of their time for me to talk with them and gain perspectives on their work.

Once I received approval for my interview requests, I typically sent the leaders or their staff an advance version of the interview guide (contained in Appendix B). My actual conversations with them occurred sometimes by phone, sometimes in person, and occasionally via e-mail exchanges. In a number of instances, I went back and asked respondents to expand on an earlier thought, to provide more context or background detail to their thinking on a particular point.

I found the leaders impressively open and willing to discuss their experiences in their first jobs. In a number of cases, my conversations with the leaders turned into nostalgic storytelling sessions in which they shared stories of first jobs, but also other interesting asides and historical context. As the research wore on, the rich details the leaders provided on the early periods of their careers helped me appreciate the diversity of their experiences. Although the ethnic diversity was minimal, tilting generally toward Caucasians, the 100 leaders profiled for the book included both men and women; those as old as seventy-nine (Dan Evans, former three-term Governor of Washington State, and U.S. Senator), and in many cases, as young as their forties; predominantly American but some international voices, including a Polish-born Holocaust survivor (Felix Zandman); people of strongly divergent political views; many millionaires, at least one billionaire, and at least one single mom. Intra-field diversity was part of the equation as well. Among the numerous business leaders interviewed, for example, I talked to leaders from industries as different as athletic apparel, health care, mortgage insurance, office-supplies retailing, soft drinks, and steel manufacturing.

Of course, the variety of professional experiences was a feature designed into my research, but I found other surprises. Besides the illustrious careers for which the leaders are already known, I didn't expect to learn about the sometimes-humorous assortment of odd jobs these people held in their younger days. Journalist Tom Hallman told me about an aimless period in his mid-twenties, when he worked as a bartender, in grocery stores, and at a car-cleaning business. Fellow Pulitzer Prize winner Paul Salopek, who treated a rootless period in adolescence as a testing ground, talked of his experiences "picking fruit, working as a landscaper, laborer, working in a gold mine, working on shrimp boats, including walk-in freezers. I mean, just a panoply of jobs."

Steve Odland, now the CEO of AutoZone, was typical in seeing his early work as training for future responsibility. In Odland's case, a paper route at the age of ten gave him great initial experience. "It taught me the basics of business. It meant that I had to service customers, I had to go out and sell to get new customers, I had to get supplies from the company in order to facilitate even the basics of business. You know, had to get a bike, the bag on the bike—they wore out, and you had to factor in depreciation. I didn't know what it was called, but I knew what it was, because things wore out. I had to make sure that I collected debts, and you had bad debts in there, people who skipped out on you and didn't pay you."

Details like this sprang very naturally out of many of my interviews. I enjoyed getting to see these people as people—human, like the rest of us, with color, texture, and personal history. In the end, learning about the essential humanity of these leaders cut to the core of my mission. While I retained a very healthy respect for the leaders, I wanted less to worship and more to learn from them. By seeing them as they really were at my age, I found the lessons contained in this book.

The book's final chapter contains personal reflections based on my own experiences, combined with the opportunity to talk with 100 leaders across different fields. Before getting to those closing thoughts, however, it's nice to remember what happened at the end of that first lunch in Seattle, when this project was born. After I had described the vision for this book to my friend, himself a young striver at the beginning of his career, he thought silently for a moment and then said, "You know, the cool thing is that I think you'll actually do it." Well, here we go.

BASICS:
FINDING ONE'S CALLING

Ride the Rocket: Five Paths to Enlightenment

How did the leaders choose their professional paths as they took their first jobs? What methods did they use to understand their strengths and weaknesses, their likes and dislikes, and to discover their identities? How did they build on that self-knowledge to begin shaping their careers?

I started with the basics. Before exploring other questions, my first curiosity was how the leaders figured out what they wanted to do with their lives. Where did they *start?* Usually, I can't help snickering at the abstract frameworks and buzzwords introduced by academic studies of leadership theory. I get turned off by the linguistic gymnastics of overly creative scholars—the kinds of rhetoric that claim to offer enlightenment in a bottle. But in this case, I was hoping for just that.

Fortunately, the 100 leaders in this book simplified things for me. The Somebodies with whom I spoke often enjoyed significant fame, wealth, and power, but their honest, straightforward stories of early adulthood helped me cut through the abstraction. These leaders worried less about one key formula to discovering destiny, and more about the fundamentals: how to be yourself, how to find yourself, and how to translate knowledge of your identity into fruitful work, for starters.

This book's lessons therefore start with self-knowledge, a concept to which we'll return many times. In this first chapter, we'll see the importance of Somebodies learning who they are. A few will tell how they steered toward their goals and where their first jobs fit in the journey.

This initial lesson sets the stage for all the others that follow, because it shows how Somebodies defined themselves and their ambitions. Their five paths to self-discovery—and dare I say it, enlightenment?—frame the rest of the book.

Ways of Finding Yourself

The first surprise in talking to my 100 subjects was the diversity of their approaches to learning about themselves and identifying their vocations. On one level, of course, I recognized the improbability of identifying a simple formula that would magically orchestrate career success from the first job onward. To become a first-rate business executive, scientist, government official, or other big success, people need good fortune with the countless little things that contribute to success, and with a few of the big ones, too. That said, maybe I did expect at least some kind of formula. The people whose views I solicited for this book are Establishment icons—Fortune 500 CEOs, not fly-by-night entrepreneurs; Nobel laureates, not merely good researchers; Presidential Cabinet officials, advisers to the President of the United States, not just county dogcatchers (apologies to the dogcatching community, of course). These were people who have cultivated expertise, relationships, and reputations, often over decades, who've typically ascended our highest ladders with great diligence and care. Wouldn't there be some formula for professional happiness in that?

Happiness might be defined as doing something we love, with excellence. In turn, the crucial question we face in starting our careers is, "At what will I excel, and love, at the same time?" I thought back on my own experiences, beginning in the ill-lit reading room in Harvard's Office of Career Services, where I flipped through drab booklets on management consulting and investment banking and listened to waves of classmates shuffle through the same room, making the floorboards creak with surprising loudness. I remember these details, rather than the rapturous wonders promised by consulting and banking, because visits to that reading room fundamentally bored me. In the near decade since then, the quest for an activity that combined passion and excellence motivated me through a series of professional experiments with different companies and industries. What did I and other small fry miss, compared to the big fish?

What I found in talking to society's Somebodies is that they are unusually good at finding and pursuing larger missions in life, but that their methods for identifying their own personal missions varied strikingly. The Somebodies I interviewed described five different ways they used to answer this question for themselves: ways I call Random Walk, Open-Ended Exploration, Closed-Ended Exploration, Killer Excellence After Expedience, and Trailblazing. This ROCKET of professional self-discovery propelled the leaders eventually to find satisfying and fulfilling work, whether or not that satisfaction came in their first jobs.

Before delving into each of the methods for self-discovery, let's consider what distinguished them. As young adults, what determined whether leaders fell into Random Walk versus some other method of self-discovery? I found a trio of key factors running through the stories I heard, which are relevant to young people today who wonder which approach is most relevant for them.

First, leaders differed in how much freedom they had in taking their first jobs. For reasons of national service (as in times of war, with the military) or economic need, some people had more constrained sets of possibilities as they started their careers, while others had more flexibility and could do essentially whatever they wanted.

Second, leaders differed in the extent to which they believed they had one clear, preset professional destiny versus several potential options. Some believed they had one ultimate destiny to which the events of their lives inexorably steered them, a line of work and identity that matched their personalities, strengths, and weaknesses. Others believed they could have ended up with a variety of outcomes, depending on a few circumstances and choices at key junctures. (I found this basic philosophical divide amusingly similar to the debate that I and many friends have had about whether there is One Soul Mate for each of us, in affairs of the heart, or whether each of us could be happy with any number of potential spouses.)

Third, leaders varied in the degree to which they consciously managed their career development and pursuit of destiny. Most were fairly focused and proactive in their career management, paddling furiously through the surf of life, but others were content to glide along, taking the waves as they came.

Method #1: Random Walk

The Random Walk approach to finding destiny is as it sounds: the least direct method, and the most skeptical of a purposeful, aggressive search for meaning. The people taking this approach tended to see the numerous ways in which luck and fortunate circumstance had impacted their careers, and while talented and passionate about their work, they did not start their first jobs with particular angst about their careers, per se.

John Sulston, an English winner of the Nobel Prize for Physiology or Medicine in 2002, explained, "Science is a random walk, and I guess most things that are worth doing are the same: the point is that the future is unpredictable, and should be approached with passion rather than career-minded worry." This attitude has been lifelong, he said. Sulston grew up the son of a Protestant minister and a teacher who encouraged his interest in the natural world and living things, from which his later vocation in biology arose. His experience was that passion, and his naturally pursued interests shaped all that followed.

"I've never taken a serious job decision," Sulston said. "'When is John going to get a proper job?' was a question that got passed back to me by teenage friends. The only answer was to find a place where I could mess about at a lab bench."

A continent away, in a very different line of work, Senator Chuck Hagel described similar feelings. To him, "Life is to a certain extent about . . . the stream taking you, the currents grabbing you. There are centrifugal forces that to a certain extent you have very little control over."

Hagel's knowledge of larger forces stemmed directly from personal experience. As a twenty-three-year-old fresh out of college in his home state of Nebraska, he felt motivated by a deep patriotism and volunteered to fight in Vietnam. Plunged along with other soldiers into a vast game of geopolitical chess, he soon found himself side by side with his brother Tom, each leading a squad of the U.S. Army's 9th Infantry division into battle. Though he survived the war, Hagel emerged with two Purple Hearts for injuries received in fierce combat, injuries that easily could have extinguished his life before he got a chance to achieve his later successes in business and government.

Maybe this brush with early death led to the dry realism in Hagel's outlook today: "I don't think there's any blueprint or road map or plan you can apply to all of us. I think we all are different not only in our makeup, in how we wander through life . . . but I've never really planned my life very much. I really haven't. I look ahead, sure, in a responsible way, and certainly as a father and husband, I do it more than I ever did, and I must, but I don't worry too much about my future career. I never have. That's probably what's allowed me to be involved in a lot of different things."

Random Walkers were defined most by the latter two variables mentioned earlier—their relatively weak belief in preset destinies, and in particular, their open-ended approaches to finding those destinies. To take another example, Bill McKibben, a *New York Times* bestselling author and environmentalist who's penned a number of books since the early 1990s, took his first job as a staff writer at *New Yorker* magazine. He wrote numerous stories for the magazine and dove into its substantial literary tradition and history. Recounting that early period of his career, McKibben makes clear that he was oblivious to some of the more practical issues. He said, "I didn't even know much they were going to pay me when I took the job. They paid by the piece, but I didn't know how much. It seemed like a wonderful place, but I fear I didn't have any long-term goals in mind then (or now, really). More of a day-at-a-time approach."

From the business side, Jay Gellert, the CEO of insurance giant Health Net, presented a similar picture in sharing how he took his first job after college with a small management-consulting firm.

"I'd done a little work with them during the time I was in college," Gellert said. "In most of my career, I've not really had a clear plan. It just seemed like a pretty natural thing to do . . . I don't think I really spent very much time thinking about alternatives."

Could it really have been so straightforward? Incredulous readers might question how people became so successful with apparently passive, relaxed approaches like Random Walk. Before attempting to answer this question definitively, let's examine the other approaches used by leaders to identify their career tracks.

Method #2: Open-Ended Exploration

Open-Ended Exploration is a second approach leaders used to discover their vocations in life. As a method for finding destiny, it is like agnosticism, relative to the atheism of Random Walk. By that I mean Open-Ended Explorers are similarly open to the surprises and quirky turns of life and actually sound at times like Random Walkers; however, they tend to be more open to the possibility that a particular destiny can or should be discovered in their life's work—that they were, in a sense, meant to do one particular thing over others to end up in a specific profession. They also tend to be more directed than Random Walkers in their investigation of options. They use their first jobs to explore possible vocations, to pursue passions, and to make early attempts at translating aspirations to achievement.

Carol Bellamy, now the Executive Director of UNICEF after stints at the head of the Peace Corps, on Wall Street, and in New York municipal government, has a breezy, conversational personality. In our interview, she laughed often, spit out a rapid-fire series of thoughts in a stream of consciousness, and told her story of open-ended exploration in an engaging way.

"I went into the Peace Corps right after college. And what was I thinking? It was a mixture of wanting to save the world, and it also sounded pretty exciting . . . I was virtually admitted to graduate school in social work"—a longtime interest—"and I totally, totally changed direction and decided to go to the Peace Corps."

Bellamy admitted freely that her momentous choice to join the Peace Corps occurred almost whimsically in the course of one fateful evening. "I was locked in the library one night [toward the end of college], and found some Peace Corps bulletins, and after reading through them, right on the spot, immediately decided that I wanted to do it." With a chuckle, she adds, "I hadn't the slightest idea what I was getting myself into, frankly, but on the other hand, I wasn't particularly worried about it."

Donna Shalala, the Clinton Administration's Secretary for Health and Human Services, coincidentally preceded Bellamy as a Peace Corps volunteer by one year and then became friends with her several years later when both were young adults living in New York City. She, too, entered the Peace Corps with some notions about law school and journalism running through her longer-term ambitions, but without very clear definition.

"I had no idea where this was all going to end up," Shalala says. "[Peace Corps] just seemed like a wonderful thing to do, and it was. It turned out to be a great adventure. I wanted to see the world. I didn't have any clear idea of what I wanted to do."

Despite entering that first job in a very open-ended way, though, Shalala learned much from her two-year stint as a volunteer. Growing up in a family of Lebanese descent, she had experienced some Middle Eastern culture before, but her work in Iran was still eye-opening. "I learned about different cultures. I learned about the kind of poverty there is in the developing world. I learned a lot about different religions. I learned that I could survive anyplace. It was just fascinating, and Iran in particular was fascinating. It's a very complex culture. Very sophisticated."

Harold Kroto, a Nobelist in 1996, viewed his first job as a chance to explore the world. While his interests in science were well developed from undergraduate studies, and he had shown enough promise to win a postdoctoral fellowship in the United States, far from his native United Kingdom, he remained open to the possibility of a mid-career switch to the graphic arts. "My science was a ticket to living in the States for two years, working with one of the top groups in the world," he said. "It was the easiest option to live abroad . . . I was pretty good at [graphic arts], but I hadn't had the training and discipline. I wanted to do it, but I just couldn't."

After the two-year fellowship ended, Kroto secured work again in the United Kingdom, at the University of Sussex, where he remains to the present day. Even at that juncture, though, thoughts of a potential career switch stayed in his mind, and Kroto treated his initial years as a professor at Sussex as a bit of an experiment. "I thought I'd spend five years and see how it goes . . . My research went very well, and I enjoyed teaching the classes I had to teach . . . There was no major problem. Now, it wasn't totally smooth—it was very tough at the start, the first three to five years, but then five to seven years in, it started to go well."

Method #3: Closed-Ended Exploration

Some of the leaders I interviewed were more directed than the Random Walkers and Open-Ended Explorers. Those who took this third approach to finding their careers, the group I call Closed-Ended Explorers, came closest to my stereotyped preconceptions of how leaders treat their first jobs. In contrast to those who waded into their careers in relatively uncertain and formless ways, the Closed-Ended Explorers began their first jobs with more specific aims. They typically started with a fairly clear idea of what they wanted to do, what fit their wants and needs, and where their passion lay. Whereas the Open-Ended types used a more inductive approach, trying a job or industry but often continuing to look at alternatives, the Closed-Ended Explorers showed markedly deductive reasoning, often evaluating potential career paths by very specific criteria.

For example, Robert Peiser arrived at his current position as CEO of Imperial Sugar through a deliberate set of career-management choices. Peiser started his post-MBA career at Trans World Airlines (TWA). He had had a pre–business school job at Hertz, and following his business-school studies, he had decided that he wanted to build functional expertise in finance. He recognized, however, that he had certain gaps in his understanding that he wanted to fill.

"I had always been interested in a career in finance and, consequently, I was interested in understanding both how the internal financial functions of a corporation worked, as well as learning the analysis and negotiations skills that were necessary for financial transactions," he said. Peiser thus treated his first job as a kind of fact-finding mission, all the while evaluating corporate finance as a profession.

The overall attitude of Closed-Ended Explorers might be summarized by David Shribman, the executive editor of the *Pittsburgh Post-Gazette* and a Pulitzer Prize winner. In approaching his first job, which in his case followed a one-year fellowship at Cambridge University in England, Shribman said, "I wanted a start in journalism, suspecting (but not knowing for sure) that that was how I wanted to live my life."

The story of Blair Kamin offers interesting additional color. Kamin, a Pulitzer Prize–winning critic for the *Chicago Tribune*, used his first job as an office gopher, doing nonserious work, to make some quite serious judgments about his calling in life. He had just graduated from Amherst College in 1980, where he had taken a class in Gothic architecture that sparked his interest. Like many young people searching for themselves, Kamin began his figurative journey with a literal one: a road trip across the country. He piled his belongings into a beat-up car and began his journey. "I took a long drive across the United States from my parents' home in New Jersey to San Francisco, where I had decided to live for no other reason than it seemed like a wild and free place where you could discover yourself."

Thus situated, Kamin decided to explore his nascent interests in the field of architecture, in which he has won his reputation and the highest accolades in his profession. "I started my climb from the bottom rung of the architectural ladder. I was an office boy for an interior design and architecture firm in San Francisco. The firm was named Whisler Patri. They had offices in an old warehouse building south of Market Street."

Kamin was determined to learn about the profession, but he stumbled upon the opportunity to do it by a stroke of good fortune. "When I arrived there in the fall of 1980, I stayed with a young married couple, Nadine Joseph and Neil Gotteiner, who lived in the neighborhood called Russian Hill. Nadine had worked as a reporter for a small newspaper in New Jersey. My father was the editor of the paper. I had worked at the paper as a summer intern.

"Fortunately, Nadine played tennis with an architect named Piero Patri. Piero's firm was about to move from one warehouse building south of Market Street to another. They needed a body to help. So while my friends from college were working on Wall Street and Madison Avenue, I was running the blueprint machine at Whisler Patri. I will never forget the smell of the noxious fumes that emanated from the blueprint machine. They made your nose wrinkle.

"My only goal was to learn more about architecture—to experience it on a day-to-day basis, not just by observing architects at work, but by talking to them and becoming part of their world. At the time, I was trying to figure out whether to try to become an architect or an architecture critic. I figured the only way to decide was to plunge right into the field."

Kamin seemed to recall those long-ago days in San Francisco's Soma district fondly, which triggered my curiosity about whether he had steadily risen at that original firm. Was this first job directly responsible for his future success as an architecture critic? No—more training and self-discovery lay ahead. "I certainly wasn't promoted to senior office boy. I wasn't promoted to anything. But I got something much more valuable than a promotion. I got a first step up the ladder—a way to learn the language and the culture of architecture."

Reflecting on his post as "office boy" later, Kamin said, "I was willing to do whatever I had to do to explore my passion—even if it meant taking a low-pay, low-prestige job. Although I didn't fully realize it at the time, it was more important to use the first years after college to explore what I really wanted to do rather than taking a more conventional path and getting a 'good job' with a 'good firm.'"

To conclude, Kamin stated succinctly: "Short-term experimentation led to long-term fulfillment."

Method #4: Killer Excellence After Expedience

Not all leaders had the luxury of dictating the terms of their first jobs. A surprising number of them began their careers with choices boxed in by some reason of personal expedience, most often financial need or other support of family. Undeterred by the sometimes mundane jobs with which they started, these leaders displayed such strong competence and drive that they boosted themselves into positions of steadily ascending responsibility. This fourth method by which leaders find their professional callings is a kind of accidental destiny, or what I (perhaps too cutely) call Killer Excellence After Expedience.

The number of even very well-known leaders who pointed to this simple approach of early-career management surprised me. While the very title of my book suggests an interest in people who started from relatively modest, or at least normal, beginnings, somehow my romanticized notion of CEOs, significant scientists, and the rest did not include a vision of them making career choices driven by basic considerations like grocery bills and house payments. Quickly, though, I found that one after another, my plain-spoken respondents pointed to real-world pressures as a major factor in their early-career decision-making. For those taking this approach, I found that society's Somebodies differed from others not so much in which job they took or why they took it, but in how they used whatever opportunity lay in front of them.

Jim Middleton, today the CEO of USAA Insurance, graduated from college just as the Vietnam War was escalating. Considerations of the military draft dominated his thinking and eventually drove him to enlist voluntarily to improve his chances at getting a favorable posting. Soon after graduating from Purdue, Middleton found himself looking at orders to report to an air base as an industrial engineer. Starting there, he worked steadily over three and a half years, getting promoted along the way to captain. His progress was not spectacular, but steady.

"We'd been through a lot of transitions on the base, and it turned out I was the guy that . . . really had the knowledge of all the manpower and books and standards and that business, so it gave me a lot of direct contact with the people who then ran it, the wing commander and the people at command," Middleton remembers.

"It just turned out at the end of that, he said, 'What would you like to do?' I said, 'I'd like to go to Germany,' and he said, 'Well, there's actually a special program that I'd like to get you into that goes to the Pentagon.' . . . He was asking me, but he was really telling me. And at that point"—just over three years into Middleton's first job—"I really thought if I didn't get to go to Germany, well, I'll just get out of the Air Force, because I'm coming up on my four-year commitment, and so I was ready to go do something else in 1971."

As fate had it, though, Middleton went to the Pentagon, worked as a staffer, and continued on to a twenty-one-year military career. His ability to manage difficult issues, communicate effectively across multiple levels of the military bureaucracy, and develop a strong professional network continued to push up his rank. Asked what it was that distinguished him from the average staffer, beyond those talents, Middleton shrugged.

"You know, I often look at that, and I often wonder, what did I do different than other people? I guess the essence of it is, while you're always nervous about things, I've never been a nervous person. A lot of being able to move had to do with communication, and how you did it, and what you said. It also had to do with thinking quickly on your feet. Always be prepared. When you take something in, you know the next four answers." In other words, Middleton excelled at the fundamentals. But starting in his first job, he certainly didn't expect the Air Force to shape his long-term future. Witness the following exchange toward the end of our interview:

> AUTHOR: What's interesting to me, also, is that . . . you went into the military initially, proactively to avoid getting drafted in an unfavorable position into Vietnam, but—
>
> JM: Exactly.
>
> AUTHOR: It ended up becoming a twenty-one-year choice. You didn't see it as a twenty-one-year choice at the beginning, but one thing led to another.
>
> JM: Yeah. You got it. That's exactly accurate.

Middleton wasn't alone. Lowry Kline, the CEO of Coca-Cola Enterprises, started his career as a trial lawyer, far from the beverage industry. Thinking back to his first job, he stated flatly, "I wanted to secure a solid financial situation personally," and only then to consider additional goals, such as a possible move into politics. Tom Clancy, the megaselling novelist, began his career as an insurance agent, focused on the pragmatic goals of supporting his family and learning a trade. He noted dryly, "I was thinking about making a living. Your first job is just an extension of school, if you're smart enough to appreciate that fact." Rather than skyrocket immediately into prominence and riches as a writer, Clancy toiled anonymously in the insurance industry into his forties.

Method #5: Trailblazing

The fifth and final way in which leaders found their professions early in their careers was through Trailblazing. The people subscribing to this approach weren't necessarily more certain than Open-Ended Explorers about their long-term direction and weren't magically free of practical needs like the Expedient, but they had strong desires to find work that suited them, and—sometimes instinctively, sometimes more consciously—essentially created jobs, companies, or market niches for themselves. In a way, these mavericks might be considered the most stubborn of society's Somebodies, the ones least willing to fit themselves to existing roles and career paths.

Wendy Kopp shows a good example of the conscious model for Trailblazing. The founder and head of Teach for America, one of the country's best-known nonprofit organizations, reflects on the conundrum she faced as a senior at Princeton: "I suddenly realized that I was going to need to figure out what to do after I graduated. I went down to our career services center, and at the time the real options for liberal arts majors such as myself were graduate school and two-year corporate training programs. I began conducting a rather ineffective job search—halfheartedly applying to a few management consulting firms, a few investment banks, a few brand management and real estate firms.

"At the same time though I was searching for something else—something I couldn't seem to find. I wanted an opportunity to assume the kind of responsibility granted through those corporate training programs while also having an immediate social impact. As my search turned up few practical options, I began descending into a funk. And I started sensing that I was not alone—that thousands of other talented, driven graduating seniors were also searching for something different.

"One day, my search and my own passionate interest in education reform—and specifically in addressing the disparities that persist in educational opportunity along socioeconomic and racial lines—led me to think of an idea: Why doesn't this country have a national teacher corps that recruits outstanding recent college graduates of all academic majors as aggressively to teach in urban and rural communities as we were being recruited at the time to work on Wall Street?

"I immediately became possessed by this idea. I thought it would have a significant impact in the short-term—through channeling the energies and talents of committed young people into classrooms in low-income communities. And I thought it would also ultimately influence the consciousness of the nation through influencing the perspective, career direction, and civic commitment of our nation's future leaders."

Passion didn't produce immediate success, though. Kopp ran into roadblocks as she pushed to translate her idea into reality, and to blaze a new trail for her own career and others. "[A]s a public policy major . . . I proposed in my thesis the creation of a national teacher corps and through my research became all the more determined that it had to happen. I wrote a passionate letter to the president of the United States suggesting that he create it as the 'Peace Corps of the '90s,' but my letter clearly fell in the wrong stack and I received a job rejection letter in return."

Kopp hedged her bets—she continued to consider more conventional first jobs that would have taken her, perhaps, along the path of Open-Ended Exploration, but she forged ahead. "As my passion for this idea grew, I was pursuing my job search and was agonizing about whether I should try to find a seed grant and get this idea off the ground or go a more traditional route. Pursuing this idea rather than a 'real' job seemed a bit scary—there were so many unknowns—and I remember asking myself on numerous occasions, 'Why can't I bring myself to just do the normal thing?' But at the end of the day, I decided to pursue my passion."

Kopp was and is a striking personality, and she'll appear again in our story. So will many of the other leaders I interviewed. The different approaches to self-discovery that we described in this chapter—Random Walk, Open-Ended Exploration, Closed-Ended Exploration, Killer Excellence After Expedience, and Trailblazing—overarch the next chapter. Self-knowledge was such an important part of leaders' makeup that they often dwelled on the subject, as we'll now see.

Run Toward Yourself, Not Away

What elements of self-discovery and identity formation appeared commonly across the five ROCKET approaches? More important, how did leaders actually use their self-knowledge at the start of their careers? What habits did they develop?

Power has run through much of Mickey Kantor's life. In the 1990s, the well-connected lawyer served as President Bill Clinton's U.S. Trade Representative, then Secretary of Commerce. He also walked the proverbial corridors of power in the national Democratic Party, chairing President Clinton's reelection campaign in 1996 and directing many of the organization's political activities as it prepared for the twenty-first century. Decades earlier, when Kantor first graduated from law school, he had been involved with power from the other side, representing underdog clients in civil-rights cases.

His choices from the beginning of his career to now haven't been as self-conscious as they might seem, though. In the early days especially, Kantor had simpler goals. "I was focused first on supporting my family, second on following my ideals, and only third on defining a vision for my own personal future," he remembered during our interview. His chair squeaked as he shifted and chuckled. "To be honest, I had my hands full at the time and was pretty busy!"

Still, looking back with four decades' perspective, Kantor did realize some consistent strands between that past and his unfolding future. He consistently moved toward the kind of work that resonated with his interests. "I don't think I was completely aware of how it all fit together, but I had strong interests," Kantor said. "I wanted to make a difference in the world. I had that idealism of the '60s, you know. And I liked working with people. Politics wasn't an extremely strong interest, but I was certainly aware of it."

Kantor's story fit the mold of many leaders whom I interviewed for this book. He showed a few signs of his talents and future path but translated his early aspirations to later achievement only with time. Leadership emerged through the 1970s and 1980s with patient work, interaction with others, and a growing understanding of himself. It sounds simple but was actually profoundly important: He moved toward his likes, away from his dislikes; toward his strengths, away from his weaknesses; and toward himself, not away.

In this chapter, we'll explore four common threads of self-knowledge in leaders like Kantor, threads that influenced their development from their first jobs on: strong self-awareness, playing toward strengths and away from weaknesses, personal authenticity or integrity, and a pragmatic decision-making process.

Strong Self-Awareness

First, and very important, the leaders often started their careers, and decision-making about their careers, with significant self-knowledge stemming from instinct or introspection. They got to know themselves. The Somebodies were, of course, generally intelligent people, but their observations and analyses were particularly insightful when trained on their own personal likes, dislikes, strengths, and weaknesses.

Senator Bill Bradley, for example, deliberately cultivated his self-knowledge through the Open-Ended Exploration model discussed previously. His first professional job after finishing his Rhodes scholarship at Oxford University was as a basketball player in the NBA with the New York Knicks. As Bradley put it, "I think from the beginning of my career in the NBA, I was preparing for the end, but I was not certain what the end would mean. So that in my off-seasons with the

Knicks, I would do things that gave me a taste of different areas of life."

His adventures were varied: "One off-season I taught school in Harlem. Another off-season I worked in a bureaucracy in Washington, at the Department of Poverty, OEO—I actually went down to work for Don Rumsfeld, who was a Congressman then . . . I worked one summer with an advertising firm. I worked one summer doing a research project on the future of cable TV. And I then began to write this book [*Life on the Run*], so I did a lot of things, tasting different things."

Later, in summarizing his experiences for young people, Bradley advised simply, "Develop your self-knowledge so that you're doing something you really want to do and not because other people thought you should do it."

The importance of gaining independence from your initial preconceptions about life and work, ideas that may have been instilled by parents or early childhood experiences, came up with several leaders. Rather than relying automatically on advice and direction from others, these were people who, over time, made sure that work fit them and their individual tastes. Kathleen Ligocki is today the CEO of Tower Automotive, but she started her career thinking she would become a professor of Chinese history. "I wanted to get my master's and Ph.D. and live the academic life. Business is something that grew on me. I didn't know it was something I would grow up to do. My father was in business for a long time, but I don't know what kind of impressions I had of it—but particularly in the automotive world, I know I wouldn't have expected to be there! I think when I was growing up and thinking of things I wanted to do, business would've been at the bottom of the list."

As Ligocki grew from her first significant job at General Motors, her self-knowledge and thinking evolved. "What I found later was that the worlds were not as separate as I thought back then. For example, I've worked a lot internationally—going places, traveling to them, and setting up businesses in foreign environments. I learned that you can bridge cultural differences by studying something about the area that you're going to or living in. Just learning something about the history, the performance arts for that culture, even contemporary sports—all of that helps you connect . . . My passions end up being shared by some of these people I meet in other business environments. In Europe, for example, many of the businesspeople are just passionate about arts. Really passionate. When I was young, I thought of business and the arts as totally separate worlds. I found, of course, that life is not so black-and-white."

To take another example, Bill Ruckelshaus had an illustrious career serving in multiple presidential administrations, at various times heading the Environmental Protection Agency, the FBI, the Browning-Ferris corporation, and a variety of corporate boards. Starting his career in Indiana, he reflected on and developed a precise appreciation for the kinds of work toward which he gravitated.

"I've had a number of these jobs, and thought about, 'What is it that makes it really appealing to me?' I sort of decided there are four things: Is the job interesting? Is it challenging? Is it exciting? And is it fulfilling? If you find a job with all four of those—interest, excitement, challenge, and fulfillment—you better hang on to it, because there aren't many like that."

Self-knowledge involved understanding strengths but also weaknesses, too. Slade Gorton, who served three terms as a U.S. Senator from Washington State after starting his career as a private-practice lawyer in Seattle, responded immediately when asked how he stood out as a young state legislator, early in his career. "I worked at it very hard. I understood the bills. I'm quite articulate. My colleagues liked to hear me speak . . . It wasn't because of my lovable personality. [Laughs] It was because people were willing to listen to me and thought I was more likely to be right [than] not."

Play Toward Strengths and Away from Weaknesses

The knowledge of their own weaknesses drove another interesting behavior among leaders. While as discussed elsewhere they had confidence in many ways, the leaders to whom I spoke often acted on the awareness of their limitations, and actively exploited their relative strengths, the areas in which they possess competitive advantages. Put another way: Somebodies tended to put ego aside and to see themselves clearly enough to play to their strengths and away from their weaknesses.

I found this surprising, in light of my own experience and the conventional wisdom one absorbs growing up. We're told to work on our weaknesses, to become better rounded, and to be "balanced" as individuals and workers. While high achievers very often do work at improving their weaknesses or flawed capabilities, sometimes obsessively so, I learned the degree to which they leverage their strengths. In short, they're not afraid to develop lopsided capabilities, if that imbalance results in a competitive advantage.

Choices of functional specialization are an obvious area where this dynamic plays out. Alan Heeger, the 2000 Nobel Prize winner in chemistry, remembered a time at the beginning of his career when he received prescient advice from an older mentor. "He did not think I would be a first-rate theorist. He recommended instead that I work with someone who does experimental work in close interaction with theory. This was perhaps the best advice that anyone ever gave me—and I followed his advice." Shifting his focus to take advantage of his natural strength in hands-on experimentation, Heeger set off a period of explosive creativity and productivity, which led in turn to his prizewinning discovery.

Similarly, the CEO of Autoliv, Lars Westerberg, concluded after just a one-year training program at his first job that "I am at best an average engineer." Rather than specializing aimlessly in an area of personal mediocrity, Westerberg learned enough about engineering to neutralize it as a major weakness. He then converted himself into a generalist, building on two key assets through the rest of his career: a "broad education" and a philosophy of "fast rather than perfect."

AutoZone CEO Steve Odland expressed most clearly the desirability of playing toward one's strengths. [Don't do just what you're good at. You've got to do what's so easy, and so intuitive, because it allows you to be great at it. What you should want to do is not something that you can just be good at in life, but something you can be great at in life] and really differentiate yourself. It doesn't matter if it's running a company, or being a doctor, or a researcher, or a politician. There's too much competition in this world for people who are good at something to succeed and set themselves apart. You've got to be great at it. And in order to be great at it, it's got to be in you. It's got to be intuitive, it's got to be something that just comes really easy to you. That's the signal that you've got a special talent in this," Odland said.

"I played the piano, and I studied classical piano, and I thought for a time, 'Boy this is great, I could become a concert pianist.' But I had to work and work and work and work and practice and practice. I couldn't memorize songs. I could play, and I was good—I was in competitions—but I never won anything. I wasn't great. Same thing with golf. I love playing golf, but I'm a terrible golfer! [Laughs] It's so hard. You have to hit so many things on every shot just right. I'm not going to be on the Tour. I'm not great at it. But Tiger Woods, he doesn't know why he's great at it. He just is. I think there's lessons in that for all of us."

Make no mistake: The leaders' focus on their natural talents produced lopsided strengths, but shortcomings, too. Nobelist Paul Nurse almost lost his chance to do great science due to what some might consider a trivial weakness. He failed the French test required for university entrance and was accepted only after the intercession of a teacher who saw his potential. Similarly, future journalist and Pulitzer winner Tom Hallman was fired from an early job as an editorial assistant at a magazine in New York, based on listless work and a lack of engagement with the job. When Somebodies like these were on their game, they could play with anyone; but when they were off, they were sometimes quite far off. It was a price they were usually willing to pay.

Emphasis on Personal Authenticity and Integrity

In terms of forming personal identity, another key characteristic described by many of society's Somebodies is the importance of personal authenticity and integrity. I define authenticity here to mean alignment between one's underlying character and externally visible statements and actions. Integrity refers to the consistency of those words and deeds, from one day or another and across different situations. Its spontaneous mention in the narratives of many of the leaders was impressive.

Lawyer Morris Dees described the grounding influence of growing up in rural Alabama: "[O]ne thing about a small town is everybody knows you. A reputation is hard to make and easy to lose. You quickly learn that you got the town drunks, and the town liars, and the town hustlers, and the religious people . . . Everybody knows you. Within twenty to thirty miles of my farm, I can go anywhere and 'You're Morris Dees's boy,' you know, my dad. So they know who you are, and your granddaddy, and your great-granddaddy. I think that gives you an enormous stability, an enormous sense of belonging."

For Grammy-winning songwriter Tia Sillers, whose "I Hope You Dance" was one of 2000's most popular tunes, work provides a grounding influence. "I always say that you become what you do," Sillers said. "Your daily actions become part of who you are, so you have to choose those actions carefully!"

Paul Fireman, Chairman of Reebok, described how he deliberately undertook exercises to reach inside himself for more personal authenticity, around the time that he founded the company that became a global behemoth in the sports apparel industry. "Philosophically, the key shift for me was a series of mind exercises I did in the late '70s. I applied those to Reebok. I got a sense of purpose, who I was, a freedom of not having to put on an act. I think it's been very effective for our consumer marketing. In the early days, our business was really in touch with our customers, because we listened to them and got the truth. It was a major advantage for me and the company."

A focus on authenticity or honesty helped guide career growth in other very tangible ways. Curt Culver, the CEO of mortgage insurance company MGIC, recounted a situation in which his dislike of a new boss, one whom he didn't view as honest, helped compel a job change. "A real key aspect [of my job change] was my boss changed—the president of the company changed, and that was my new boss, and I didn't trust him. I talk to the kids when I lecture on this, too: as you deal in life, honesty has to be one of the keys to your success, both personally and corporately, because if you don't have the trust with the person you work for, they will ruin your career."

Physicist Bill Phillips talked about the importance of openness, trust, and resulting professional collaboration in his career. Given the highly competitive nature of research science, I was surprised by his thoughts and pressed him to elaborate. He gave me a direct example from the laboratory in which he worked as a graduate student, at the start of his academic career.

"At MIT, while I was a graduate student there, we were looking forward to a visit from this guy in Germany. And one of the students who was there working on a particular project was talking to Dan Kleppner [the lab's leader] about this impending visit. Thinking about the capabilities of this German scientist—capabilities we knew very well because we knew about the kind of things he could do in his lab, the kind of equipment he had, and this student was thinking about the kinds of things he himself was working on, which were things that this other guy could do very easily . . . And he said to Dan Kleppner, 'When this guy comes, I don't want to talk about this work we're doing, because if he gets this idea that this is something that's good to do, he could do it a lot faster than we can.' And Dan's reply was, 'No. That's not the way we do things here. If somebody comes to visit us, we show them what we're working on. That's just the way it is: we're completely open. It's what we do.'

"I've always thought that was very good advice, because I really do think that in the end, you accomplish more by being open than you do by being secretive . . . I think that not only is this right for science, because I think science is best done in as open an atmosphere as possible, but I also think it's best for you individually to be as open as possible— because if you've got an idea, and it's a good one, the chances are that other people have this idea as well, and are thinking about it as well. It may very well be that if you express this idea, being completely open about it, it won't be news to everybody—but at least if you're open about it, and tell what you've been thinking about it, you'll at least get credit for having the idea . . . And chances are pretty good that if you had it first, you've got a good enough head start on other people that you're going to get there earlier anyway, so if it's not so, well, [laughs] at least you get something out of it."

In contrast to the example set by Phillips and his long-ago mentor in the lab, of course, is the deceit perpetrated recently by a few scoundrels in the corporate world. The central importance of authenticity led Daniel Burnham, formerly head of defense, electronics, and technology giant Raytheon, to view those events incredulously. "You can be smoked out in a nanosecond by the people on whom you rely . . . [T]he core strength of any senior executive—I know this will sound trite and hackneyed, but it's very true—is integrity, no question about it. People will follow you, as long as you're honest. If they smell that you're just in it for yourself, no one will follow you. The thing that has shocked me the most, looking at things like the Enron situation, is how these guys got to senior leadership positions with a lack of integrity. How did they get people to follow them? How were they able to hide their lack of integrity for all of those years? I just can't imagine how they managed to get ahead acting with those values!"

For Kathleen Ligocki, CEO of Tower Automotive, trying to trick people is futile in any case. In a crucial early-career experience managing a factory for General Motors, she relied heavily on the expertise of her peers and even direct reports to help her get up to speed in her job. She was open about the limits of her knowledge, so she would be taken more seriously in the areas where she did have expertise. She concluded, "In general, people around you know when you don't know much. So if you spend a lot of time trying to tell them how they should work, it's just makes you look bad."

Pragmatic Decision-Making Processes

As the Somebodies told me more about their openness to life's unpredicted turns, and about their willingness to stray off conventional paths, I became increasingly interested in how they made their big decisions. Was there a specific way in which they evaluated their options or thought about trade-offs? Were they particularly quick or slow? How did their foundation of self-knowledge influence their choices?

In terms of decision-making speed, I found that leaders varied widely. Some talked about making significant choices with just a day of consideration. For example, Raytheon CEO Daniel Burnham discussed his move from one business at Allied Signal to another early in his career: "I had at least to go through the motions of thinking about it. I told my boss I wanted to negotiate, and he laughed. He told me, 'The negotiation is over. You're going.' I had a chance to run the biggest part of the company, and to learn something I'd never learned. Now, it wasn't easy, because the Allied [chemical] and Signal [aereospace] people didn't mix. The very fact that I was coming from the HQ , also, was not going to make me popular. But after I talked it over for a night with my wife, I was ready to go."

Donna Shalala had a similarly efficient decision process when she was wrapping up her work in the Department of Housing and Urban Development in the Carter Administration. She found herself choosing among several attractive options. She had started conversations with the Kennedy School of Government at Harvard, the editorial board of the *Washington Post,* and Hunter College in New York about the latter's presidency. Shalala chose the Hunter job within days. She remembered her decision as taking "Not very long. Maybe a week. And I didn't consider it very painful."

Others, of course, did take longer. When MGIC CEO Curt Culver was deciding to leave his first job to go to a bigger company, within the same industry, he mulled it for about a month. Others took several months; CEO Jim Middleton pondered at length his switch over to business after a twenty-one-year military career. So did Pulitzer Prize–winning journalist Bill Dietrich, when he was deciding to leave an early job in the Washington, D.C., bureau of Gannett News Service in favor of returning home to the West Coast.

In some cases, the decision took much longer—up to a year or more. Bob Catell, today the CEO of utility company Keyspan, had been at what was effectively his first employer for twelve years when he came to a decision that he considered at length. His process for sorting through options is interesting. "I did come to a little bit of a crossroads in my professional career in the early '70s . . . I was kind of looking around and I was at that point in my personal life. I had a young family, and I had to make a decision as to whether my future was here, which was in Brooklyn Union, before it became Keyspan, or whether or not I should look around, to see if there were opportunities where I could do better. So I did some of that.

"I looked around and I then actually sat down with [two of the top executives], and I discussed with them what my future was here if I stayed within Brooklyn Union. They were frank and honest. They told me that they couldn't promise anything, but they thought I did have a good future here, and that before I make any rash decisions and leave and go someplace else, I should give it a little more time here to see how things worked out."

When asked if he actively considered any alternatives, Catell replied, "Yeah, I did. I looked around, I looked at ads in the papers. I sent some letters out with my résumés, to see what was out there. And I got some responses, too. But didn't really aggressively pursue them. Had some conversations with folks, again, testing the waters, so to speak, if there was something that might be more attractive to me somewhere else, so I did that over a year's period.

"I think everybody gets to the point in your life, I was there, probably in my mid-thirties . . . and thinking about, 'Is this going to be it for me forever, or do I need to look someplace else and make a move?' I decided to stay here, obviously, and it worked out okay."

Regardless of the time they took for their crossroads decisions, though, the Somebodies I interviewed spoke repeatedly of a pragmatic reliance on gut instinct, on trusting themselves and not getting overly bogged down in analytical exercises with pros and cons for every possible contingency. This gut instinct rested on strong self-knowledge.

Sierra Club President Larry Fahn started his career as a lawyer and had a tempting offer a few years later to move into the Foreign Service. He would get the chance to influence U.S. government policy on the environment, which was already a strong interest of his, and he thought hard about it. "It was very attractive to me. I would get to work on things that mattered to me, in an important job," Fahn remembered. After wrestling with the choice, though, he ended up turning down the offer. He had just moved to California and bought a house and felt that the surroundings there fit his lifestyle desires. "It was such an ambient atmosphere . . . I really liked living there, and had a feeling it would be a place for me in the long term. So even though it wasn't easy, I turned the Foreign Service down."

When Bill Mitchell, now CEO of Arrow Electronics, chose his first job, he didn't obsess too deeply about the decision. "I quite frankly don't remember making this into too big a deal. This wasn't a huge analytical exercise. I came out and interviewed for a bunch of companies. At that point in time—this was 1967, 1968—and jobs were reasonably plentiful, I had technical training and engineers were in short supply, so there was a certain amount of market opportunity. So I went and interviewed with a bunch of companies that looked interesting to me. They were all over the map. They were small companies and big companies, all over the country, from different industries. [I] did a lot of interviewing. And it ultimately came down to, sort of, I liked the people, I liked the industry, a lot of things lined up, but it wasn't a big analytical process where I lined them up and did weightings, pluses and minuses, and things like that. At the end of the day, it met a lot of my criteria, and there were those pluses and minuses, and the chemistry seemed to be there—it felt right. By the way, I've come to believe that a lot of decisions get made on that basis, particularly early in your career."

At times, hearing narratives like this, I wrestled with disbelief. I assumed that society's big leaders, its top achievers, would make more decisions based on highly thoughtful, structured processes, but repeatedly, the leaders themselves disabused me of this notion. For example, CEO Kirk Thompson told me he had joined the JB Hunt trucking company in 1979, just before the trucking industry was deregulated in 1980. Hearing this, I asked him if the pending change in laws, and the resulting revenue growth it enabled for JB Hunt, spurred him to change jobs. "Not really," Thompson murmured. "You know, at the time, I'm twenty-six, I've got two kids, I'm staying away from home too much. I'd like to make more money so my wife can stay home from work—you know, it was less strategic and more the here and now, frankly."

Ultimately, I concluded that leaders aren't necessarily faster or slower, more structured, or more apparently logical than average people in their decision-making. Their responses varied according to the situation. Instead, leaders' decision-making stands out due more to three other factors: first, their clarity of self-knowledge—their understanding of their own wants and needs, which may differ from others; second, their tendency to act decisively once decisions are made; and third, their ability to conduct internal dialogues, continually assimilating new information and ideas that they find in the wider world—in other words, their capacity for change. Each of these is addressed more later.

In closing, a recurring theme in my conversations with leaders, and thus of this book, is of how self-knowledge provided the groundwork for smart decision-making and other instances of personal change and growth. Before we move on to later chapters, it's helpful to consider one more example of personally driven change and the internal dialogues necessary to drive the change: that of civil-rights lawyer Morris Dees, who grew up in 1940s and 1950s Alabama. Talking about his early-career entrepreneurial exploits, Dees displayed much of the instinct-driven decision-making seen in other leaders. "I didn't just one day decide that I wanted to start a business . . . Some [people] might sit around and decide, 'There are five different fields of endeavor that I'd like to undertake, and I think computers are the best one this year, so I'll get in my garage, and I'll set up a little computer research lab' . . . [Not me]. I just wanted some money. My folks were poor."

As his career involved, Dees turned from business to the nonprofit civil-rights law that has given him some measure of public celebrity. His Southern Poverty Law Center has won several major judgments against hate groups, for instance. Dees hardly foresaw such a destiny in his youth. "I grew up with a segregationist attitude. Everybody else did. Clearly was no racist, though . . . First whipping I ever got was for calling a black person a nigger. My daddy gave me that whipping. We weren't liberals, though—just typical white Southerners.

"Then I began to develop my attitudes about race in college, when they tried to integrate the university while I was there, and were unsuccessful. I saw a mob beat back this young black woman. Then I reflected back on things that my daddy showed me that were fair. I just happened to grow up . . . went to high school during *Brown v. Board* [the Supreme Court decision mandating school desegregation], and then got out of college in 1960, when ahead of us, we had the Selma march, and the bombing of the 16th Church [in Birmingham, which tragically killed four young girls and pricked America's conscience]. I think I was beginning to change my attitudes. In fact, in the 1965 Selma march, Millard Fuller and I actually hauled marchers from Montgomery to Selma in our car. That might not seem like much to you, but if you step out of line as a white person in Alabama, and then you've got to go to court and represent people? Hell, the black people sat on one side of the courtroom, and the judge called the black lawyers by their first name, not Mister. He'd never say Mister. So that took a little bit of, you know, stepping out, so to speak."

In response to the various stimuli, then, Dees evolved as an adult, which led him to his calling with the Southern Poverty Law Center. He founded the nonprofit organization and drove it to its current position atop the nation's civil-rights legal establishment only after undergoing substantial evolution in his understanding of himself and his ambitions. Things were far different when he started. Dees remembered with a chortle, "I wasn't born a full-blown civil-rights lawyer right out of law school. I went to law school because my daddy said he'd never seen a cotton boll weevil [a vestige of farm labor] . . . never saw one in a law book." Like other leaders, Dees's personal growth and capacity for change rested on his strong sense of himself and his experiences.

Pay the Rent First, Conquer the World Later

What were leaders' mind-sets as they started their careers? Were their dreams and ambitions as large as their eventual achievements, or were they stead-fastly grounded in the here and now? Did they have an inkling of where their remarkable careers would take them?

In the spring of 1973, when Daniel DiMicco was a senior at Brown University, big headlines dominated the newspapers and nightly news. The Vietnam War, high gas prices triggered by an OPEC squeeze, and the early twinklings of a scandal called Watergate all intruded on the nation's consciousness. DiMicco, though, had his own urgent questions and concerns as he prepared to finish his undergraduate years. Where would he go? What would he do? Who would he become? Letters from graduate schools and prospective employers would give the first hints about his path, and he was eager to learn them.

Today the CEO of the country's largest steel producer, Nucor, DiMicco was at the time undecided even about whether to go into business or engineering. He did eventually choose to earn a master's de-gree in engineering from Penn, and the program at Penn would lead in turn to a job as a research metallurgist and onto his career in the steel industry. At the time, though, this path was anything but clear.

"The first thing I looked at when I got accepted at Columbia and a few other business schools, and I got accepted at a few engineering schools—I looked at the business schools' letters, and they said, 'We'll be happy to loan you $5,000 for the school year.' And I looked at the engineering schools' letters, and they said, 'We'll be happy to give you a full scholarship plus a stipend of $333/month, plus books.' I looked at that, and being that I didn't have a really strong focus just yet, I thought, 'Let me go to the engineering schools.' This may sound like a crazy way to make a decision, but that's how I did it!"

DiMicco's practicality stayed through graduate school. By then, he'd started a family, and his role as the breadwinner strongly influenced his thinking.

"[W]hen you're twenty-five years old, you're looking for your first job. You're not necessarily thinking of becoming CEO of the largest steel producer in the United States. [Laughs] What you're looking at is, okay, you're married, you've got a young family, and you're just getting started in life. You're looking for a job that pays well, with potential for growth opportunities, hopefully in the field that you've developed your expertise in, through the education process."

DiMicco's story was not unusual. Years ago, when today's Somebodies were Nobodies, their egos weren't inflated by mystical confidence and grandiose visions for their futures. They didn't often foresee the professional recognition, the newspaper headlines, and the money that would come their way. They didn't start their first jobs with maps to the tops of their respective professional mountains. Instead, they were more likely to be thinking about earning enough money to pay the rent, to stay current on their other bills, and perhaps to start building some small savings. They were hustling to lay the foundations of their lives, without necessarily knowing how the full blueprint would look. When they started their careers, in other words, the Big Shots were pretty much like the rest of us.

Many of the leaders I interviewed said that they had nursed quiet but intense hopes, clear glimmers of ambition, as they took their first jobs. Those dreams, though, had to compete with more immediate concerns. Scientists were more likely to worry about paying for their notebooks than they were about eventually winning the Nobel Prize. Future business leaders thought less about becoming Fortune 500 CEOs than they did about their FICA tax withholdings. If anything, the fear of mediocrity and failure provided more fuel for these people's motivations than did aspirations to greatness. When the stories of their lives were just beginning, after all, they had no way of knowing how things would turn out. So they started by putting one foot in front of the other and not thinking too far into the future. They paid their rent first, and conquered the world later.

Everyone Has Bills to Pay

With very few exceptions, the leaders I interviewed took their first jobs with an understanding that idleness was not an option. Typically, their families simply weren't affluent enough to offer the choice of whiling away post-college years in endless considerations of "What do I want to be when I grow up?" This didn't mean that all leaders fell into the category of expedience-driven career discovery, as with Dan DiMicco, but they typically had basic financial and family obligations to meet. It's not a sexy formula for success, necessarily, but important to remember for the many young people today who are afraid to commit to an initial career path for fear of shutting off more attractive alternatives. Somebodies usually didn't have that luxury. They didn't necessarily want it, either. Senator Chuck Hagel, who grew up in Nebraska and volunteered for the Vietnam War while still in his teens, described how "people become paralyzed too often when they think too much about consequences, and the future." Hagel and others like him jumped into their first jobs without worrying too much about distant, metaphysical concerns.

Another example comes from Paul Norris, the CEO of WR Grace and Company, a multibillion-dollar specialty chemicals company located in Maryland. He's a sophisticated business executive who's traveled the world and grappled with a highly dynamic company in the midst of a fast-changing industry. But life for Norris started in much simpler circumstances. He grew up in the same backcountry area as his future wife, and when he was starting his career, he felt genuine pressure to develop independent sustenance for his young family.

"We both came from the same rural community. Her father was a lawyer; my father was a farmer. I probably grew up in a little more the traditional rural background than she did, but we both came from a very small town . . . We didn't have a safety net. We probably did have a safety net—in other words, I don't think our parents would have let us starve to death [laughs]—but we didn't really believe that . . . I think my kids . . . know that if something happened and they needed support, we would clearly be there. It wouldn't even be a question. Now, I suspected my parents would be there, my wife's parents would have been there, but it wasn't such an obvious conclusion as it is today."

Several CEOs I interviewed aimed for goals that sound, especially with decades of subsequent inflation, hilariously modest. Asked about career milestones he sought in his first job, Keyspan Energy CEO Bob Catell laughed and said, "Yeah, when I came to work for Brooklyn Union—this was in 1958—my initial goal was to make $10,000 a year. That seemed to me to be an interesting number, because when I started, my salary was much, much lower than that, as you can imagine. So I really didn't have visions of being chairman of the company . . . I wanted to advance to some sort of a management position, and I think $10,000 a year, a five-figure salary, at that point was my goal."

MGIC's Curt Culver actually chose against money, opting for a significantly lower-paying job with a company in Madison, Wisconsin, where he could be near his friends and family, over one in Chicago, Illinois. Still, the figures remained in his memory decades later. "I was just more interested in working, at the time, and then as you start working—I came out and made . . . $800 a month. So it's $9,600 [a year]. So my first goal was to make my age in money . . . Six months after I started . . . because I did a good job, I got reviewed again and they bumped me to $12,000. That was huge for me, [making] a thousand dollars a month."

Even Vishay Intertechnologies CEO Felix Zandman, who had enough confidence in an invention to break away from his first job in his twenties to start his own company, had relatively small forecasts for the future of his business when he courted investors. "To tell you the truth, my plan in the beginning when I came to my relative, and he asked me, 'Do you have a business plan?' and I said, 'Yes'—I said, 'The business will make maybe $2 million a year. And that will be quite good.' So I didn't have any vision of that. I was not after the money so much. He said, 'You know, you never know what can be.' He was quite a guy, my partner. 'You never know what it's going to be. Go ahead and do it. I believe in you.' And then he made a fortune!"

The modesty went beyond mere dollars. Many leaders were young people who were still defining what they wanted to do and how far they thought they could go. Bill Mitchell, today the CEO of Fortune 500 company Arrow Electronics, started his career at a small business called Raychem Corporation. He had just graduated with an engineering degree from the University of Michigan, and moving from the Midwest to sunny California, he took a job as a production supervisor in a wire and cable plant. Entering the job, he said, "There wasn't a burning desire that said, 'I have to put myself on a path to be the CEO.' I barely knew what a CEO was at that time. What it was was, 'Gee, here's an opportunity. I'm getting out of school. I can actually make some money and have two cents to rub together. And maybe I'll get some promotions along the way.' It was pretty vague at that point in time as to what it was I was going to do."

Coping with Insecurities— and Sometimes Using Them for Motivation

Leaders showed strong modesty early in their careers in part due to another trait that many of them shared with the rest of us: basic insecurities and inexperience. Early in their careers, as they began like everyone else as so-called Nobodies, they did not sail through work and life without doubts. A number of these high achievers shared the stories of their early diffidence and uncertainty; their nervous gulps before big meetings; and hard, lonely work trying to find novel advances with their ideas.

Years before he won the Nobel Prize, English cancer researcher Paul Nurse had to fight off depression and lags in his motivation during research work. The sandy-haired, ruddy-complexioned Nurse appears now as the picture of good cheer and health, but he was considerably less jovial as he struggled with the difficulties of his early academic career. Studying for his Ph.D. at the University of East Anglia in England, he encountered typical difficulties. "Like many students, I found the drudgery of real experiments and the slowness of progress a complete shock, and at my low points I contemplated other careers, including study of philosophy or sociology of science." Nurse learned to find alternative sustenance—in his case, social interactions—to cope with the difficulties. "[T]his experience did teach me the need for sympathetic support of scientific colleagues, because at the forefront of research there are so many difficulties that depression and low motivation are a constant danger."

Nurse's situation in that first lab mirrored those of many of his scientific colleagues and seemed to arise from the circumstances characterizing his life at the time: hard work, poor weather, little acclaim from the wider world. Even more interestingly, a few of the leaders I interviewed, like scientist Doug Osheroff, confessed native insecurity. Osheroff is himself a Nobelist, served as the chair of Stanford's physics department, and worked as part of the blue-ribbon panel analyzing the *Columbia* space shuttle disaster. Despite these sterling credentials, Osheroff struggled for self-validation in his early days.

"I wasn't a person who ever really had a great deal of self-confidence. I think I recognized that in myself at a rather early age. For me, it was very important to push myself to accept new opportunities, which I probably wouldn't have done otherwise. I daresay, when they invited me to be a member of the board investigating the shuttle accident—even that was . . . kind of a double-edged sword."

In short, leaders have their frail moments and insecurities, like others do. Looking at the examples of Nurse and Osheroff, they used their self-awareness of these insecurities and developed effective coping mechanisms: for Nurse, immersing himself in a supportive community, and for Osheroff, deliberately pushing himself beyond his normal comfort zones. A third method of coping was the use of insecurities and professional inexperience as extra motivational fuel. It was a kind of psychological judo, by which leaders used their insecurity or inexperience as an extra spur to action.

As he entered his first post-MBA job, in finance for airline company TWA, Robert Peiser, who is today CEO of Imperial Sugar, said that he remembered "feeling somewhat disadvantaged relative to my contemporaries in that I had graduated from the Harvard Business School, which, as you no doubt know, focused on a case method of teaching. While that has provided me with a great foundation for general management, it did not prepare me for the quantitative requirements of my early jobs, at least compared to others who graduated from Columbia and U of Chicago. That forced me to work that much harder to catch up in learning certain quantitative techniques and probably created an extremely strong work ethic that has continued to this day. I believe it also fostered an attitude that I wasn't quite up to the tasks at hand without the greater effort that I would have to make, and that insecurity has also remained and driven me to work that much harder to achieve my personal and corporate objectives."

Interestingly, Peiser even recognizes the peculiarity of his insecurities—that they were probably unfounded, and that a Harvard Business School graduate was hardly at an actual disadvantage, but perception fueled real reactions from him. "I was a young man striving to overcome certain perceived disadvantages that probably didn't exist as much in reality, but which forced me to work that much harder, hone my analytical skills, and develop an aggressive negotiating style."

Bill Phillips, a Nobel Prize–winning scientist at National Institute of Standards and Technology in Gaithersburg, Maryland, described a similar experience when he finished his undergraduate studies at a tiny liberal arts school, Juniata College, and began graduate work at MIT. "There were certainly times when I was thinking, 'Gee, I must be in over my head here.' Because it always seemed to me that I was surrounded by people who were a whole lot smarter than I was, and I needed to work really hard to get myself on the same level they were. I remember lots of very long evenings working on homework problems with other graduate students, struggling to understand things." Phillips's insecurities spurred him in those early years.

At this later stage of his career, journalist and Pulitzer Prize winner Tom Hallman actually welcomes the nagging doubts and negative voices in his psyche that accompany big projects. He described candidly how he was hampered by doubts early in his writing career, but how he came to recognize them as part of the creative process. "[T]he journey—I love the process of taking something, feeling those doubts. If you want to call me a Somebody, I feel honored. But what people should realize as they read this, is I'll bet that every person that you say is a Somebody, there's a big part of them that still thinks that they're Nobody. Because once you start believing you're Somebody, you're not. So for me, it is that journey: Can I do this? Can I do this next story? Can I report?

⌈"The doubts and fears become a part of the process, where as a young person, those doubts might cripple you, now they're like old friends. I'm not saying I want to have them, but they're going to be there. If you ever don't feel those doubts, then it's over."⌋

Earning these epiphanies was a very conscious process for Hallman. He bounced around among multiple low-paying jobs between the ages of twenty-one and twenty-six, without yet settling on his eventual future as a writer. He worked during the day and stayed up late at night reading. The books he devoured by lonely lamplight became an inspiration.

"I became really interested in biographies," he said. "I started to read—I realized how little I knew about WWII, for example. So I started to read about the war, and I became fascinated with some of the leaders in the war, and I ultimately became really fascinated with Winston Churchill. As I read about his life, I took lessons from the way he lived, his failures and successes, and saw how these people that we look at as great, they had tremendous ups and downs, doubts . . . I continued to come back and read about John Adams or great men and women in history. They are so similar to us. They're not born geniuses . . . That's what I got a lot from reading these books on history, that these men and women were real. They had doubts, they had low moments. They had all those things that made them so human, and I could see myself in those lives, the good and the bad."

How Leaders Moved Beyond Paying Rent—and on to Conquering the World

Some of the stories above hint at the larger ambitions to which leaders aspired in their early days. Even with the pressures of day-to-day responsibilities and bills, leaders didn't completely shut off their dreams and hopes for a better tomorrow. Once at work, they often spotted opportunities—or created them for themselves—and jumped on them. Returning to business leader Kirk Thompson, today CEO of trucking company JB Hunt, we hear a typical story. Thompson faced plenty of pressure in his first job, which began under very difficult circumstances, but he didn't let that deter him from self-improvement. When he was nineteen years old and a sophomore at the University of Arkansas, his father died. He dropped out of school, got married, and began interviewing for jobs. Thompson got a job with a small trucking company called JB Hunt—a firm that grew into a multibillion-dollar business, and which he now heads as CEO. That first job and a restirring of academic interests combined to make life grueling.

In his comfortable Southern drawl, Thompson recounted, "I started at the very bottom, in the accounting department, making minimum wage, and after about—oh, I guess maybe a year of that—I decided this was not going to cut it. I needed to go back to school. So I talked to the people here, and they said, 'Well, don't quit. Why don't you just go back to school, and work here full-time, and go to school part-time?' So that's what I did, but it took about—because I changed my major and the whole bit—so it took . . . five years more, because I graduated in '78, of working full-time, and doing correspondence, and taking 7:30 classes, and going all through the summer, and night classes that were available. There weren't all that many, and meanwhile, I worked here."

Thompson realized that he was responsible for his own destiny, and this understanding provided all the motivation he needed for his job. Asked what drove him also to resume his education amid the rigors of his first job, though, he replied, "I think . . . the thing that motivates a lot of people is I was on my own, and if I was ever going to 'make something of myself,' in terms of being able to support my new wife and then when we had a baby in '76 . . . a family. So I had to support the family. So the motivation was to get a . . . degree because I'd always been a good student, and I guess the great American dream." Thompson thus began with the most basic and simplest of intentions—to take care of his loved ones—and built on that foundation with the classic desire for self-improvement.

Returning to Dan DiMicco, the head of steel company Nucor, we hear a similar story of gradually escalating ambition. DiMicco, remember, started his career focused first and foremost on earning a living and supporting his family. Seven and a half years after exiting graduate school, though, he had gained enough confidence and perspective to move from his first job at Republic Steel to Nucor. In part, he felt dissatisfaction at the culture of Republic, which he felt underutilized the talents of him and his colleagues. More important, though, Nucor itself held major allure for DiMicco.

"You'd read all these stories about Nucor, Nucor, Nucor, Nucor—and a buddy of mine who was there with me, same age, we'd always talk about it: Wouldn't this be a great company to work for? They really had their [stuff] together. They pay you based upon how you do your job, your performance, you know? . . . They're looking for entrepreneurial, aggressive people who think for themselves—Wouldn't this be a great company to work for?

"Well, he left and went to business school, and after a couple jobs, ended up working for Nucor. He called me up and told me about a job opening in Plymouth, Utah, as a metallurgist . . . for the plant . . . [S]o I interviewed for it, thinking, 'Hey, Utah's a long way from New York, but this is the kind of company I want to work for,' so I left research and went into very practical application of being plant metallurgist and manager of quality control for a brand-new steel mill in Plymouth, Utah."

As he entered his thirties and made this move, then, DiMicco's mind-set shifted. His aspirations and ambitions grew as he saw the path actually to achieve them. He notes, "I started to set some attainable goals—I wanted to move into management of the company, and manage the operations—that's were all the action was. Gradually the opportunities came about."

Stories like these arose regularly in the interviews. Even when pressured by and fully taking care of the same financial and personal obligations that all normal people face, leaders also maintained a quiet eye on bigger prizes, on opportunities for growth. In a few cases, leaders actually put aside their immediate needs and obligations to focus more on their longer-term ambitions. Daniel Burnham, who eventually rose to become CEO of industrial giant Raytheon, was actually laid off from his first job at RCA Computer Systems. He heard the news not from his boss or other direct company communications, but from a radio broadcast to which he was listening in his car one day. Despite feeling significant financial pressures, Burnham juggled his anxiety with the desire to maintain high standards in his resulting job search.

"It was a major shock, no question. I had a child, and my wife, and I had another [baby] on the way. I had *no* money, you understand. It was a very, very tough time. I moved into my parents' basement to save money. We were down there only four or five days, which was good, or we would've killed each other! [Laughs]

"[To move forward, I] just looked at the newspaper ads, dusted off my résumé, and started looking around. I remember standing in my mother's living room, and the phone rang, my mother answered, gave it to me. The job offer came through, and I said no thanks. I hung up, and my mom said, 'Who was that?' I told her what it was, and she said, 'I can't believe you didn't take it!' She was really unhappy about that."

Burnham concluded, "I didn't want just any job, even then. I wanted something that would excite me and keep me engaged. I ended up with a great company, one that's not around anymore, but it was a Fortune 250 company."

I found that as leaders grew from coltish college graduates into later adulthood, they came to balance their immediate obligations with longer-term ambitions in a variety of ways. For some leaders, it wasn't conscious—the blissful ignorance of inexperience helped open up possibilities naturally. They described the oddly liberating effects of not knowing (and thus being able to ignore) conventional wisdom. For example, Owens-Minor CEO Gil Minor found that his youth left him fearless to ask questions and to grow his knowledge.

"I just wanted to learn the business, especially with the customers. But I didn't know anything, and sometimes not knowing anything is a good thing, because then you can ask questions, and you can be humble about what you don't know—if you are prone to doing that, and I am, because that's the only way you're going to learn," Minor said.

Sometimes ignorance led to bolder action, too—helping young leaders move beyond the proverbial paying of rent, and onto bigger, broader moves. Former Cabinet Secretary Dan Glickman took his first job in Washington, D.C., after graduating from law school, but after a short time, moved back to his native Kansas to pursue political ambitions there. After a successful run for a high-visibility school board position, Glickman entered a Congressional race as a dark-horse candidate against an established incumbent, with Glickman himself at the tender age of thirty-one. He believes his relative inexperience gave him the necessary confidence to forge ahead with his campaign.

"[W]hen you're younger, you're willing to take risks that you do not take when you get older," Glickman began. "You're . . . not encumbered or burdened by life experiences, both good and bad. You haven't had a lot of experience, so you [are a little naïve], but you also haven't been burned! In later years in life, when I thought of doing other risky things in politics, I ultimately said no. Like I was going to run for the Senate against Bob Dole, or do other kinds of risky things, which I didn't do, because I had too much experience behind me. And back then, when I decided to run against this guy, a lot of people in the community said, 'No, no, no, you don't have a chance.' I didn't even listen to them. 'That's fine, where do I go tomorrow on my campaign?' But later on in life, I began to listen to them."

Ultimately, leaders like Wendy Kopp, the founder and CEO of nonprofit Teach for America, recognized the two-sided nature of inexperience, both the upside and downside. It helped her think big but also resulted in avoidable mistakes. Kopp began building Teach for America after a letter she wrote to the President of the United States, sketching out her idea and proposal, met with polite dismissal. "Recognizing that the federal government wasn't going to make this happen, and blessed with the tremendous advantages of inexperience and naïvete, I started imagining that I might be able to start it as a nonprofit organization," Kopp remembered. Despite being just a senior in college, she pursued her vision doggedly.

She went on: "Some college students ask me now whether it's better to dive in and pursue their 'big ideas' or get experience—or go to graduate school—first, and I'm genuinely torn. In my personal case, I felt that the timing was so perfect to launch Teach for America that I simply couldn't wait even a year or two to start it. And I do think I benefited hugely not only from good timing but from the advantages of naïvete. At the same time, however, there were very real disadvantages to inexperience. Teach for America could have jumped over so many learning curves if I had myself taught successfully in an urban or rural public school, and if I had learned how to manage an organization."

Unlike Kopp, most leaders, as we saw, did in fact pay their proverbial rent and build significant domain expertise in their respective fields before jumping into their career-defining work. Still, Kopp wasn't alone in her capacity for surprising accomplishment. In the next chapter, we'll learn more about the roots of the dynamism and confidence that helped leaders move beyond paying the rent.

Become the Big Fish by Mastering the Small Pond

How did leaders gain the confidence to raise their sights? After many leaders started their careers with surprisingly pedestrian goals, what boosted their outlooks and gave them the ability to dream bigger dreams?

Colonie, New York, is a sleepy suburb just northwest of Albany, the state capital. Unlike the hustle and bustle of cosmopolitan New York City about 145 miles away, Colonie has a Yankee simplicity to it. With just over 75,000 people, most of whom are a bit older and wealthier than the national average, there's a settled, comfortable feeling to the town—great for those seeking a quiet life; terrible for a new journalist seeking big, exciting stories.

Still, when Alan Miller showed up in Colonie in 1978 to work at the city's newspaper, he didn't care. The rookie reporter was hungry to make a name for himself and to begin his climb in the journalistic profession—"chomping at the bit," he says now—and he was eager to work with Harry Rosenfeld, an older *Washington Post* editor who'd left the fast pace of the nation's capital for a more relaxed life. Within weeks, Rosenfeld had Miller busy with a wide variety of writing assignments, and the young reporter was dashing around the area, writing copy and piling up bylines. Sensing the deeper ambition in Miller, who went on to win a Pulitzer Prize in 2003 for investigative reporting, the wizened editor shared some prescient words with his pupil.

Miller recalled, "My first beat was covering zoning meetings, the police blotter, and other developments in the suburb of Colonie, where the *Times Union* was located. When I began Harry told me: 'One day you will cover Moscow better than anyone else because today you've covered Colonie better than anyone.'"

Therein lay a profound lesson. The confidence to achieve great things springs from successful achievement of smaller tasks. Confidence is a delicate thing, after all. Even for the most accomplished leaders, it can be fleeting, difficult to maintain in the face of the world's indifference or worse, outright rejection. It's critically important to success, yet elusive—particularly for people just starting their careers. Leaders aren't the exception, as we saw in the last chapter. They didn't start their first jobs magically blessed by the belief that they could achieve anything. Like everyone else, once they paid their proverbial rent, they needed to build their confidence for bigger achievements.

What marked leaders was precisely that ability to find confidence. In turn, their confidence fostered ambitions. Again, though, there was no secret potion involved. Despite differing circumstances in their personal upbringing, their field of work, or their relative enjoyment of their first jobs, leaders almost invariably built confidence through the same basic pattern: they began with small successes in highly localized settings, then used the knowledge, contacts, and above all, confidence gained from these experiences to replicate larger successes on a broader scale.

Civil-rights lawyer Morris Dees, who went on to found the Southern Poverty Law Center, began his entrepreneurial career with a business he started in college. The business delivered birthday cakes for parents who wanted to send a nice gift to their children at the university. Fondly recalling that experience at the University of Alabama, Dees drew a clear link between the cake business and a much larger direct-mail company he would eventually sell for millions of dollars to a large media company in his early thirties.

Dees narrated how his confidence grew from early college days: "I've got this birthday cake idea, and so then I maneuvered around, and got a mailing list of parents with kids' birthdays . . . I remember sitting at the table—we got married when we first got to college—and my wife was licking envelopes . . . We mailed the letters about thirty days before each kid's birthday . . . Every thirty days, I'd drop the birthdays, the people who had birthdays thirty days hence. Just a good guess, you know. I didn't take any courses in direct mail—just a typical letter."

Dees continued his stream of consciousness: "So the trends set there . . . Maybe 800 envelopes for that month . . . Transcend that to mailing 20 million pieces. There's no real difference. There's not a bit of difference in having an idea, wrapping a direct-mail or direct-marketing concept around it, whether it's a brand-name concept, and mailing 50 million pieces. One day, I was sitting watching a big mailing machine with a big mailing we were doing with 25 to 30 million pieces for some book offer, before I sold my company to Times-Mirror . . . I thought back to sitting at that kitchen table and licking that one envelope.

"The things that I started were small things, and each one gave me confidence I could do something bigger. You learn what to do and what not to do. Because all businesses basically have the same problems: people problems, personnel. That's the foremost issues. Then obviously, you've got to keep good records and produce a good product, and you've got to keep your costs in line, and you've got to make a profit. Then you've got to find what the market wants, et cetera."

Similarly, Nobelist Rich Roberts described how his confidence sprouted when he went to Harvard University on a postdoctoral fellowship after switching subfields within science and found himself doing work alongside the top people in his field. "Everything was new, I didn't know what I was doing, I felt like a fool for the first year or so, but it was tremendously exciting. Just the name Harvard had a certain thing going about it, and so I felt very good because I was there, but also [I had] some trepidation, because only good guys were around. But then once I got there, I discovered that I was actually probably as good as most of the people around me . . . That period in Cambridge was a major turning point right there."

Across all fields, the same dynamic appeared. Leaders learned to swim in bigger ponds by mastering small ones first. Bill Dietrich described his growth as a writer, from his first job working for a small newspaper in Bellingham, Washington, near the Canadian border, to his current position at the *Seattle Times*, with a Pulitzer Prize in tow:

"[M]y ambitions have evolved over time. I think some kids, they grow up and they want to be an astronaut, or they want to be President, they want to be the Great American Novelist. And they carry that goal forward through their whole lives. My ambitions have been more, as I've achieved one thing, what else can you do? Or how . . . much further could I advance, or so on? So it was to get a better newspaper job, then it was to, oh, maybe I could write a book. Oh, if I wrote that book, maybe I could write a better one. And if I wrote those, maybe I could write a novel as well as nonfiction, and so on. So there's been this sort of slow progression to my career planning that I think is different."

Given stories like these, it's not surprising that first jobs often hold prominent places in the psychology of society's Somebodies. Years or even decades later, they remembered seemingly unimportant events, conversations, glances, and people who had influenced the crucial first steps in their professional development. These were the groundwork for future success.

Once armed with confidence, leaders had the strength to follow their intuitions instead of conventional wisdom—to make their moves, to advance their novel ideas, to fight for their beliefs. Numerous stories offered by the leaders showed how their steady, sometimes quiet, but often fierce confidence in the face of adversity helped their careers.

Paul Norris, the CEO of WR Grace and Company, described the period just after business school, when he was helping Grace—his first as well as current employer—shut down a subsidiary for which he was working. His confidence played a key role in his ability to push forward. Norris had surveyed the situation and decided that the best thing for the company was to get out of the business, despite the fact that this recommendation went against his own self-preservation within the then-current organizational structure—as well as his own wife's fervent advice.

"My wife was saying, 'You're crazy. This thing is going to shut down, you don't have a job, they haven't offered you a job, and we've got a kid and a mortgage.' So I said, 'Look, I'm learning a lot'—this whole divestment process, we also negotiated a license agreement. I had a crusty old guy about sixty-five who'd bought and sold more businesses than I'd even dreamt about. So I was supposed to be the content guy, and he was the process guy, and I was learning a tremendous amount about how you bought and sold, negotiated license agreements, working with the legal group. So I told my wife, 'This is all going to work out. I'm confident.' [Laughs]"

CEO Felix Zandman, in his decision to quit a prosperous first job to start his company, encountered similar concerns from his spouse. Today, knowing that the start-up company has grown into a multibillion-dollar enterprise that made Zandman and all his investors very wealthy, it's easy to vindicate the decision. Back then, though, when he was still a young man with a mortgage and a young, growing family, the logic was far from clear for Zandman. But strengthened by his teenage experience as a Holocaust survivor, when decisions carried impact far more serious than a quarterly earnings statement, he went ahead. Zandman decided to bet on the value of his invention. "It was just a very strong feeling internally that this was the right way to go, and don't pay attention to the money. My wife was very upset. I quit from a job that was very well paid—'What are we going to do with the kids?' and so on."

Career transitions, which will be discussed in more depth in the next chapter, are obvious junctures during which confidence is tested. Many leaders pointed to successes that they had in their first jobs as keys to their confidence during these trying times. As he moved from a twenty-one-year Air Force career—his first job, so to speak—over to civilian life and a job at USAA Insurance, future business leader Jim Middleton realized a huge change. "It was a hard decision. I went from having a great network—I mean, I could pick up the phone and get tons of stuff done—to I walked in, and I came to work at this company as pretty much a senior analyst. So I went from full support [from] tons of people to 'type your own stuff Monday morning' kind of thing. It was a big change."

To get through this transition, Middleton relied on his early experiences in the Air Force: "I figured . . . I have enough ability and I know enough that it won't take me long to make a mark. To be honest with you, I never thought I'd get a shot at running the company, but I thought I could get into the senior management piece of it, which—it all worked. I never really looked for coattails, I don't think I ever had them. But I was fairly strong on issues that came about."

In some cases, of course, leaders simply had more innate confidence than others. While most of the people I interviewed explained how their first jobs helped build their confidence, a few indicated that their success stemmed from a natural optimism and self-belief. Recalling his mind-set as he entered his first Congressional race at the age of thirty-one, Dan Glickman said, "I basically took this on as a challenge, that I was not afraid of this challenge at all. I can honestly say that I was—I viewed this as a climb, probably a mountainous climb, but it was nothing I wasn't prepared for personally, spiritually, and emotionally. I mean, I was ready for this, even as a kid. And there's just something in me that made me ready for this."

Pulitzer Prize–winning photographer William Snyder concurred in his description of the large projects he's undertaken in his career over the last couple of decades: "Whether it's just naïvete on my part, or huge ego, I always felt that if I put my mind to something, I could do it. There wasn't anything that could keep me from doing it."

Most leaders, though, didn't start with any inherent advantage over their average peers. They needed to become big fish by swimming in small ponds. Ann Richards, who worked as Governor of Texas from 1990 to 1994, inserted one of her characteristic zingers as she closed our interview and addressed some advice about confidence to young people starting their careers: "Be proud of who you are. Don't always think that someone else is doing something better or smarter. Be proud of what you are. Be broad. Be *big*. Don't let anybody put you down. Most young people that I know are more cautious than I think they need to be . . . Never say no to a new experience, unless it's *seriously illegal*. [Laughs]"

KEYS:
CHASING THE DREAM

Learn When to Stay and When to Go

Once under way in their early careers—having paid their bills and gained an initial base of confidence—what career moves did leaders make? How long did they stay in their first jobs? When and why did they leave?

A key moment had arrived in Brad Anderson's career, and he knew it. As the 1970s drew to a close, the future CEO of retail giant Best Buy, which today grosses more than $21 billion in revenues, was a scruffy stereo salesman in his late twenties. He was working at a small electronics store that he laughingly describes now as "real glamorous—it was built out in a space previously occupied by a [convenience store]." Anderson had started working at the store a year after college "because I could listen to music and get paid at the same time." Now, seven years into the job, having advanced little since he joined, Anderson had confrontation thrust on him.

"The founder of the company came out to the store that I was working in, and I thought he was coming out to fire me," Anderson said. "I didn't see him much, and I was kind of a long-haired—the last thing I looked like was any kind of corporate individual. He came out and asked me to step outside, and then I knew for sure that I was getting canned.

"Actually, when I stepped out on the sidewalk, he said, 'You know, I'm really not happy with what's going on, and I don't have any confidence in the leaders, and I'm thinking about making a change.' He said,

'I've got these three people I'm considering for the job, and I want to know what your opinion is.'"

Suddenly, Anderson's perspective shifted wildly. Instead of worrying about getting fired, he realized that he might be losing his best chance to make a difference in the store's operations and to try some of the ideas he'd developed after working there for years. He was shaking physically, and nearly overcome with nervousness, but he couldn't help blurting out an impulsive thought: "Well, I think I'm the right person for the job, not the three [other people] that you're considering," he said. Anderson now calls the move "completely out of character" but knew that his moment had arrived and that he couldn't waste it. Anderson looked into his boss's face to try to gauge the man's reaction, and saw that the sudden burst of audacity "took him aback pretty substantially. I thought he was going to fall off the concrete step."

On that day, at least, Anderson did not get the satisfaction of an immediate answer. His boss did not respond to his request then, instead backing away and driving off with hardly a word. Anderson recounted the story: "But he obviously thought about it, because he came back and wound up dividing the [management] job into two positions. He left me with this responsibility for the store, but also gave me some corporate responsibility, and did the same with another person in another store. We sort of shared the management underneath the founder and tried to turn this thing around."

At the time when Anderson won his newfound responsibility, his location was part of an eight-store electronics retailing chain that grossed $4 million in annual revenue and actually lost money. This chain eventually became Best Buy. (Today, of course, it's more than 5,000 times larger in revenue.)

Asked what compelled him to volunteer for the management role more than two decades ago, Anderson responded with what might be called brute modesty. "I thought I could make better decisions for the store, but really didn't have the point of view to put myself forward for it," he said. "So [the conversation with the boss] was just like, it fell in my lap. Even though it was out of character, I just jumped on it."

As they define their professional identities and begin building their careers, how do leaders like Anderson know when to stay and when to go? When do they make their career moves, and why? A Machiavellian reader might assume that successful achievers advance their careers through intricate, carefully plotted plans, and that supercompetence and hard work alone do not explain success. Career moves can be a critical part of professional growth, after all—they allow people to experience new things, meet new people, and place themselves in the path of new opportunities. High achievers might naturally be expected to make unusually adept moves, then.

This expectation, which we'll examine through the rest of this chapter, is both right and wrong. On one hand, leaders' approaches to career management did not have quite the flavor of backroom scheming that some people may imagine. Looking back on their careers, these outstanding men and women loved their work first and foremost, and didn't particularly relish fancy maneuvers among jobs or organizations. On the other hand, it's true that the leaders I interviewed often described conscious and savvy ways of managing their career development. The next chapter will drill into *how* leaders made their moves and what tactics helped them stand out from their peers. In this chapter, we'll look at the timing and reason behind career moves—what made leaders move on from their first jobs, for example, and *when* they chose to hop jobs.

Patience—or Lack Thereof

Before getting to how leaders made career moves, it's helpful to start by looking at when they made those moves. Were they impatient and eager to move on from their first jobs, or relatively relaxed? Looking at my own peers, I see pervasive restlessness influencing their thinking from their first job on. In some people's eyes, the latest generation of twenty- and thirtysomethings are the poster children for job-hopping and the resulting mess of entries under the "Experience" section of our résumés. Would leaders be noticeably different? Yes, to a degree—I found that leaders were a bit more patient than most of us in their approaches to their first jobs. Some left within a couple of months, when the job was an obviously poor fit. Many, though, stayed longer, in some cases even for decades, and more important, they seemed to have a different mind-set than many young people do today.

Of course, it wasn't as if the leaders I interviewed were passive observers of their own careers who simply sat back and awaited action. A number of leaders did not necessarily express impatience, for example, but did indicate that when they were growing up, they were very aware of their progress relative to typical milestones of age. They didn't want to fall behind a normal "curve," certainly.

Other leaders professed a good amount of patience—or at least a conviction that they didn't find the need to agitate for promotions or new types of work, as their careers naturally evolved on their own. Bob Catell of Keyspan joined a company called Brooklyn Union for his de facto first job after a very brief stint at AT&T, and he worked there for fifteen years before even becoming an officer.

Looking back now on his start at Brooklyn Union, Catell said, "I wouldn't characterize [my rise] as all that rapid. I spent two years in the meter-repair section and then moved into what was called—still is—the distribution department, which was really the outside-construction department. I spent about the next ten years in the outside construction department . . . advancing from a position as a field engineer, as they called it, up to the next level, which would be a field superintendent and assistant manager, and eventually manager. Then I was transferred out of the construction department into the engineering area of the company, again getting a promotion as I moved into that area . . . I'm trying to think when I was promoted to my first office position as Assistant Vice President. It took me almost fifteen years to rise from a junior engineer to an officer. I don't know if you consider it a meteoric rise or not. It seemed like a long time to me at the time!"

Still, Catell did not feel particularly impatient during his early career. "I wasn't impatient. I was enjoying every job. One of the basic principles I tried to follow in every job I had was to do the best I could in that job. I also never really worried about the politics. I figured if I did a good job, that would be recognized, and that would provide an opportunity for advancement."

Catell's comments echoed those of many others who stressed the importance of excelling in one's current job, and doing it to the best of your ability. Some interviewees argued vigorously that professional excellence grows directly from patience and perseverance.

When I asked journalist Tom Hallman what was most important to his turnaround from a period of aimless career wandering in his twenties, he answered immediately: "Number one, staying on the path. Not quitting. If I look at the people I knew who I went to school with, or who went to other journalism schools—let's say you take one hundred of them—over the maybe six to seven years out of getting out of college, people got maybe discouraged or wanted things too fast. I'd never had any expectations of doing anything, so it was not like I was disappointed, because I said, 'Hey, I've got a job!'" Like the tortoise to others' hares, Hallman steadily improved his work toward the ultimate reward of a Pulitzer prize. "I never expected to be anything, so I wasn't impatient. I never felt like anything was owed to me. So I just kept plodding along."

Slade Gorton, who started his political career in the Washington State legislature and did not enter the national political stage to begin his eighteen years in the United States Senate until more than two decades later, believed that overeager careerism actually hurt people's potential progress. A thoughtful Gorton took off his glasses and leaned back in his chair as he described some colleagues from his early days in politics: "I started in the Legislature in a very interesting time, with a lot of very able people. I think there must've been a half a dozen people whom I started in the Legislature who *knew* when they were going to be Governor or Senator or even President of the United States. They had a career in politics that was just set. When they were going to do what.

"I observed fairly early that that was a great disability, that thinking about . . . how what you did today was going to affect when you went up the ladder—disabled you from doing well the job you had at the time. And most of them, obviously, almost every one of them, did not succeed . . . The people who got somewhere were the ones who concentrated on the job they had."

For a number of leaders, patience did not come naturally, but was learned as an adaptive skill within large organizations. USAA Insurance CEO Jim Middleton described a stint in his late twenties, when as a young Air Force officer he was staffed in Washington, D.C. He was a rising young officer on a hot career track but felt like he was cooling his heels a bit within the capital's bureaucracy. "As much as I disliked my early years in the Pentagon, they did me a lot of good in terms of understanding how to play the plate and patience, because I've never had inherently a lot of patience, but I've learned to have it. I've learned you have to have patience."

Varying Tenure at a First Job

Translating this general talk about patience into the specifics of career moves, I was curious to know how often leaders changed jobs. The average college graduate today will change jobs more than ten times and work in potentially three to five different careers.[2] Before starting the research, I suspected that leaders were more likely to have linear career paths, with extended tenures at their first job. What better way to develop expertise and contacts, and rise to the top, than staying put and building expertise and contacts within a specific domain?

Again, these ideas were at least partly right. The Somebodies I interviewed typically committed to a job or company for a moderate length of time, at least five and often more than ten years—longer than the averages for many of today's young people. Reasons for this are open to speculation; presumably, earning the helm of a large corporate enterprise or government institution requires specific knowledge and contacts, and a personal gravity built only through repeated demonstration of competence over time.

In certain fields, though, such as arts and entertainment or to a lesser degree science, leaders often displayed more career mobility than I expected. When the proverbial knock of opportunity came to their door, they answered it. Even in business, when people stayed put, it was usually because their jobs metamorphosed to the point of being virtually new roles. It was rare to find leaders who'd simply dedicated them-

---

2. Source: Esquire Group, "The Importance of Networking and Relationship Building"

selves to a particular job or institution and never wavered from their initial paths.

The longest tenure I found for a first job—in other words, staying with the initial employer, even as roles evolved—was thirty years. Lowry Kline, now CEO of Coca-Cola Enterprises, graduated from law school in 1965 and joined a law firm in Chattanooga, Tennessee, as an associate. He steadily built a practice in trial and corporate law, making partner and staying with the firm until 1995. After three decades, Kline needed a change. As he put it, "I began to experience burnout. I joined my present company in 1995 and moved gradually to the business/management side, where I gained renewed incentive."

While Kline's tenure was unusually long, a number of other leaders did work with early (if not their first) employers for well beyond a decade. For example, Reebok CEO Paul Fireman stayed with the olive oil company where he started as a warehouse laborer for more than seventeen years. Tower Automotive Kathleen Ligocki, after doing a six-month archaeological dig in Mexico and then working briefly at a low-paying job in a government agency, took a position with General Motors, which she intended to last only a short time, to help her earn money for graduate school. She ended up staying for fifteen and a half years. Similarly, Jim Middleton joined the Air Force, intending to stay for just a few years and weather the storm of the Vietnam War, and twenty-one years later, he left with a full pension, only to begin his second career in business. Two Pulitzer Prize–winning photographers, April Saul and William Snyder, started with smaller newspapers where they stayed for only a couple of years and then moved to larger publications—Saul from the *Baltimore Sun* to the *Philadelphia Inquirer,* and Snyder from the *Miami Herald* to the *Dallas Morning News*— where they've each worked for more than twenty years.

In each of these instances of extended tenure, the key to longevity appeared to be rotation through different roles. The chance to try new activities and learn new skills kept the future Somebodies interested and engaged. At the olive oil company, Fireman moved into sales, then management, and even did brief stretches helping with finance. For GM, Ligocki began as a factory supervisor, switched after a time to sales, took a sponsored detour to get her MBA at Wharton, and continued to rotate through different functions as she climbed the corporate ladder. The others' stories are similar. Again, leaders often stayed with their organizations for extended periods of time, but typically, those stays involved job changes to the point that they may have seemed almost like new jobs. Even (or especially) these scions of stability and responsibility thirsted for change and personal growth beyond their first jobs. Perhaps the most meaningful lesson was that they often sought and found those things within their organizations, without needing to transfer among multiple organizations to get those benefits.

It should be noted that by itself, the picture of early-career stability is not complete, either. Ligocki arrived at GM only after the archaeological dig and trying the job at the government agency. Bob Catell, Bruce Karatz, and Parker Kennedy, the eventual CEOs of Keyspan, KB Home, and First American, respectively, each settled into lengthy, multidecade tenures at their current companies, but only after taking first jobs at other places. Catell started as an engineer at AT&T and stayed only six months, while Karatz and Kennedy both began as lawyers in private practice for the clients for whom they went to work.

Leaders in nonbusiness fields showed a similar pattern: eventual stability in a couple of key roles or at key organizations, but only after some early-career experimentation. Almost all the Nobel Prize–winning scientists and academics I interviewed had long CVs full of institutions where they had held fellowships, temporary teaching positions, and other relatively short-lived postings. Tenured positions at academic institutions naturally reduced movement, but they usually came only after several jobs in different environments. For example, William Sharpe, the Nobel Prize–winning economist who created the Sharpe ratio for assessing investment portfolio risk, followed his academic studies with a stint at the RAND Corporation, a private think tank in California that he remembered fondly. Sharpe greatly enjoyed working in the private sector, but after several years, felt the desire to advance his academic career. He thus left RAND to take a junior faculty position at the University of Washington, in Seattle, but a few years after that, he returned to RAND to build on his independent research. Though he settled at Stanford later in his career, Sharpe has maintained active outside activities, including a consulting firm he helped found.

Nobel laureate Paul Nurse displayed a similar adaptability when faced with a major opportunity at the age of thirty-one. For the previous six years, he had worked very comfortably as a research fellow in the Department of Zoology at the University of Edinburgh, in Scotland. The posting was his first job after finishing graduate studies, and he says himself that the time was "pivotal for my entire research career." In Edinburgh, Nurse benefited from a masterful mentor: "He gave me both complete support and total freedom, spending hours each week talking with me . . . An astonishingly generous supervisor, he never once was coauthor on any of the papers I produced . . . His laboratory was an exciting environment where I had many interesting colleagues."

Despite this anchor of stability, Nurse had the perspective and restlessness that led to professional change. "I thought it was not advisable to remain in one academic environment, and the long, dark winters in Edinburgh could be rather dismal. I also thought that the next stage in cell-cycle analysis required molecular genetics, and . . . so I looked for an environment that would make this possible." Sentiment aside, in other words, Nurse moved from that first job when he realized he needed additional professional and personal stimulus. This kind of narrative was common among the scientists with whom I spoke—and somewhat contrary to a picture of those scientists as stodgy, ivory-tower intellectuals outside the normal bustle of life.

Even some future government leaders, like former Cabinet Secretary Donna Shalala, described a varied path for their early careers. After Shalala finished her two-year stint in the Peace Corps, she returned to the States with hopes of entering journalism. But as she put it, "I couldn't get a job. *The New York Times* wasn't hiring. I would've had to go back to Cleveland to work at the *Cleveland Press*, and I didn't want to do that. There just were not a lot of journalism jobs. So I started out being an academic." Shalala finished her academic studies, became an assistant professor of political science at City University, and eventually moved to Columbia. In addition, she began building her network of contacts, fellow young professionals in New York and Washington who would be highly relevant for her future entry into the Clinton Cabinet. She found that working in a well-networked and intellectually vibrant environment produced a rich abundance of opportunities for professional growth.

"My field was public policy, and I just kept getting invitations to do things, to help a governor with a transition, to sit on the New York . . . Municipal Assistance Corporation . . . I was hanging out with a crowd in New York . . . of young people who were just starting out in politics and journalism, and it was just opportunities that were offered to me . . . I also met Bill Clinton around that time. He was a friend of mine in New York. I met Bill and Hillary Clinton in the '70s. Then Hilary and I ended up in the '70s and '80s sitting on the board of the Children's Defense Fund. Hilary did work for Marian Edelman for a while. I met Harold Ickes during that time. I mean, I knew—I met Bob Rubin during that time. I knew all of these people."

Congressman Chris Bell of Texas had an especially interesting narrative around the timing of his early career moves. He studied journalism at the University of Texas, and his first job after graduation was with the tiny television station in Ardmore, Oklahoma. Asked why he chose that job, he laughingly alluded to the highly competitive nature of broadcast journalism: "It was the only option!" From Ardmore, Bell moved on after only eight months to a larger station in Amarillo, Texas, and worked as a reporter there, quickly winning recognition and becoming one of the anchors. A couple of years after graduating from college, the young up-and-comer was nudged by local Democratic Party operatives to run for Congress in 1984, at the tender age of twenty-four.

Some might assume that the 1984 race thus started Bell's inexorable rise in politics, but they'd be wrong. Bell lost that race after a hard-fought nine-month campaign and then he entered what he forthrightly termed "a little bit of a rudderless period" lasting for the next four years, through his mid- and into his late twenties. Bell returned to journalism, but encountered the kind of difficulties that many people face, both in the office and at home. "I decided I'd like to move up in journalism and get to a different market [than Amarillo]. I was sending out tapes [of my work], and that wasn't happening. I ended up getting married, in a failed marriage, that lasted only a few months. It was really heartbreaking, something that I never expected to happen."

Ultimately, of course, Bell did get elected to the U.S. Congress, where he served from 2002 to 2004. He was a highly successful radio reporter and lawyer before then, but only after holding a number of different jobs during his twenties. Rather than gloss over the uncertainties and anxieties of that period, he spoke frankly about them. "I think the time from when you're twenty [years old] to thirty can be extremely hard," Bell said. "That old saying that it's always darkest just before dawn is oftentimes true."

Again, the lesson was that across fields, there was no one length of tenure, or straight-line path characterized by job stability, that stood out as a magic catalyst of success. For every leader who stayed with an organization for decades, there were others who tried a number of roles before settling down.

Emmy Award winner Gordon Clapp started his acting career, for example, with a small theater troupe he and some friends created in Williamstown, Massachusetts. He was there three years, far from Hollywood or Broadway, before he got his break in higher-profile roles like the hit television series *NYPD Blue*. Clapp traveled with the group in low-glamour circumstances. Still, he loved the work.

"The value of that was that I really got to do a lot of different, really diverse roles, just got a lot of stage time, so that I became as comfortable onstage as I was offstage . . . The game face became part of my life . . . I was working all the time. Not all the material was completely gratifying [laughs], doing three shows a day of a children's play . . . We were all thinking eventually of going to New York or someplace [bigger], putting ourselves on the open market," Clapp said. From that initial group, Clapp then moved on to a stint with a small theater in Halifax, Nova Scotia, and only after that to the more established environment of Hollywood.

In summary, then, the leaders I interviewed turned out not necessarily to be the paragons of early-career stability I expected. They did typically commit to jobs and institutions to a greater degree than most young people do today. However, when circumstances dictated it, they showed a fair amount of mobility, too. What specifically broke through the inertia of complacence, the inertia that keeps people in their first jobs? Eventually, what factors caused them to move? The answers to these questions form our final topic of the chapter.

What Compelled Departure from First Jobs

Few people work for the same company, university, government agency, or entertainment group throughout their entire careers anymore. Yet the decision to leave the first job and begin the sometimes decades-long slalom through a professional career can be a difficult one, especially for relatively young people. When is the right time? What are the right reasons? Leaders were no exception in wrestling with these questions as young people. Even when they remembered their first employers fondly, however, or spoke of the valuable lessons they learned in their first jobs, leaders departed their first jobs for a variety of reasons. The most common one? It was limited opportunity for advancement and professional growth.

Keyspan CEO Bob Catell, who stayed at AT&T for only six months before departing, felt significant pressures to provide for his wife and mother at home. He lacked the personal safety net of his more affluent peers. Still, Catell had the temerity to seek out new employment based on his quick assessment of career prospects with Ma Bell. "It was a huge company. And I was a junior engineer, and they had me working on testing long-distance circuits. I realized pretty quickly that someone like myself in a company that at that time was probably a couple hundred thousand people would not have a great opportunity, I didn't think, to be recognized and to be advanced. So I started looking around and found that there was a company in Brooklyn called the Brooklyn Union Gas company that was hiring engineers. So I applied to the Brooklyn Union Gas company and fortunately I was hired. Brooklyn Union at that time was a company that had about three thousand employees, so I felt it was a lot more opportunity for someone like me perhaps to get recognized. I would have an opportunity for advancement . . . it didn't take me very long to decide that, and look for something else [beyond AT&T]."

Like Catell, Paul Norris felt compelled to leave his first job when opportunity appeared limited. He actually has worked for WR Grace and Company at three separate stages of his career, interspersed with stints at other companies: he was at Grace first as a student intern, then as his first job after business school, and most recently as CEO of the company. While retaining an obvious affection for the company, he has experienced life in other organizations, as well. For the purposes of our interview, we treated the first full-time stint with Grace, after business school, as his "first job." He described starting in 1971, rotating through a variety of roles, and leaving in 1981 for Engelhard, as he began entering the middle phase of his career, at age thirty-four. Norris remembered wanting to grow his capabilities at the time and finding Grace too limiting.

"I felt at the time I left Grace that the ladder to continue to grow was more limited at Grace, because at that time—I'm talking about something that was embedded in the culture, and I'm still trying to change today—there was a tendency that if you were in one group, one business or one division, that you were limited to the opportunities in that group or that division. There's not as much cross-company move or cross-company development of people. I felt that I was ready to learn different things.

"The fundamental reason I think you change [positions] early in your career is to provide yourself with different learning opportunities, and to continue to challenge yourself. I don't think you ever want to be comfortable. You always wanted to be stretched. So when I felt that I was no longer going to be stretched and I was too comfortable, and opportunity came [for] a big sales and marketing job for Engelhard, it seemed like a good way for me to grow. Significant opportunity to learn. One of the things that I didn't realize is that I got the opportunity to learn a new culture . . . I was much closer to the top levels of the company, so I learned a lot about strategic management, and human resource management—much more of the corporate kinds of activities, versus the . . . product-line management opportunities.

"Then I went to Allied for the same reasons: different business, bigger company. I felt over a long term, more opportunity to learn, to grow, and to develop, and then when [legendary CEO] Larry Bossidy came, it was a dramatic shift. It was, you know, the accelerated development that you get as we moved from Allied Signal to a more GE-type culture and environment. That was the most invigorating—I probably learned more in those eight years than I did in the prior twenty."

Symbol Technologies CEO Bill Nuti sounded similar notes. Asked about key crossroads he had faced in his career, he talked about leaving his first job as a salesman at Big Blue. He struggled with "whether to leave the safety of IBM and venture into the unknown with a small telecommunications company in a different industry. I came from a family who treasured job security and long-term careers with a single employer. This was not intuitive to my family. It turned out to be one of the best decisions of my career. Not that staying with IBM would have turned out bad—they are a great company—[but] the other company just afforded me the opportunity at a young age to personally and professionally develop at a more accelerated pace."

Sometimes, the decision to leave the first employer hinged on the availability of specific jobs and promotions. Imperial Sugar CEO Robert Peiser started his career at TWA and specifically cited two mentors above him who significantly aided his early professional development and who themselves went on to senior positions at TWA, one as Chairman and CEO, and the other as Vice President and Controller. The quality of those in front of him was ultimately a factor in Peiser's departure from the company, as he saw the logjam developing ahead of him.

Peiser said, "The biggest choice was leaving that job to become Assistant Treasurer of Hertz in 1977 [after five years at TWA]. I had been very successful at TWA and no doubt had a bright future, but it appeared that the promotional path was about to slow down, simply because of the quality of those above me and their relatively short tenure in their positions."

Spotting potential slowdowns in a rising career motivated other leaders to change their paths, also. Craig Sturken, CEO of Spartan Stores, was blunt about how prospects for advancement influenced his thinking on career moves. Asked what prompted him to leave his first job, Sturken replied, "Primarily the opportunity to move forward where

I was . . . That's really what drove me to look beyond that company [throughout my career]. I was at a crossroads. I was at a situation where I just had to make the decision, because I knew that I was at a dead end. Sometimes because of political issues—politics play a huge role at all big companies . . . [I]n one case . . . I chose to leave [a company] because it was clear that the future CEO of the company had already been chosen, and he was a competitor of mine, in that we both had the same job. The existing CEO, the incumbent, had made the choice to go with the other man."

Wanting to understand better the timing of his move, I pushed Sturken further:

AUTHOR: So you saw that—

CS: I saw the handwriting on the wall.

AUTHOR: And felt, what's the point in sticking around?

CS: That's right. I'm not going to be #2—I want to be #1.

AUTHOR: What was your thinking in terms of timing of those things? Did you typically wait for a while, or was it a situation where you were—

CS: I'll tell you, in every case, it was always like a bell went off in my head, like a gong.

AUTHOR: So things would build up over time, but then you'd have that moment of realization?

CS: Finally I came to the conclusion, or an opportunity jumped into the road in front of me. While I'm pondering, "What should I do? Should I hang around here any longer?" lo and behold, an opportunity presented itself, and I chose it.

A final example of this dynamic comes from Arrow Electronics CEO Bill Mitchell, who talked about a switch he made in the middle of his career, after his first job but before he reached his current situation atop Arrow Electronics. Mitchell was then working at a company called Raychem, and his awareness of time's passage underlay his thinking. "I really did want to become a CEO. It was pretty obvious I wasn't going to—that that wasn't going to work at Raychem, just because of the timing. I was too close in age to the guy who'd been named CEO, and by the time he would've been through his thing, I would've been past the age, and so it was time to go look for something else. So I did."

Not all career moves were made with the same motivation in mind, of course. Particularly in nonbusiness fields, leaders' reasons and methods differed. Ultimately, though, the hunger for excellence was common among all leaders I interviewed. As they moved from Nobodies to Somebodies, it became part of their identities to find ways over, around, under, and through obstacles to success—and this included career moves beyond the first job. Some leaders were consciously self-aware of this fact; others learned it over time. For all, though, it played a basic and essential part in the journeys of self-discovery early in their careers. In the next chapter, we'll explore the actual steps that helped leaders reach for excellence—not just when and why they made career moves, but specifically how.

Learn How to Stay and How to Go

What kind of moves did top achievers make? On a tactical level, how did they manage their careers? How did they stand out?

John Lithgow was a young man who grew up fast. Raised in a theatrical family, the actor who's won a Tony and four Emmy Awards, in addition to numerous other laurels, knew early that he wanted to make his living in the dramatic arts. He starred in numerous student productions at Harvard, where he attended college, and extended his interests through a postgraduate academic fellowship in Europe. Returning from Europe after his studies, Lithgow knew what he wanted; he just needed to learn how to achieve it.

Lithgow had married young, a month before his twenty-first birthday, and had a son soon after arriving back in the United States. He started his work in Princeton, New Jersey, in his father's dramatic troupe, and enjoyed the versatility of work for about a year. At that point, however, he became restless.

Lithgow said, "I worked for him for a year, directing two major productions, playing several major roles . . . I just worked and worked and worked. I also designed the sets . . . I had it easy—I had a dad who would employ me. But at the end of that year, as much as I'd enjoyed the work, I just made the conscious decision, 'I've got to work for somebody other than my dad.' He wanted me to continue working."

Asked what compelled him to leave his nest, Lithgow replied, "Just the lurking unease that in the company of these actors . . . I couldn't help feeling that a lot of other people felt that I had this important position in the company because it was my dad's company. I was uncomfortable with even the smell of nepotism, even though I was doing a good job . . . Some of it had to do with . . . a young man's rebellious instinct . . . I wanted basically to go to New York and enter the most demanding, the most competitive marketplace."

Lithgow faced feelings similar to that of many future leaders—as well as the rest of us—in their twenties and early thirties. How far was he meant to go? What were his limits? What would help him grow as an actor and fulfill his potential? His response to these challenges characterized many other leaders I interviewed: first, he strove for visibility; second, he cultivated broad functional expertise; third, he strove for positions that would stretch his capabilities, rather than simply being glamorous or good "résumé builders"; and finally, he was above all thoughtful about his choices. Lithgow, like many other leaders, made conscious trade-offs in an effort to reach his goals. We'll return to his story later, and learn how those trade-offs paid off. In the meantime, Lithgow and other Somebodies' approach to career moves gets our attention.

Raising Professional Visibility

Leaders often showed a knack for getting noticed early in their careers and using the extra visibility to learn about or create new opportunities for themselves. Bill Bradley was perhaps the most celebrated of the 100 leaders at an early age, owing to his all-American status as a basketball player at Princeton, his membership on the gold-medal winning team at the 1964 Tokyo Olympics, his Rhodes scholarship to Oxford University in England, and his return to the States as a pro basketball player. Bradley certainly experienced some of the difficulties brought on by fame, but it helped him, too. Before entering the NBA, for example, he benefited from wise counsel he received at a special dinner.

Bradley recounted: "I remember when I was considering whether to play professional basketball, [Senator] Morris Udall in Washington had a dinner of people in Washington, friends of his that were going to give me advice as to whether to play basketball or go to law school, if I wanted to be in politics, that kind of thing . . . And the people who were there were Byron White, who was on the Supreme Court [and had won the Heisman Trophy as a college football player], [and] Paul Sarbanes, who was then a Congressman . . . [The dinner] was a tremendous gift [Udall] gave me, and that was because . . . I had met him when he came for a conference at Oxford."

Not all future leaders had opportunities for high visibility as obvious as Bradley's; still, when chances came, they were rarely squandered. These Somebodies usually delivered steady, highly competent work in the tasks and roles assigned to them, and then they also stepped up when they had the chance to do higher-profile work or come into contact with top people in their fields.

Former Raytheon CEO Daniel Burnham began his career at RCA but was laid off from that first job as part of a general company resizing. Burnham started over at Carborundum, a then-Fortune-500 company no longer in existence. As events moved rapidly at Carborundum, Burnham gravitated to the heart of the action through strong performance.

"I guess I lucked out in that I had a couple of senior guys who tripped across me. You've got to be visible, and I had that. I got involved in putting together the business plan for this division. Again, it was one of those experiences where you just have to jump in and do the job. I don't know how I did it. The CFO liked [the work I did], and brought me into corporate staff, and I started getting into business planning.

"To make a long story short, I was corporate controller at twenty-six or twenty-seven. Then in 1978, a tender offer was made for us—unfriendly. So we went out to try to find a buyer . . . It was critically important for us to find a good buyer, and so they put the COO, the CFO, and me on a team to sell the company. We had about a month to do it, and we did it. By coincidence, the company that I became the primary interface with ended up being the one that bought us. I had to put together a business plan on the whole company, present it, and then put it into action.

"I'll never forget—the first pitch I made was to [legendary investment banker] Felix Rohaytn—I had to pull this whole business plan together, all the notes, everything. It was a lot like 3M would do it. A lot of businesses, lot of data, a lot of marketing, too. The meeting was supposed to start at 9 A.M., and the books were all assembled at ten [minutes] to 9. I thought the CEO was presenting. Well, the CEO asked me to sit down, introduced me, and then he told me to present. I had to present for an hour! As you can imagine, that was a bit of a surprise, but off I went. Felix came up to me afterward and said, 'Kid, that was a hell of a job.' That felt damn good." Burnham had been ready and eager to answer the door when proverbial opportunity knocked.

Not all visibility stemmed directly from work. Curt Culver, now CEO of MGIC, started his career at a smaller mortgage insurance company and gained extra exposure to the CEO due to his background as a competitive collegiate golfer. Culver said, "One thing maybe that also helped, was because I was such a good golfer, and our CEO was, too. Here I was, a peon in the company, but I was golfing with the CEO once a week . . . so I got the attention of people, I guess for things outside my work abilities. But then I think on the golf course you demonstrate so many . . . qualities that may be attractive to him, to learn more about me, that helped me in my career . . . If you have the attention of senior management, things happen."

Cultivation of Broad Functional Expertise

Another career move cited by many top leaders, particularly in business, was the cultivation of broad expertise. While narrow specialties often propel early career successes, Fortune 1000 CEOs often pointed to cross-functional perspective as a key aim of early jobs. Kirk Thompson, the CEO of trucking company JB Hunt, joined the company for his first job when it was in the range of $10 to 15 million in annual revenue—a fraction of what it's now become as a multibillion-dollar business. His skills grew along with the company. Thompson said, "[T]he fact that I'd done so many different things [in growing the company] broadened my perspective and allowed me to be, I think, more ready and prepared for the CEO job, as opposed to somebody who was in a single-line trajectory. Had I come in as CFO, say, when we were $250 mm, it would've been different than being in the trenches, doing the job—you understand what makes money, and how the business operates, and what's out there, what the environment's like, and what makes things tick. Until you do that, you're going to be less successful, I think."

Asked to elaborate, Thompson continued, "Yeah. I'm saying, if you come in, let's say you either come in through finance—you graduate with an MBA from Harvard and you come in as a financial analyst, and then you're a controller, division controller, and then you're CFO. You will be prepared, you will have learned a lot along the way.

"But if you have been in a variety of positions, in operations, in sales . . . cross-pollinized, you're going to be *much* more effective and much more prepared. I've seen it happen many times. It's true in spades in my case. Getting to know the business from the ground up and how it operates. Now I would say, too, though that if you've got to pick one or the other, you need to understand economics and how money's made, if you're going to be in a for-profit organization. A lot of times you get somebody who's come into the sales organization and all they want to do is sell, sell, sell. Well, that's wonderful, but you've got to make a profit on it. Someone who can analyze and understand—maybe that's my bias, but an industrial engineer, or an accountant, or somebody who's got that kind of training and discipline, is a valuable individual. Now, it'd be nice to have some social skills . . . It's good to have a base of economic understanding and analytical skills, but you need to be more broad than that as you go through life and your career. It'll pay off big-time for you if you are."

Paul Fireman, who had a similar experience with his first job, helping run a small family business for nearly two decades prior to founding Reebok, said, "All the experiences we had in that [olive oil] business were not fancy, but they provided very good lessons. Most people have very linear, singular experiences in business. You get started, and you get very good at a very narrow slice of running a company. That wasn't me. One day I was shipping, the next I was selling, or doing financing, HR—so in a sense I touched all parts. When you're in a company that size, you have a more rounded résumé. By necessity, you have to do a little bit of everything. You have a patchy résumé, but you have more to offer than someone who's just been in his slot at a bigger company."

Even in a more corporate setting, Lars Westerberg, now the CEO of Autoliv, sought his first job specifically for its breadth. He joined ASEA/ABB, competing hard for a spot in an eighteen-month training program split between Sweden and Brazil, because he wanted "the chance to get broad exposure—sales, engineering, et cetera." He knew that "As a trainee, you get exposed to many different fields," which was important to him as he began a twelve-year stint at the company.

Similarly, Paul Norris of WR Grace aimed for a big-picture perspective as he started his career. "The thing I liked about the company was the combination of technology and marketing, because we make some fairly sophisticated technical products, and we supply those to sophisticated industries like the refining industry. It's the ability to understand that technology-market interface that I thought was pretty interesting. I did that throughout my whole career. I always felt that you could have a good technical capability, or a fundamental strength, but if you can't find a way to translate that into a customer value, you won't be successful."

Of course, the lessons from cross-functional learning weren't always easy. Ron Sargent, the CEO of Staples, took his first job at Kroger's grocery company after getting a Harvard MBA. Like all new employees, he dutifully rotated through stints in store operation and management. At times, the experience left him wondering if he'd made the right choice relative to more specialized businesses like consulting or banking.

"In my first six months, I remember talking to one of my friends who was on Wall Street. He had called me at the store, and he was telling me about his first big deal, where he was involved in a [mergers and acquisitions] project. And that day, I'd cut up, I don't know, probably twenty-five to thirty boxes of chicken, in a meat department, and I had blood from my neck to my knees. And I'm thinking, 'Hmmm, I wonder if I made the right move, the right career decision.' [Laughs] I mean, he's telling me about his first Wall Street deal, and I've been cutting up chicken all day in this forty-five-degree meat department!"

Stretching Capabilities, Even If It Means Sacrificing Some Glamour

Sargent's story about the Kroger meat department exemplifies another key career move from the playbook of many leaders: choosing roles that offered high growth, even at the expense of high glamour. Leaders recognized the need to extend their capabilities, for example by broadening their perspectives, or by shouldering unusual responsibility.

For Shirley Tilghman, who has served as President of Princeton University since 2001 after being a professor of molecular biology at the school since 1986, growth at the start of her career meant a step off the beaten track. After graduating from Queen's University in Kingston, Ontario, Tilghman went to the West African country of Sierra Leone for two years as a science teacher. From her undergraduate studies, Tilghman had a good sense that she would eventually return to research and academia, but she needed the mental change of pace the two years in Africa gave her.

"I started filling out applications probably in the middle of the winter and very quickly came to the realization that I couldn't possibly imagine going to graduate school—that I had had the experience of working in labs every summer when I was in college, and also doing research projects in faculty labs during the year. So I knew perfectly well that if I started graduate school, I was on a treadmill that would be unrelenting and would never let me get off, and that if I was ever going to do anything in my life other than be in a laboratory, I was going to have to do it right now, when I graduated," Tilghman said. "Those two years that I taught high school in a little village were the only two years in my life where I didn't feel as though I was striving to excel and having to work really hard to excel. It was a vacation from life—and I loved every second of it."

In the business world, sacrificing glamour for personal growth often meant that leaders started with line management instead of staff positions. They started work in the trenches of a specific subsidiary business or product line, in other words, rather than at corporate headquarters as aides to senior executives. Many of the CEOs whom I interviewed came out strongly in favor of line responsibility. These leaders tended to value direct responsibility for a specific segment of a business, because of the accountability and strategic thinking it breeds. While a staff advisory role to executives can bring high-level visibility, it results in less-concentrated responsibility and, thus, learning.

Norm Axelrod, CEO of Linens 'N Things, chose his first job after business school from among three options: consumer marketing at a company like Procter and Gamble; market research at Yankelovich Partners; and retail management, which he ultimately chose, at Bloomingdale's. He opted against consumer marketing relatively early, which left Yankelovich as the choice besides Bloomingdale's. Axelrod chose the latter because, as he said, "I felt at Yankelovich that I was more desk-tied and report-driven, and I thought that it wasn't as meaningful a first-level assignment. It was almost too strategic and not enough line responsibility."

When I returned to that point later in our interview, asking him why he preferred line to staff work in that first job, Axelrod answered, "No matter how good your recommendations are, you still have adjustments to make along the way. I think the guys who have taken responsibility for their decisions, and learned that the world's not perfect, and relationships are important—facing negative decisions is important in your career. I don't know anyone who's been enormously successful and not had some setbacks."

IKON CEO Matt Espe faced a similar choice early in his career at his first employer, General Electric. Like Axelrod, he chose the line position, in part because he felt it brought him closer to customers and the actual action of the business. "I was presented with two opportunities— one was a regional management position, and one was a somewhat more glamorous staff position. After careful consideration, and considerable input from mentor and friend Steve Bennett [now the CEO of software company Intuit], I decided to take the line leadership role, which was a better fit with my long-term leadership goals. Field leadership roles can provide invaluable experiences and prepare you to make more informed decisions in staff roles as your career progresses."

Espe also pointed to the importance of line experience in promoting ongoing learning for leaders like him. It helps keep perspectives fresh and in-tune with realities. He said, "My field experience has served me well over the years; in fact, to this day, I make sure I'm out in the field as much as possible at IKON, to keep my finger on the pulse of the company."

In summary, leaders often saw line management as a key step to maintaining their longer-term growth potential. After his first major job at Carborundum ended in the company's acquisition by Kennecott Copper, future Raytheon CEO Daniel Burnham was given a lofty title, pay, and office, but he felt stifled by the new role. "I became head of planning there. I didn't want the job, but they offered a lot of money. I had just a huge office in New York City, absolutely huge, but I hated it. When I was asked to go to New York, I remember asking my boss at the time about it. I said, 'Hey, I don't really want to go out there.' He told me to put an outrageous salary demand on them, so that they'd turn me down. I was making $50,000 at the time. I asked for $70[K], and they offered $72! Well, at that point, I couldn't really say no."

Still, Burnham eventually took a nearly 30 percent pay cut to get back into line management. "[A]fter a while, I really didn't like the job, even with the office and the salary and all that. I called Carborundum, which was then a . . . subsidiary—and I told them I wanted to come back. Well, they said they couldn't afford to pay me what I was making. They offered me a product manager position, but said, 'There's no way we can afford to pay what you're making now.' I kept asking how much they would offer, though, and they finally offered $50[K]. I took it . . . I came home one day and said, 'Guess what? We're going to Buffalo, and my salary's going from $70 to 50[K].' . . . [Chuckles]

"But at Kennecott, I wasn't connected to anything! I wasn't managing a product. Here I was in the world of Felix Rohatyn [the major investment banker mentioned earlier], walking with the giants, so to speak—it was very exciting and all that, but it wasn't what I wanted at the time. Sure, I was making less money [in Buffalo], but I was still learning a lot of new things in the new job. I went into marketing, and from there became a GM. [Even at $50K], I was still making more money than I ever expected, so that was a hell of a cool thing."

In Burnham's view, the less-traveled path of line management and assumption of responsibility comprise an intrinsic part of a leader's growth. "What makes a guy feel like he can run a big organization if he hasn't risked something for that position? If you haven't put it all on the line [yourself], you're going to be a bureaucrat, not a builder of organizations, not a leader! If you haven't faced risk yourself, you're not going to have the confidence and decision-making ability to do well in a position of responsibility."

Conscious Management of Career Moves

Ultimately, in discussing career management with leaders across different fields, what I learned was this: almost all enjoyed their work with a passion. At the highest levels, you can't fake it. Combine passion and intelligence, and you get excellence on the immediate tasks and roles assigned to these people. Beyond that, a few approached their careers fairly blithely—on a conscious level, at least—relying on sustained, strong performance and a faith that mentors and the overarching system of meritocracy would reward them justly. A few others wanted to view their career in terms of free spirit, intense passions, and lucky breaks. Most, however, did acknowledge some level of conscious planning to their careers. As Carol Bellamy described one of her career transitions after her first job in the Peace Corps, "[M]ost of life is quite considered, but then you have to have a little sprinkle of luck. If it's just running around chasing your tail, that won't work. So I thought about it, certainly."

Therein lies the ambiguity, though—just what kind of planning they did was among the most interesting topics in my conversations with the leaders. They consistently denied doing extremely precise, structured career planning based on preternatural knowledge of the future. When discussing expertise, relationships, and events spanning decades, rather than days, they insisted, quite fairly, on the impossibility of overly detailed planning. Unexpected turns occurred regularly. At best, it's clear that leaders' techniques of career management, combined with outstanding personal qualities like willpower, were less like the precision-guided laser bombs of today than the overwhelming but relatively imprecise munitions of long ago. They aimed with a general awareness of their career goals and vague hopes for hitting the bull's-eye, but not necessarily knowing how close they would come. Hence the focus on broad fundamentals like those described throughout this book.

With that context, and the appropriate caveats, in this section we examine some of the more specific, conscious career moves made by leaders around their first jobs, to understand what young adults today might glean from their elders' examples. In politics, for example, I found that a number of leaders chose their places of residence with at least some eye toward future electoral prospects. Dan Glickman, who served nine terms in Congress before joining the Clinton Cabinet as Secretary of Agriculture, remembered the transition from his first job after law school back to his home state. "I worked for the government as a lawyer for about a year in Washington, after law school. Then I decided to go back to Kansas, where my parents lived. I'm sure one of the reasons why was because I felt like that was a logical place to start a political career, if I was going to be involved in a political career. So then I went back to Kansas and practiced law there, and I was also involved in the family business there. My folks had been very active in the community for a very long time, so we had a pretty well-established name in Wichita, although they had never run for office and were fairly apolitical."

Similarly, Senator Slade Gorton chose to move to Washington after graduating from law school at Columbia for partly political reasons. "I had literally never been in Seattle before I finished law school. And I had picked it out of an atlas and almanac. Between my second and third years of law school, I had a summer internship with Ropes and Gray, which is one of the most prestigious Boston law firms . . . But I had really more on my agenda than just being part of that kind of law firm. I was very interested in politics. And it didn't take much imagination to know what kind of future an impecunious Yankee Republican Protestant had in Boston. [Chuckles] So I turned down Ropes and Gray."

Gorton, now a firmly entrenched member of the statewide political establishment in Washington State, began from scratch. "Seattle law firms didn't customarily interview at Columbia then. I think I may have had one interview. So the day that I received my law degree, I had a one-way bus ticket to Seattle, and about $300 in my pocket, and came out here . . . I knew very, very few people here."

Besides the beauty of the physical environment, Gorton listed three key factors in his decision, all of which related directly to his future ambitions: "First, it was a very open society. So many of the people in my profession and others came from somewhere else, like I did. It wasn't like a Southern or Midwestern city where everyone has grown up there, and their parents have grown up there, at all. The second is that when I came here, very much unlike the present circumstances, even the good downtown business law firms were very small. I think the largest law firm in Seattle had something like thirty lawyers. And San Francisco, by contrast, already had very, very large law firms. That I found extremely attractive—that you'd get to know people much more rapidly. And thirdly, it seemed to be politically open. It was a two-party state, unlike Massachusetts, where I was from, and just as it was easy to get into the profession and meet new people, it seemed to me that it would be easy to become a participant in politics."

For business leaders, too, the dawning of ambition led them to start structuring their activity around specific capabilities they knew they would need. Arrow Electronics CEO Bill Mitchell reached that point in his late twenties, after he left his first job with a company called Raychem and began working at ExxonMobil. "[A]t that point I started to say, 'Hmm, there's this thing called a career that you've got to worry about, and you've got to do some career management and check some boxes . . . ' That became *very* obvious in a place like Exxon where it was a very stable, well-organized—with very prescribed paths that you got from point A to point B. I got on the Exxon track, spent a couple of years in New York, then got transferred down to Baton Rouge, Louisiana, because one of things they said was [that] you couldn't spend all your time in a corporate-planning department. You had to get some operational experience.

"So I went to a refinery and was able to use some of the technical background. At that point in time you became aware in career types of things that there are some boxes you have to check. Maybe you need some international experience, some financial experience. That's about the time that I started to say, 'Hmmm, you've got to think about some of these things.' Still had no thoughts of how far it might go. It was still, do a good job, try to get recognized, enjoy your surroundings and environment."

For AutoZone's Steve Odland, the goal of being CEO was very explicit and guided his actions from early on, when he worked at consumer-foods company Quaker Oats. "I said very early in my career, 'I want to be CEO of a public company, a major public company, someday' . . . When I was in my mid-twenties, I said, 'I love doing this. Someday, I don't know if it's going to be Quaker Oats—which happened to be a $5 billion company—but this is really great. As a CEO, you can make a lot of money, you can get involved in society, you can be an inspirational leader to thousands of people, you can create a lot of shareholder value.'"

Odland described several choices he made very carefully with his longer-term ambitions in mind: the timing of his children's births, for example, and the decision not to go abroad to get experience with international marketing. He professed a very strong awareness of consequences for actions dating back even to his first job and earlier. "Life is like a long hallway, with doors. Some of them are locked, some of them are open, and you have to determine which doors you're going to go through in life, and it's hard for a child or a young person to think through, with any level of maturity, the consequences of going through those doors."

At times, leaders made specific career moves to exploit niches that others may have overlooked. Well before Dan Glickman moved back to Kansas to start his political career, for example, he said, "I think I knew it at a young age, like in my teens, I knew that this was part of it. We lived in a small state, that was—I remember going door to door for candidates in the past, and I worked on some nonpartisan races. I think I saw an opportunity there. I saw an opportunity where I didn't see a lot of very, very aggressive, young, bright people entering the picture, either. In some sense, there was kind of a void."

The same kind of understanding of strengths and weaknesses drove the choice of industry for some leaders. Spartan Stores CEO Craig

Sturken admitted openly that competitive factors weighed in his consideration of his first job. "I worked part-time for that company in high school and college, and I saw the company and the industry as an opportunity for someone who did not have a Harvard MBA. You know what I mean? I just had a plain old college education."

Ron Sargent, the CEO of Staples, went to Kroger for his first job out of business school in part because of his potential edge in the retail industry. "When I was graduating from business school in '79, there were a lot of people going into consulting, a lot of people going into investment banking—maybe that's still true today. Not a lot of people [were] going into retail, maybe a handful in my class, and I thought that would present a great opportunity to apply some of the things I'd learned in business school to a less sophisticated kind of business."

In returning to the story that opened this chapter, we find an instance in which a leader realized that he faced stiff competition in his industry of first choice, but persevered through initial difficulty. John Lithgow had, in his early twenties, left his father's theater in New Jersey, and decided to move to New York City in search of acting jobs. He lived on the Upper West Side, attending numerous casting calls, interviews with directors, and other meetings, all in an attempt to break out and establish his reputation. For two years, he found little success.

"There we were, a family of three, [with] a little baby, in a West End Avenue apartment, and I had no work . . . I even screwed up, because I hadn't registered as a New York resident during my working year [there previously]. I had no unemployment insurance in New York City. I was so naïve—I had no job and no income at all, and I had no money . . . It was two years of practically no acting work, and quite pathetic auditions for commercials and soap operas and regional theaters, just getting nothing!"

On the verge of giving up his quest for acting, Lithgow received an offer to be associate art director for a small theater in Baltimore. It would mean giving up acting, but it would be a steady job in the arts. Somewhat unhappily, he accepted it. Then, two weeks later, an acting offer arrived, and Lithgow's dogged determination for the past two years suddenly paid off.

"I was asked to go to work at Longwharf [Theater] for an entire season. I pulled out of the Baltimore job, took the Longwharf job, and I've always regarded that as one of the major decisions of my life," Lithgow said. "If I had stayed with the Baltimore job, and honored that commitment I'd made, I would certainly have gone on to become a director, and not an actor. It was a tough decision, and I was very guilty, because they were furious in Baltimore . . . It was god-awful. But I just felt that I had not had my acting job yet, apart from working for my dad."

As soon as Lithgow arrived at his new job, though, he realized that he had made the right move for him: "It was thrilling, I have to tell you. I went off to Longwharf, and the first rehearsal with that company, I was so ecstatic. I felt, 'This is the company I want to work with forever.' I was really happy I'd made the choice."

Continuing his narrative, Lithgow then revealed the shocking turn of events that then occurred. "And the second show I did was an American production of a British play called *The Changing Room*, in which I had this very unusual and stunning role—really a one-scene turn in a big ensemble play. That show came to New York, to Broadway, intact . . . It started at Longwharf in September . . . In March, it came to Broadway . . . It opened on, I think, March 7, and on March 25, I won a Tony Award for it—three weeks after my Broadway debut!

"It was incredible. I'd never even pictured myself on Broadway! I imagined myself a journeyman repertory theater actor, very much like the actors that I grew up with, who worked for my dad. This was so thrilling for me . . . There I was, at age 27, and I was a Tony winner. It would always stay with me."

Not every Somebody had a tale of early-career maneuvers that ended as neatly as Lithgow's. Their approaches often bore similar traits, though. As discussed, many leaders achieved visibility within their organizations or fields, developed versatility in their roles, challenged themselves with capacity-stretching jobs, and made thoughtful career choices. But the last habit, thoughtfulness, shouldn't be confused with risk aversion. Leaders didn't always take the preset, obvious, well-beaten path—far from it. As we'll learn in the next chapter, the people I interviewed displayed an impressive flexibility early in their careers, an ability to read situations, react to them, and change paths as opportunity rose or fell.

Don't Let Old Plans Get in the Way of New Opportunities— or Luck

Were there any wild cards? Did leaders ever jump off the beaten track, and not pay their rent or not develop confidence through early successes? Did they ever see an obstacle in their career path and just step aside from it? Did leaders ever allow themselves to get swept up in unplanned fate, luck, or contingency?

The story of Pulitzer Prize winner Paul Salopek's entry seems to come straight out of the pages of a Jack Kerouac novel. The soft-spoken Salopek had gone through a rebellious adolescence, roaming across countries and through a disparate collection of odd jobs, when he stumbled onto the opportunity to rekindle his lifelong love affair with writing. He was in his early twenties and had vague notions about going back to school to become a scientist, when a series of chance experiences changed his mind.

"I was going to go work in the shrimp fisheries in the Gulf, to earn some money and to go stretch my arms and legs a little bit before getting back into academia. And my motorcycle broke down, halfway across the country in the Southwest, in the small town of Roswell, New Mexico. At the time, I think it was about 40,000 people . . . I had about $60 on me, and I thought, 'Well, I'll just stay a week or two, doing odd jobs, enough to buy the parts that I need to repair the bike.' Stayed at a real flophouse hotel and started working during the days at a meat market, cutting meat, and at nights, at a doughnut shop. So I pulled sixteen-hour days, just anxious to move on. I moved out of the hotel when I saw an ad in the local newspaper for a room for rent that was cheaper, and moved in with this old lady who was living alone in a house out among the tumbleweeds, who turned out to have worked as a young woman for the *Saturday Evening Post*.

"So . . . when I got home from the meat market, and in between that job and going out at night to work at the doughnut shop, turning in the graveyard shift, we would talk about stories. We'd talk about writing . . . I'd never really given that up. I was always still just a fanatical reader, and was—I would inhale books. In a certain way, even by then, as much as I'd imbibed the subculture of academia and science, I think I still was structuring the way I looked at the world through words, and through stories, and did not realize how powerful that yen or yearning was, until this woman, this old woman, said, 'Look, you're making minimum wage at these two jobs. Why don't you go bump up and add two dollars an hour and take a job at the local newspaper?' which was then looking for a piece reporter. I had never worked at a newspaper before. She knew sort of my plan to leave as soon as possible, but that didn't deter her from giving me a recommendation.

"So I went there one day, and they hired me on the strength that I had a college degree and started reporting. And the idea then became, 'Well, maybe I'll do this for a month or so. It's something new, another challenge, before moving on to the Gulf.' I never looked back. At that point, I discovered the beauty of, and the power of storytelling. I was good at it, very good at it, and never took a second look back over my shoulder about going back into science."

Salopek's experience—finding his professional destiny after his motorcycle broke down in a dusty New Mexico town—is obviously not a common one. Most of the time, leaders made career choices that optimized their chances for success in an observable, relatively direct way. These decisions weren't always formulaic, because they sometimes cut against the grain of conventional wisdom, but in hindsight they made sense for people who were set on achieving big things. At other times, though, achievers like Salopek actually took the flying leap off into the wild blue yonder. They breathed deeply, thought hard, weighed possibilities and consequences . . . and let go. They opened themselves to chance and didn't let their preconceived plans get in the way of unexpected opportunities or luck.

At some level, I began this project with the suspicion that Fortune 500 CEOs' jobs, government posts, and top prizes in scientific and artistic fields went to the risk-averse, rather than the risk-acceptant—or at least [were] fairly tied to a disciplined track from the beginning of their lives. Again, I thought of these people as sober stewards of the Establishment, rather than swashbuckling risk-takers—but I was at least partly wrong.

Having now done the research, I wouldn't characterize most of the leaders as crazy in their risk acceptance, but they weren't extreme in the other direction, either. Intuitively, it seemed, they grasped the notion that those who take no risk enjoy no reward. Many had stories of jumping off the well-beaten track of things they "should" do, to try fortuitous new possibilities instead.

Leaders are leaders in part because they hone a good sense of when and how to embrace risks. With remarkable regularity, leaders described times in their lives when they left safety and conventionally prescribed paths to try something their background or circumstances or simple desires demanded. In some cases, they viewed it almost as a risk *not* to try something new; in others, they displayed a refreshingly casual openness to new possibilities.

"I've always thought that one should be prepared to take risks and not be confined in some totally predictable way," said Carol Bellamy, today the global head of UNICEF and previously the director of the Peace Corps. "There are extraordinary opportunities out there; look for them, and try to take them! You're going to fail sometimes."

Bellamy herself exemplifies this ethic, as she chose her first post-collegiate job, in the Peace Corps, when she got locked into her college's library one night, and while waiting to get rescued, began reading a pamphlet on the then-new organization. She sped through the entire pamphlet, became fascinated by the notion of joining the Peace Corps, and decided on the spot to defer plans for graduate school in favor of this adventure abroad. Upon returning from the Peace Corps, the pattern continued: Bellamy entered law school in response to ambitions she had hatched while abroad. She then went to Wall Street but was pulled into New York City government by several colleagues, and she ran twice for mayor, unsuccessfully. Her profile had been raised, though, and led to further work on Wall Street, and then the Peace Corps and UNICEF. At each point in her career, Bellamy left herself open to suggestion and new ideas, both from her own curiosity and from others, and has thus woven an unpredictable but rich tapestry of experiences.

Several leaders echoed this idea that many of their best moments in life came from reacting to the unexpected. By remaining open to surprises and letting life unwrap gifts of serendipity, the Somebodies launched new episodes in their lives. For example, chemist Harold Kroto argued for the futility of trying to induce the kind of insight that produces a Nobel Prize. For his own discovery, innate curiosity combined with hard work and a bit of luck.

Kroto said, "I also tell students that if they want to win a Nobel Prize, forget it. Sometimes they just ignore me, and who knows, maybe one of them will be successful. But if they do go for the Prize, they'll look around a priori for a project that they think will have that kind of importance, and they probably won't find it. You just can't force that kind of serendipity to occur. My own discovery [for which he won the Nobel], I would've never thought it'd turn out the way it did. When I started, I most definitely was not thinking I'd win the Nobel for it—it just wasn't in my mind. I explored the problem, and then some serendipity hit . . . I do the sort of science that interests me. I think if you do that, and do the work to the very best of your ability, the serendipity will take care of itself. Things will happen."

As Kroto and others suggest, leaders adapt well to the unexpected twists that life can take. Rather than torture themselves with anxious worry, they relax and surf the waves of change. AutoZone CEO Steve Odland said simply, "One of the other things I've learned in life is to embrace change, and embrace what I call possibilities. Everything in life is a possibility; it's just a matter of what you seize on." Similarly, civil-rights lawyer Morris Dees described a long string of entrepreneurial ventures he had organized as a young man, and when I asked him how he spotted the opportunities, he highlighted the importance of being open to possibilities and seeing the potential inherent in each situation. Not everyone can do that skillfully—Dees acknowledged, "I guess everybody looks at a situation and sees different things."

In many cases, leaders absorbed career risk in a fairly thoughtful way, understanding that short-term sacrifice might lead to long-term gain. This relates to some of the themes in the last chapter, around career moves, but it's interesting to focus specifically on the openness leaders showed to uncertain outcomes. They sacrificed short-term comfort, in other words, even knowing that they wouldn't necessarily enjoy a long-term payoff.

Ron Sargent of Staples had an instructive story. After graduating from Harvard Business School, he spent his first ten years of work at Kroger, steadily climbing the ranks of the grocery giant, as it grew from $25 billion in annual revenue to $45 billion. Yet, when a headhunter came calling about a young office-supplies company, he listened to the pitch. "This thing at Staples kind of intrigued me. It was a company that wasn't making any money, was only a couple of years old at the time . . . Was just kind of an idea that was just getting started . . . [N]ot only was it a new company, but a new industry. It was a little bit the Wild West, but after looking at it, I said, 'This is one of those things where I could be really happy [if] I joined this start-up thing, or I could be unemployed in a year, with this wonderful career at Kroger behind me."

Sargent's ability to accept risks rested on a clear-eyed assessment of his personal situation, confidence in his own abilities, and frankly, acceptance of risk with the possibility of reward. "Kroger was a big company, and it was a company that I was going to get increasingly more responsibility and bigger impact, but . . . it was a little like shoving an elephant around. You didn't see the quick, daily impact I thought you'd see in this start-up thing. I knew it was a risk but at the time, I wasn't married, didn't have any kids, and I had enough confidence that if it didn't work out, I'd do something else."

Sargent's story was similar to those of a number of leaders who took roundabout paths with their first jobs. This came as an intriguing surprise. With the great ambitions harbored by these people, what compelled them to step sideways or even backward from conventionally attractive options? Tying back to my own personal experiences, this is one of the trickiest decisions that young people face. Hard-won gains early in your career may seem laughably small later in the future, when perspective changes, but they're hard to give up in the beginning.

For some leaders, these decisions to forego opportunities or to take the proverbial path less traveled had to do with personal desires—a weighting of private factors over conventional career wisdom and an impressive patience. Curt Culver took his first job in Madison, Wisconsin, which he favored over another offer in Chicago that would've paid twice as much right away. "I wanted to stay in Madison, frankly. I was offered a job in banking coming out of graduate school that paid twice as much as the job I took at Verix, but the job was in Chicago, and I was more interested in being in Madison, thinking economics would take care of themselves, if I do a good job. Also, it was a smaller company in Madison, and one that I thought I could make a difference. Although I've got to tell you at the time, I don't think I thought of that."

At other times, a competing professional passion pulled leaders away from seemingly exciting opportunities. Bill Bradley ran for Senate in 1978, but he passed on a potential run for a Congressional seat four years earlier, in 1974, when he was still playing in the NBA. It was difficult to pass. "I was in the middle of writing *Life on the Run*. I felt I had something to say that probably no one else would say, because no one else could have the experience and actually write it, put it down. And so I passed on that experience in '74. When I did it, I thought . . . I'd lost my opportunity to be a senator. That's where I wanted to be, because I always thought you ran for the House, take four years, then run for the Senate. But I felt I was following my deeper impulse, my true self, by staying playing and writing. So that's what I did."

Similarly, music critic Lloyd Schwartz, who went on to win a Pulitzer Prize writing for the *Boston Phoenix*, said, "I think one of the most crucial turning points in my whole life was turning down my first job offer." Having grown up in New York City and then attending Queens College in Manhattan, Schwartz's long-time ambition was to return to the city with an academic job. As he finished his graduate studies in English at Harvard, in Boston, he received an offer to teach at well-respected Fairleigh Dickinson, which is located in New Jersey. As Schwartz recalled, "Most people who teach at Fairleigh Dickinson live in New York City, live in Manhattan. So here was my chance, my big chance to return to New York City. And I turned it down. People thought I was crazy to do that, mainly because . . . to land a tenure-track job in a very good school in the vicinity of greater New York was a real coup."

Schwartz took the so-called "crazy" choice because he had fallen in love with the arts community in Boston. He had become editor of a small literary magazine, which gave him an outlet for poetry that he enjoyed writing, and he had also crossed paths with a talented troupe of actors that loosely included at various times Stockard Channing, John Lithgow, Tommy Lee Jones, and James Woods. His passion for these different activities made the job at Fairleigh Dickinson impossible, in his mind, to take.

In some instances, also, leaders didn't necessarily stray from their chosen career path, but they made significant sacrifices in other professional arenas, choices that might have looked counterintuitive to others. For example, Honolulu Mayor Jeremy Harris had begun working in the 1970s in Hawaii both as an academic, teaching at a local community college, and also in politics, on the Kauai County Council. A political opponent sensed opportunity from a potential conflict of interest and drove a change in the law, which prevented full-time university employees—institutions funded by the state—from holding political office at the same time. Harris remembered, "The Board of Regents passed the rule change, known as the 'Harris Amendment' "—because of its obvious targeting of him—"and everyone expected me to step down from the Council. Instead, I quit my teaching job and devoted myself to the part-time Council job, which paid just $16,000 per year."

The examples of Schwartz, Harris, and others illustrate an important point: while society's Somebodies did enjoy interesting opportunities and to some degree good luck, they also made decisions that were *right for them,* if not in line with conventional wisdom, at critical crossroads. Like the Somebodies profiled here, many young people feel the pull to take the so-called right job, as Schwartz did with the faculty position at Fairleigh Dickinson, or to maximize their salaries, as Harris did with his teaching job. Few, however, have the foresight and strength to weigh the options in such situations, think through whether they're ready and eager to make the sacrifice, and chase the opportunities Fate has presented. Knowing just when to shirk conventional wisdom often distinguishes the great from the mediocre, as we will see again in the following section.

Discipline in Listening to Inner Voices and Intuitions, and Following Dreams

When we talked, Pulitzer Prize–winning cartoonist Mike Luckovich described to me how he ignored the typical post-college path with his own career, when his target was a first job in the cartooning industry. Denied in his first few attempts to break in with a respectable paper, he forged ahead. "It was very simple, almost primitive. 'I have to keep drawing and drawing and drawing in case a job opens up, and when that job opens up, I'm going to send them my stuff.' My first job [which I finally got] at the *Greenville News*, I applied to them, and sent cartoons, but also what I did is, every few days, I would send them fresh batches of cartoons, so they could see, as the news was occurring that week, what I was working on. It's just this drive I had . . . I just couldn't have taken failure. I got frustrated that it wasn't happening quicker, but I just knew this was what I had to do to achieve that goal of getting a job."

Felix Zandman, the CEO of Vishay Intertechnology, faced a somewhat similar career path, forsaking his first job at an industrial company to pursue his dream. In his case, Zandman wanted the chance to start a company around a personal invention, an industrial technology, he'd created in his spare time. "I knew internally that I had to do it. So I quit. I quit a very important job. I was making a fortune at that time—director of research, big company, New York Stock Exchange company. And I went on my own! So it just was an internal feeling that I invented something important, and I felt that I had to do it."

I expressed fascination at this ability to hear his inner voice and to heed it. I asked Zandman, a Holocaust survivor who lost his entire family in World War II, and who had survived himself only by hiding from the Nazis under the house of a benevolent Polish family, how he had understood his deeper impulse. He replied simply, "I always felt internally, when I felt I had to do it, I did it. During the war, you know, it was the same way. Sometimes . . . the decision to go to the left or the right was life or death. And I kind of knew by intuition which way to go. I escaped several times from a concentration camp—several times that happened to me."

Sometimes a dream or vision need not be an immediate call to action, but more a whisper in the ear, something to keep in the background. Senator Chuck Hagel described such an experience when he first moved to Washington, D.C., in April 1971, as a twenty-four-year-old. He was completely new to Washington, a young man looking to find work and learn more about the government, but he had a midday reverie.

"The Sunday that I arrived in Washington, in April, and it was 1971, I checked into a hotel, and I walked around the Capitol that afternoon. It was one of those bucolic, perfect spring afternoons. I was just completely consumed with the Capitol, and the beauty, and the grandeur, and the history, and it . . . was just in every pore of my being.

"I walked across the street from the Capitol, and walked up the steps of the Russell Senate Office Building, where I am now. It is one of the closest [buildings] to the Capitol. And as I walked up the steps, of course the doors were locked, but I sat down on the steps, and I looked back at the Capitol. I don't know how long I sat there, probably a good half hour, just all by myself, very quiet, looking at the Capitol, thinking about this country—and thinking that maybe someday I could come back here. Maybe someday—and I was trying to get a job. I didn't have any grand plans for myself. But I thought, the privilege of being a United States Senator would just be something I couldn't imagine. But I thought about it a little bit.

"Every day, when I walk up and down those steps [now]—out that door, down those steps, coming back when I vote in the Capitol, back up those steps—I think of 1971. That beautiful April Sunday afternoon, sitting there on those very steps, looking at the Capitol."

For Hagel and many other leaders, the capacity to internalize such experiences and react to them was critical. Whether through inner intuitions or more obvious external stimuli, leaders learned from their experiences—and adjusted their behavior. They frequently found success by adjusting to new, unexpected paths, and leaving stale, old ones.

Work Hard, Work Smart, and Work Some More

How much substance lies behind the facade? When the klieg lights go off, audiences dissipate, and the din of incoming calls, faxes, and e-mails subside, what makes up these leaders? Were they thinkers, or doers? Were they the hardest workers or the smartest? Or both?

The voice came like a jolt of electricity through the telephone. I was interviewing entrepreneur and civil-rights lawyer Morris Dees on his experiences building the Southern Poverty Law Center, and when we got to the topic of "book learnin'" versus direct experience in the world, Dees's opinions were clear. His intensity jumped a couple of notches as he compared his own work experiences out of college with some of the more comfortable, affluent students he sees entering the job market now.

"[Y]oung people today, shoot, they're not hungry. They got some idea that they're going to devote their life to some business career, but they ain't suffered a day in their life. They went to Columbia or Harvard or Yale, MIT or someplace—not that they're not smart—but at least my motivation was not—I did not even dream, when I was doing all those things, that I would end up selling a company for what today would be $25 to $30 million bucks. I had no idea. I didn't even think about it.

"It was just one thing leading to another, and I think along the way, you have to have enough sense to ferret out the wheat from the chaff."

To separate the proverbial wheat from chaff, Dees advised real-world effort and experimentation over Platonic philosophizing. "I find this with so many people. They have an idea to do something, but they just talk about it to everybody. The difference, I think, with an entrepreneur is getting an idea and doing something about it. Clearly, you fail with some of them, but if you haven't failed, you haven't tried many."

Dees's beliefs were perhaps more intense but not altogether different from those of many leaders I interviewed. These people expressed appreciation for formal education, but even more for actual, hands-on experience. I found most (though not quite all) leaders to be overwhelmingly oriented to action—to working hard, working smart, and then working some more. Quite simply, these were rarely lazy or complacent people.

Owens-Minor CEO Gil Minor described his first job after business school, when he went to work integrating a recent acquisition, rather humorously called Acme Candy Company, into his larger parent company. Fresh off his MBA, Minor was surprised by what he found: "All the fancy footwork that goes with an MBA—the application of those principles and all those things I learned didn't . . . help me one bit. What I did learn from the Acme Candy Company was about people; about how people work with other people. And how someone who doesn't know about a business has to learn about the business. It was the most humbling and most wonderful experience of my life, as it turned out. I was down there for two years doing that."

For Minor and many other leaders, professional expertise and personal wisdom were cast in the crucible of real-world experience and hard work. "I didn't help that business for all my MBA training. What I learned about was people," Minor said. Asked what kinds of things he learned about people, Minor went on, "Well, the people that do the work, the . . . hardcore workers who are coming to work every day, who are earning the wage, who care about their families and all that—they put in the time, and they're the heart and soul of the company. I don't care how big the company is, or how small it is. The people who do the work are the ones who know what the problems are, they know how to solve the problems. Generally, all managers need to do is ask them, and they'll tell us. That's the bridge of communications.

"But I went down there as management, but I found out very quickly that that status wasn't ever going to help me. If I'd kept on saying, 'I'm management; you guys will do it the way I want you to do it,' we would've gone under water so fast that it would've made your head turn. But I just loved these people. I saw what they were doing, so I just rolled my sleeves up and worked with them. It was a great experience, with the families and everything."

Nadine Strossen, President of the American Civil Liberties Union (ACLU), shared Minor's appreciation for real-world experience over formal titles and honors. Strossen has enjoyed a long and distinguished legal career by any Establishment standard: she worked early in her career at the distinguished firm of Sullivan and Cromwell, authored a number of well-received papers and books, and served as a tenured faculty member at New York Law School, in addition to her work for groups like the ACLU. Still, when she attended Harvard Law School, she chafed under the routine.

"I hated everything about law school except the credential," she said with a soft laugh. "I wanted to get out and get the experience. I loved *being* a lawyer, but not going to school to become one. It was very surprising to me when I decided later to join the faculty here [at New York Law School]. The academic environment wasn't something I really liked when I was younger."

As we saw earlier with the ROCKET framework, of course, not all leaders chose their hard-won experience. Some were pushed into situations, by expedience or otherwise, that demanded action and difficult effort. But the crucial point was that they responded to these opportunities and worked extremely hard at pursuing them. Former Texas Governor Ann Richards started as a schoolteacher, raising a young family with her husband, when she found herself pushed by some political allies to run for a county commissioner's seat. She had worked on behalf of other candidates, in particular female candidates, but the outspoken feminist-in-the-making hadn't expected to be thrust into the political arena herself: "I just had to do it, though, because the guy who was in there [in office] before me was just *so* bad. I don't think I had a grand plan, but once I started, I ran [for the office] hard."

In the rest of this chapter, we'll explore several different aspects of leaders' orientation to action: their decisiveness after making crossroads decisions, their sheer relentlessness in terms of work hours, their commitment not just to hard work but smart work, and finally, their delivery of quality output. Competence and long hours weren't necessarily sexy, but they formed key buttresses of many Somebodies' careers.

Once Decisions Are Made, Decisive Action

Put simply, without action, the most elaborate strategies and best-laid plans produce no change. Many of society's Somebodies grasped that presciently. They showed an impressive ability to marshal decisive action after big decisions. They might wrestle with uncertainty at key crossroads early in their careers, but once those decision points are passed, leaders described an impressive capacity to throw overwhelming resources and attention—everything they had, essentially—at the challenge to be conquered.

In 1978, when Bill Bradley left the Knicks and pro basketball and decided to run for the Senate seat in New Jersey, he committed himself fully to the effort. He had hesitated before, and ultimately passed on a potential run for Congress in 1974, but four years later, he went in with a clear head and heart. "I was running against a so-called icon, a Republican, Clifford Case. And the most important thing when you decide to run for politics is you have to have your internals right. If you want to do it, your internals are right, and things will turn out all right, even if you win or lose. I knew that was what I wanted to do more than anything else at that time in my life."

Bradley entered the Senate race in 1978 without knowing how he would do, and took his bearings early in the contest. "[L]o and behold, we took a poll and it showed that while Clifford Case was very well known in Washington, people in New Jersey felt like he had forgotten them. So I felt I really had a chance against Clifford Case—nobody else did—but someone else thought he had a chance against Clifford Case [also]. A young conservative, and he beat him in the primary. So I ended up running against Jeff Bell in the general election, in New Jersey against a far-right candidate at that time, and did well. I got 54 percent and was elected.

"It never would've happened had I been testing the waters," Bradley said. "I decided this was where I wanted to make the jump, this was what I wanted to do and be, and therefore I was going to try to do it. That and everything after that flowed from that decision. If I'd said, 'Gee, do I talk to 100 politicians, "You think I have a chance to beat Clifford Case?" 'No!' You know, they'd say no." Bradley describes in his memoir, *Time Past, Time Present,* how he put in eighteen-hour days on the campaign trails and debated his opponent nearly two dozen times, moving with a vigor that exceeded even that of other first-time candidates.

Paul Fireman similarly described the depth of his commitment after leaving his first job, at a family-run olive oil company, to found Reebok. Fireman had been restless for some time and was looking for an opportunity that would allow him to switch careers, when he stumbled on to Reebok at a trade show. The initial products and brand had been created by a small United Kingdom–based company—and Fireman plunged in.

"I was picking a subject matter that I thought had potential, and I liked the focus. I could see the little business had gotten started, but there was a lot more that could be done. I had an intense focus, not so much to become wealthy, but to set up a productive business. It became obsessive, where you don't see the negatives. Probably one you wouldn't see done by too many people today. But all I wanted to do was succeed. There were constant naysayers. And it was tough going. After about a year, I was going backwards, and I needed to make payroll. I needed to get over the hump, as they say. But as I said, it wasn't really a thought [to give up]. I didn't create it so much out of practicality." Fireman had three children then under the age of six, but he would not be deterred. Essentially, failure was not an option—he had committed himself decisively to this path and needed to make it succeed. There was no back-up plan.

Owens-Minor CEO Gil Minor had no timetables or exit plans in mind when he started his first job, either. Because it was a company his own family had started, he knew he would be making his career there. That outlook produced a deep commitment from the beginning. "I just volunteered for things and worked a few extra hours. I was going to devote my life to it, and felt like that then, and still do today. So this is the ground floor. This is the foundation of what you're going to do the rest of your life, so do it right," Minor remembered.

Wendy Kopp sounded a similar note in her summary of her first job, founding Teach for America. She was fresh out of Princeton, with little in the way of real-world experience or savvy in establishing new non-profit organizations, but she had determination and a strong bias for action. Once committed, she said, "I had no real option but to fully throw myself in, be absolutely relentless, and pick myself up after mistakes with a commitment to learn from them. I think in many ways this way of operating has probably been the key to my success."

Sheer Relentlessness and Dogged Work Ethic

William Snyder showed up for work at the *Dallas Morning News* in 1983 as a twenty-three-year-old self-styled "hotshot." He'd had a good couple of years as a young photographer for the *Miami Herald*. He'd traveled the country, won a few small prizes for his work, and begun to build a reputation within his profession. He felt on top of his game.

Looking back now, he cringes in knowing how much he didn't know.

Snyder was just beginning the professional odyssey that would eventually win him three Pulitzer Prizes. Through some bruising political battles in the newsroom, to the difficulties of balancing work and personal life, to the usual ups and downs that confront all creative people doing intense work, Snyder persevered. The kind of toughness Snyder developed in doing his work was apparent in his sometimes blunt speech.

"Most people in my business . . . obviously the intelligence is there. But the thing that separates people who are successful from people who either are not successful or are not that successful, is just the ability and the desire to work that much harder, and to make appropriate sacrifices. I sacrificed a lot of things."

Bringing in an analogy to sports, Snyder said, "I mean, you see guys with huge amounts of potential, and they just don't work very hard! You know, then you see someone like Larry Bird, who just worked on every aspect of his game throughout his entire career, or Michael Jordan—I mean, Michael Jordan sucked from medium- to long-range when he first came in. He wasn't a very good defender, and he worked and he worked on those aspects of his game. That's why he was as good as he was. He had that little bit. You know, he made sacrifices throughout his life, because there were hours and hours and hours he spent on the court. Yeah, he had God-given ability, but a lot of them do, and he did something with it.

"I think you know, just somewhere along the line, that clicked for me. I was willing to . . . stay at a scene five minutes longer than my competition. I was willing to push the deadlines as far as I possibly could, to get the picture better."

There was no magic to the work ethic that many leaders described as central to their success. By itself, a regimen of long hours didn't suffice, but it served as basic ante to the poker games of professional life. Repeatedly, across a wide variety of fields, personal circumstances, and other variables, leaders stressed the importance of consistent effort and strong performance in basic tasks.

Like Bill Bradley, for example, politicians Dan Glickman and Slade Gorton described spotting opportunities and then pursuing them with extraordinary fervor. They both remembered their initial campaigns for public office as contests of energy. They outworked their opponents with long hours of phone calling, doorbell ringing, and handshaking. Glickman's first job was as an intern in the D.C. office of a senator from Colorado, where he got an early glimpse of some of the behind-the-scenes drudgery required of public servants. As he recalled, "I worked for him doing, oh, pretty much intern-type work, but I did it for two and a half years. I used to come in some mornings very early in the morning, open the office, open the mail, sometimes answer mail, and so that was all part of this same kind of experience being in Washington."

Undeterred, Glickman then moved back to his home state of Kansas and launched an ambitious campaign for the Wichita school board. The job provided media exposure in his home district and allowed him to do substantive work on the key issue of education. He visited every school in the district, more than 100 in total, and worked extensively to build ties with the media, despite the fact that the school board position was not even paid. This set the stage for Glickman's first campaign for Congress.

"When I ultimately ran for Congress, I was thirty-one, and I ran against a guy who was—I think he was sixty-four at the time. A very nice man, he was an incumbent Republican Congressman. His name was Garner E. Shriver, and he'd been in Congress for sixteen years, but he was the antithesis of me as a personality. He was lethargic, and quiet . . . and I was energetic, and frenetic, and I ran that kind of a race, and it was in the post-Watergate era, and it just worked out perfectly for me. It was a nonideological race. The race was based on style, and who was going to fight more for the district, and not based on philosophy at all . . . I spent a lot of time going door to door. I walked about 50,000 homes. I mean I spent a year doing nothing else, and the whole campaign was based on energy and vitality, and just, it worked!"

Senator Slade Gorton had a similar story. His opening came in 1958 when a seat in the Washington State legislature became available. Gorton had patiently laid the groundwork for a political career throughout his twenties, and a redistricting battle had created an opportune situation in a district with favorable political inclinations and no incumbent. Gorton recounted, "I didn't know anybody in the district, but campaigning then was basically going from door to door . . . [W]e got a handful of friends, and we went door to door more than anyone else in a big race. There were ten candidates, and I ended up winning."

Oscar- and Emmy-winning director David Frankel responded quickly when I asked him toward the end of our interview about the keys to his success with *Sex and the City, Band of Brothers,* and other productions on which he's worked. "When people ask me how to make it in Hollywood, I tell them, you've got to have stamina—just the ability to keep going, keep working, taking feedback and making your stuff better . . . I mean, it's not easy. You can tell when you produce something and there are forced smiles. People don't want to hurt your feelings, but you know when you've got to make it better." Frankel certainly put in his time—he joined an entertainment company called Telepictures for five years after graduating from college and juggled his day job while writing scripts at night, searching for his big break.

Like other leaders in his field, Frankel understood the particularly tantalizing nature of success in the hit-or-miss entertainment industry. "A friend once told me that everyone's got one script inside of them— the ability to write at least one good screenplay," Frankel said. "And some people have two. But the people with three, they're the ones that'll go the distance. They're the ones that just have that stamina and that sheer drive that enables them to be successful . . . And the thing about Hollywood is, there are barriers to entry that, ah, can seem slim, but are at the same time overwhelming. You just need to write that first good thing and get it in the hands of the right person who'll believe in you and can help you. But of course that's not easy . . . If you can get your foot in the door, it'll crack wide open. People are so hungry for talent all the time. But to get that foot in, you've got to create something really good, and get noticed. And creating that one good thing, that's where all the work, all the hours come in."

Leaders from every discipline were the opposite of slackers, often offering colorful descriptions of the long hours they endured. Matt Espe, the CEO of IKON Office Solutions, began his career at General Electric and took his work ethic to what he now recognizes as humorous extremes. As he explained, "I have always worked hard and applied myself to tackle every challenge and opportunity. Especially early on, I always tried to be the first in the office by at least half an hour. In fact, this caused an interesting unspoken rivalry between me and another highly motivated colleague during my first assignment. I would end up getting to the office at 5:30 just to ensure that I was the first one there!"

James DeGraffenreidt, CEO of Washington Gas, told me that even today, he typically sleeps only five hours a night, devouring three daily newspapers and checking his e-mail before leaving for work—at 6 A.M. ACLU President Nadine Strossen explained for her own night-owl habits: "I just have a high level of energy. Back then, I didn't usually need more than four hours of sleep a night. It's not quite like that now, but even today, I often wake up without an alarm clock. My eyes open, and . . . I'm thinking of what I need to do."

Gander Mountain CEO Mark Baker spoke of how he often hears the morning paper arrive, and described how even during a sleep-deprived period early in his career, he took flying lessons for fun.

Such around-the-clock intensity surfaced in story after story. Before joining USAA Insurance in the business world, Jim Middleton's first job was in the Air Force, and at the age of twenty-six, he was transferred to a staff job in the Pentagon. Looking back on that time, he said, "Those were some of the busiest, I would say *the* busiest—the Pentagon years were unquestionably the most stressful, the busiest—you were literally on call all the time—weekends, nights, everything, and we worked a lot of that. Those kinds of routines. It was really hard having, the first ten years, having much of a life other than just, go work." Middleton was learning tremendously valuable lessons about organizational behavior and decision-making during that time, some of which we'll explore later, but to gain the insight, he needed to put in the time.

Smart Work—Recognizing Key Moments, and Seizing Initiative

Of course, simply toiling away without thinking about the ends can waste effort. As Clinton Cabinet member Donna Shalala said, "People hire you for your judgment, not just for your stamina." Besides working hard, the Somebodies I interviewed provided several examples of how they work smart, recognizing key moments and rising to the challenge, or seizing initiative in situations of ambiguity.

Going back to photographer William Snyder, we hear the story of a key photo shoot he did in Romania, which led to one of his Pulitzer Prizes. In the situation, working smart meant preparing for an opportunity and taking full advantage of it. "[W]hat I did not realize when I attacked this story—and I really mean attacked this story—I was very, very well prepared before I got on the plane. It wasn't just a matter of going to Romania and taking some pictures. It was making phone calls, sending faxes, researching where I wanted to go. I only had about two and a half weeks, and finding the right people, talking to people who had been there and worked on similar stories—where do I go? Who do I talk to? . . . Working smart is also very, very important. If you're not prepared, if you don't know exactly what you're going after, then all of that hard work is not that important."

To Snyder, working smart also meant not faltering in the key moments—the critical moment at which earlier work culminated. "[W]hat happens in our business a lot is that you have to go across the country, or somewhere, and you have to take a photograph of some big important person, say a CEO or an NFL star quarterback or something. And you literally have thirty seconds to a minute to actually shoot them. The logistics and everything of getting to that point to take those pictures is just mind-boggling to a lot of people.

"What I find that a lot of people do, and what I've done in the past is, you know, you go through all these machinations to get there, and when you get that thirty to forty-five seconds, you're so relieved that everything has gone right up to that point that you lose focus for that minute and a half. You come back, and you look at the pictures, and they're boring at best. And it's because you did all this other hard work, but you really weren't smart about it once you got there. . . . [Y]ou have a stand-in, you found the perfect location, you put in lights, maybe you've added some other things, you've got a cool idea, you've got assistants standing around, this, that, and the other—they usher the person in, bang bang bang bang bang, you're so excited, and you come back, and it's nothing. That's another aspect of working smart—being able to take a deep breath under pressure."

In certain environments, working smart can mean overt use of rhetorical tools like logic. Jim Middleton indicated that he strove for transparent logic in his decision-making, as a young military officer in the Pentagon, because in addition to improving the quality of his decisions, it also reduced the politicization inherent in his job. He explained, "[W]henever I came down on the side of an issue, I tried to do it based on a logic stream. I tried to make it, no matter who looked at it, this is how you'd logically end up on it. I was always careful not to get too hooked up with—you know, Middleton is making it because Joe Smith is pulling him along."

Paul Norris took a similarly fact-based approach with a situation familiar to many people starting their careers: salary negotiations. When Norris received his first salary offer for a job he held during business school, he wasn't ungrateful necessarily, but he followed up in a structured way. "They offered me a salary, which I thought was a little low, and so I did some research, and I found out that the salary they offered me was about, oh, 6 to 7 percent lower, I guess, so it wasn't huge—than the average salary for people with MBAs and technical degrees. So I went in and said, 'Look, I really want to work here, I really like you guys, blah blah blah, but here's my research that says your salary offer is a little low.' So they gave me the average! . . . [T]o me, it was not a confrontation . . . It's just that, 'I don't know if you were aware. I did some checking'—and I think the Conference Board was the basis for the information so, you know, it was a credible source . . ."

For Chip Pitts, President of Amnesty International USA, hard work and smart work went hand in hand. His day job as a corporate lawyer helped his after-hours involvement with a wide range of humanitarian causes, and vice versa. Pitts became a partner in one of the world's largest law firms, Baker and McKenzie, by billing a huge number of hours to his clients, but he also attracted new clients who respected what he was doing for groups like Amnesty International.

"At my peak, [managing the workload] was a real challenge," Pitts said. "One year I billed 2,500 hours, and at the same time handled something like 300 pro bono cases. Now, of course I had people who helped me, but still, it was a constant grind. It was nice when some of my [corporate] clients heard about what I was doing on the pro bono side and supported me in those pursuits."

Somewhat similar to Pitts, Kirk Thompson, CEO of JB Hunt, viewed hard work and smart work as integral parts of a whole. Thompson believed that neither is sufficient without the other. "I think it's a combination recipe . . . [Y]ou can have a mediocre game plan and still succeed. It's why sometimes less talented teams beat more talented teams. It's because of execution and will. It's all wrapped up in there together. Sometimes you can out-execute people even if they've got a better deal going. And even better people, and you just out-execute them, and part of that is that will. So it's a very big part of it. But I don't think you can overcome a poor plan, or a poor product, or a poor formula completely."

Related to Thompson's idea is the notion of honesty with oneself; that is, you can work as hard as you want, but you need to be realistic about the ultimate potential of your output and how hard you're actually working. Cartoonist Mike Luckovich expressed frustration with the unrealistic expectations that he sometimes encounters in young people looking to enter the field. "When it comes to something like cartooning, you have to be able to look at what you're doing and look at what's out there, established cartoonists, and think, 'Am I doing as well or better than what I'm seeing out there?' So you have to be realistic with yourself. I often have young people come into my office, and they've done a couple of crappy drawings of Snoopy, and they think—they ask me, 'Am I good enough to be a cartoonist?' Well . . . you're not putting out much effort. You really have to put out the effort, and you have to be honest with yourself."

Another key aspect of working smart, echoed by many leaders, is seizing initiative—in other words, working hard at tasks assigned to you, but also at self-created tasks that solve pressing problems. IKON CEO Matt Espe advised simply, "display initiative and a lot of energy. Listen to those around you and look for things that are broken. Then, come up with a solution, go to the boss, and get it done."

Journalist Bill Dietrich remembered having to fight for one of his early award-winning efforts to write about the deinstitutionalization of mental health patients across the country. "I heard about this and could see that it was going to be a major change. Some of the big mental hospitals were going to close, and there were going to be more mentally disabled people walking the streets, out in society. I said, 'Hey, we should do a bunch of stories about this.' The city editor said, 'Well, this paper doesn't do big stories. We've never done a series, we're never going to do a series, so forget it. Go and cover the council meeting instead.'

"So what I had to do was do a lot of the reporting and writing on that on my own time, then bring it to the paper as a fait accompli, and say, 'See, isn't this interesting?' And with it, they said, 'Well, yeah, it is interesting, and since you already did it, we'll run it.' It won some awards, and got me recognition, and that's sort of how you advance yourself in the newspaper industry . . . I also learned at that first job that you can't wait for people to invite you to do things. You have to take some initiative and push yourself. That's what I've also tried to do subsequently in my career."

Photographer William Snyder told a similar story of doing guerrilla work to pursue his interests, for one of the assignments that actually won him a Pulitzer. His editor specifically rejected Snyder's proposal. "So I said, 'Do you mind if I freelance it?' So he said, 'Yeah, sure.' So I don't remember if I was clear, but I freelanced it back to the newspaper, to our Sunday magazine and a couple of other things, and just pieced it together. I had a little money saved away, and I took vacation time, and some of this money, and the money I was getting from the paper, and from another wire service to cover their elections, and went and did it on my own, and then proceeded to get as many pictures published in the newspaper as I could, in just about any avenue I could.

"I would win contests with the stuff. That's the other way you get your name out there, in my business, is win contests and peddle your pictures around. It's far easier now, because of the Internet. You can create an entire Web site and put up your stuff and figure out ways to drive people to it, but this is 1990—the late '80s and early '90s—and you really couldn't do that . . . I continued to do stories on my own for a couple years after that. It was just the best way to do it."

Sometimes initative is needed to create the first (or early) job. When Chuck Hagel went to Washington, D.C., in April 1971 as a complete newcomer to the city, he was hustling like any other young person today might. "I'd never been here. I didn't know anybody. I went door to door for a week and must've left 100 résumés, and that's how I got to Washington. So I did take the initiative. You can't in most cases, I believe, just hang back and say, 'Well, the opportunities will find me.' To a certain extent, that's true, but you still have to step up a little bit and grab life a little."

Similarly, Eric Freedman, now a professor at Michigan State University and formerly a Pulitzer Prize–winning journalist, urged young people to stand out through initiative. In his own first job, as an intern to Charles Rangel in the U.S. House of Representatives, Freedman gained extra responsibilities by recognizing a need and meeting it. "Seize the initiative. Volunteer, repeatedly if necessary, to do more than is asked. Exceed expectations. Be curious. Many, perhaps most, interns wait to be told what to do and settle too often for menial—or at least routine—tasks, instead of actively seeking to do more. When I was an intern, Rangel—as a junior member of the House—was on some committees that didn't interest him—one dealt with NASA and space, the other with public works. I volunteered to monitor some hearings he couldn't attend and to prepare a statement for him to read about a public works project near his district. When our caseworker quit, I immediately asked my boss if I could fill in."

Excellence in the Task at Hand

Like decisiveness after crossroads decisions, hard work, and smart work, a final habit, doing the best possible work in the task at hand, came up spontaneously with an impressive number of the people I interviewed. While these high-achieving stars certainly understood longer-term ambitions and career maneuvering, a key point they often underscored was the need not to trip on the first and most basic step in one's professional journey: the one right in front of you. This relates to the book's third lesson, about paying one's rent first, but it deserves a bit more attention here.

Bill Ruckelshaus tied his perspective from service in two Presidential Cabinets and a variety of corporate assignments back to his first job after law school. "The mistake that more people make than not is when they get one job, or one assignment, they immediately begin thinking about, 'What's my next step?' And they forget that if they don't do the job they have in a superior way, there won't be any next step. That's certainly the advice I've given my children when they were quite young. I really believe it. I've had several experiences in my own life where you're given something to do which . . . you may think at the time is not fully up to the capabilities you could bring to something bigger—but if you just pay attention to the assignment you've got, and do it to the absolute best of your ability, people just pile assignments on you! They just give you more and more to do.

"Let me give you an example: I had an early experience in the Indiana attorney general's office, when I first got out of law school. I came back to Indiana and was practicing with my brother and my father, practicing law, and at the same time was working in the Indiana attorney general's office. You were able then under the rules to have an outside practice as well as the government practice, as long as you didn't have a conflict of interest. I went into the attorney general's office with maybe fifteen other people. The national highway system was being created at the time, and they needed a lot of young lawyers to try these condemnation cases, where they were building highways and taking property from people . . . I wasn't working on highway cases, but most of them went over to this separate office where they were working on these highway cases, and they developed this level of cynicism about what they were doing, and about the attorney general—just a poisonous atmosphere!

"I was lucky enough to be assigned to the state board of health and have a normal relationship with the attorney general's office, and I kept asking for more things to do, and boy, they just kept piling them on me. Three years later, I was the chief counsel in the Indiana attorney general's office, and there were about eighty-five lawyers reporting to me. A lot of that was luck—other guys left. People that were much more qualified than me to do that work by virtue of their experience weren't around, so he gave me the assignment. These other guys I came in with were still trying highway cases, just as they had when they had come in. My sense of it was, they just didn't pay enough attention to the job they had, and concentrate on doing it really well—or they would've gotten more assignments."

CEO Jim Middleton understood that this kind of focus on one's immediate job requires belief in the meritocratic system: "I really had faith that people would look and say, 'This guy's got some capability.' The thing that upset me the most would be to watch guys and their whole focus, and nine-tenths of their effort was on trying to look good so they could go to some other job somewhere. I always thought, that is really goofy. Why don't they do a really good job in what they're in, and somebody will figure that out? It worked for me . . . I never really ever, even in all the jobs I've had here in the company, I've never lobbied for, 'I want this one, or I want that one' . . . I felt like if what I got asked to do was clean coffee cups every day, then somebody figured out that that's what the most important thing to do was."

To encourage the habit of excelling in your present role, Senator Chuck Hagel encouraged young people to recognize that the seeds of opportunity often lay right at their feet. "You have to be careful that you don't paralyze yourself by planning too far out. I've seen too many people make too many mistakes tripping over what's in front of them now, by reaching too far, and thinking too much about future and consequences. I've always believed that you should enjoy as much as you can what you're doing today, and if you do enjoy it, you believe you're doing something that's worthy, and you're doing it the best you can, the future always takes care of itself . . . Does that mean every job is perfect? No, there's no job that's perfect. But just focus in a way that you need to focus, and do the best job you can today, and you will have plenty of opportunities."

Hagel continued, "Life connects. The thing that you're doing at that time puts you in a certain universe—that's a universe of contacts, of relationships, of awareness, of knowledge. That always comes together in a way that presents opportunity." Hagel's words referenced his own experience in his twenties. Once he returned from his war service in Vietnam, he worked in local media in his home state of Nebraska, then moved on to to work in a Nebraska Congressman's office in Washington, D.C., then from there into the government affairs division of Firestone Tires, back into the government as part of the Veteran's Administration under President Reagan, back home to Nebraska to co-found a wireless telephone business, and so on. At each juncture, knowledge that Hagel developed and that people he met were helped set the stage for the next episode in his career.

Paul Norris of WR Grace used an approach that sounded counter to the others, but may have produced the same effect. He said, "I think that the key there was to always try and do whatever you did in the way the person who was at the next level would do it. It was always to try and think and act the way you should think and act if you were at the next level. In other words, if I was an analyst, and my boss was a business-development manager, try to understand how he would think and act. And learn and conduct myself in a similar fashion." Norris thus seemed to advocate thinking and acting *beyond* one's current role—but listening to him further, you hear his basic point that you do that to develop greater effectiveness in your current role. He continued, "I think that's the way you develop the fastest—you have to convince people to have confidence in you. I think that's an important thing, to watch how other people are behaving and make sure that your behavior is consistent with that if that's what you want to do."

Not surprisingly, working hard, working smart, and working well comprised a major component of leaders' success. The strength and persistence that enabled leaders to do these things sprang in many ways from within themselves. That said, competition with others brought out another dimension of leaders' motivation, too. We turn to this now with our next lesson.

Be Productively Competitive

Do leaders strive for some abstract, objective standard of greatness, or do they measure themselves more directly in comparison to peers and competitors? Do they ever get caught up in the smarmy games that people play in the trenches of organizational behavior? Or do they somehow manage to stay above the fray?

Talking with Nobel Prize winner Harold Kroto can feel like running alongside a sprinter. The British-born scientist speaks rapidly and changes direction often, perhaps befitting his wide and diverse interests. Though a chemist by training, he still maintains an active interest in graphic design and the visual arts. As we talked about his early career, Kroto digressed several times to describe his unfulfilled interests in graphic design and even pointed me to a website that displays his work. A single-minded focus on science alone can be "boring," he told me with a soft sigh.

Yet make no mistake: In his scientific research, Kroto fully appreciates the commitment and drive needed to be successful at the highest levels. He became markedly more animated as he described how even those with outstanding training and talent need to labor to keep up with peers in the highest echelons of his field. "Research itself is a full-time occupation. You're competing [with] people who're working twenty-four hours a day, people who are fantastically clever. To do that, you've got to be very, very dedicated yourself, and work fifty-six hours a day, or whatever. I don't do things unless I can do them as best as I can."

When Kroto made the discovery that ultimately led to his Nobel Prize, a strong competitive streak in his personality gave him the fuel to follow all the way through with the difficult work needed. It sounds odd, but it's important: with competition from an external source, fellow scientists pushed Kroto to reach inside himself and fulfill his own innate potential as a researcher. He had been spending long hours in his lab just before his big discovery and was near physical exhaustion, but Kroto insisted on seeing the data firsthand so he could make the best possible inferences.

He recounted: "With the discovery [which led to the Nobel Prize], I got a phone call saying, 'Do you want to come [and observe the experiment firsthand], or just see the results of the experiment?' I jumped on a plane and was there the next day! That was very important. If you suggest an experiment, as I did, and you don't go and do it, you can't take ownership of the idea as easily. There are follow-up questions to be asked, other work to be done, and if you're just looking at someone else's results, it's hard to have the same kind of insight."

As with Professor Kroto, across almost all the leaders interviewed, I found a strong taste for being the best in their given fields, a taste that translated into raw drive. It sometimes lurked near the surface of leaders' consciousness, sometimes not, but it was almost always present.

For Daniel Burnham, who eventually became CEO of Raytheon, a streak of latent competitiveness he may not even have recognized in himself surfaced in one fateful moment less than two years into his career, and lit the proverbial motivational fire. He had just joined a team of analysts at a then–Fortune 500 company called Carborundum.

Burnham said, "I was only there [at my job] for nine months, twelve months, and I was walking over to eat lunch with three or four analysts at my level. I remember this very clearly. They tended to hire from good schools, most of these guys were from Harvard, Dartmouth business schools. I remember this Harvard guy talking about how good it was to have excess, ah, funds, and I was thinking, 'Hey, I don't have any extra money!' You've got to understand, we were really on a tight budget in those days. Well, I found out that this guy made $100/month more than I did. I remember this day like it was yesterday. I felt like I was every bit as good as this guy, and by God, it was like turning a switch in me. 'Goddammit, I'm every good as this fellow.' I really remember thinking that! I became very competitive at that point.

"Up until then, I think I was a little more passive and took what came to me, but I realized then that maybe I needed to be more aggressive. I remember this all, that day, like it was yesterday. Now, understand, I don't think that was the biggest of moments! [Chuckles] I think I could've gotten my motivation in a better way, and I think I was a little more provincial in my thinking then. But boy, I do remember it like it was yesterday!"

For other leaders, like Curt Culver of MGIC, competitiveness has provided a lifelong wellspring of motivation. Culver's older brother is himself CEO of a good-sized enterprise, a family-run restaurant business, and though the two maintain very strong, healthy relations, Culver chuckled as he pointed to the friendly competitiveness as a spur. "[H]e's two years older, but I was always the better athlete, a real good golfer, as I mentioned. I played competitive golf, and he's a good golfer, too. I think because of that, he got called my name a lot, even though he was two years older, and that always made for a competitive situation. Even today, with the restaurants, [which my brother runs and] which I'm a part owner of, so I'm a very happy shareholder, there's still a—you've got to be competitive." (Interestingly, in September 2004, Culver's golfing prowess pulled him ahead not just of his brother, but of all Fortune 500 and S&P 500 CEOs—*Golf Digest* magazine named him its top CEO golfer, over Sun's Scott McNealy.)

The competitiveness appeared in all different personalities. Kirk Thompson, CEO of JB Hunt, was generally good-natured and relaxed throughout my interview with him. When I asked him what differentiated him as he began his first job, though, his drive surfaced. He said, "I think this is true for most people who end up being CEO or coach or upper management of any kind—you've got that competitive drive. When you were in school . . . it wasn't always okay for me to make an A. I wanted to make the highest grade in the class. That kind of idea. I think there's that drive, that ambition, that competitive nature, whatever you want to call it. The will to succeed. I hate to lose." I asked Thompson where he had originally gotten the drive, and he professed not to know, but he did say it had been lifelong. "A little kid, yeah. I just hate to lose, so you just keep putting out the effort, because be-danged if I'm going to lose."

A slight variant on raw competitiveness that appeared in leaders' stories was the desire for independence from others' sometimes-arbitrary whims. Leaders were often independent-minded and spirited people, and not surprisingly, they disliked having their professional fortunes flutter around at the direction of some random boss or organization. They described the drive for self-determination in competitive terms.

For example, Deborah Blum, today a journalism professor and earlier a Pulitzer Prize–winning reporter, found that allowing others to dictate her writing assignments left her dissatisfied. She had moved through three different newspaper jobs after college, taking on a variety of reporting beats and winning several local-level awards, but she came to a crossroads in her late twenties. Her passion was writing about science, but in the daily to-and-fro of her job, she wasn't able to pursue quality stories. She would walk into the newsroom each day, and before she could sit down at her desk to reflect on potential story ideas, her editor would have an assignment waiting for her.

"I realized that I was really going to have to say, 'What do I really want to write about here?' Or I would rattle like a bead in a box, around these different beats, indefinitely, with editors picking my path. I didn't want that. I wanted to pick my own path." Until Blum seized control of her career from the direction of others, she felt frustrated. For her, the answer lay in returning to graduate school, to focus on her passion and to reset her career direction with a new job after getting her master's degree.

Civil-rights lawyer Morris Dees also needed a strong sense of self-possession to conquer some of the challenges he faced in starting the Southern Poverty Law Center. He recounts in his autobiography, *A Season for Justice,* how he faced death threats and other scary moments in tackling rogue organizations like the Ku Klux Klan in court. As we discussed some of Dees's life experiences that had helped forge the steel in his personality, he hearkened back to his early entrepreneurial work, and how it had been driven at its core by a desire for self-determination. As a sharecropper's son, he had witnessed firsthand the difficulties of living under a landlord's direction.

Dees told me, "[T]he bottom line was, I wanted to buy land, because I wanted to farm. My whole goal was to purchase land. My dad didn't own any land. He ended up getting a little 110-acre plot. I guess in the South, people are kind of measured by the land they own . . . So I guess I wanted the land, but I wanted the independence. Because see, we had always rented, we had always been sharecroppers, and we moved from farm to farm. If you re-read that personal section of my book, you'll see that motivation. I wanted nobody to be able to tell me that I couldn't live there. Nobody could move me off. That's what happens if you're a tenant farmer. You're at the mercy of the landowner. If he had some kid that decided that he wants to farm, the kid got the farm, and off you go. That happened to us on two separate occasions, so finally my daddy got a place and built a house. So I guess I was doing all that work to acquire some assets."

In response to these feelings, Dees worked at a huge array of self-created ventures at different times in his Alabama boyhood: raising chickens and pigs, selling scrap tires, recycling sawmill pulp as planting mulch, driving a gravel track, surveying land for the state government, and serving as a legislative page in the state capitol. By the time he graduated from high school, despite growing up in a basically poor, rural community, Dees told me that he had compiled $10,000 (in 1950s dollars) in his bank account.

In a very different time and place, but with the same tones, Staples CEO Ron Sargent talked of how competitiveness influenced decisions early in his business career. Sargent has a low-key personality, easy to laugh and to establish a bond in meetings with strangers. His ambition was clear, however, even as he took his first job after business school at Kroger's grocery company. "I'd looked at retail as an opportunity to run a business one day. I looked at consulting or investment banking as opportunities to advise people who run businesses. I guess my makeup was always, 'How do I lead this thing?' "

Jim Hagedorn, the CEO of Scotts Company, used an analogy to describe himself similarly. Referring to his riding hobby in high school, he remembered, "I had this horse who could not stand to have anyone in front of him. You know what I mean? He would just—you would just walk up alongside of him, and he'd take off running. I love that attitude. That's kind of the way I am. I don't like to be in the pack. I want to be out front. And I think I'm pretty good at that. I like leading."

Hagedorn went on, "I think that if I stopped working, I would still have to run something. If I didn't run something, I think I'd go bananas and six months later, people would look at you and say, 'He looks like Saddam Hussein. What happened?' [Laughs] You know? When they dug him out of that hole, he looked a bit disheveled. I don't want to be Saddam Hussein, crawling out of some hole, where people say, 'That's Jim Hagedorn? No way!'"

Not all Somebodies expressed themselves as colorfully as Hagedorn, but the point stood nonetheless: leaders had mental compasses pointing up. They weren't necessarily egotistical in a smarmy, off-putting way, but they channeled competitive feelings. They used their pride, in other words, to push themselves to do better and to reach higher.

Find the Social Animal Within

How did leaders relate to others? When they were Nobodies playing anonymously in the sandbox of life with the rest of us, were the future Somebodies bossy, friendly, or lonely? Which social skills were most important? Why were they important? Most important: How did leaders who weren't naturally outgoing build the social sides of their personalities?

It was immediately apparent in talking to successful leaders across different fields that they are almost all social animals. By this I mean they benefited strongly from relationships, whether they were naturally introverted or extroverted. Obviously, not all leaders are extroverted social butterflies. Some people make it to the top of their fields while maintaining quiet, reserved personalities. In a few cases, it was precisely the cerebral detachment in their personalities that enabled leaders to succeed where others faltered. In most situations, though, leaders were outgoing people who engaged others easily and often. Certainly in business, government, and nonprofit organizations, it takes people with substantial social skills to climb the ranks of leadership. Even achievers in presumably more solitary fields, however, like science and arts and entertainment, benefited strongly from an ability to teach others, to be taught, to communicate clearly, and to establish relationships of trust and caring.

This chapter explores several aspects of leaders' social interactions. It begins by describing the benefits leaders enjoyed as a result of their strong social ties. It then analyzes four ways in which leaders built those ties: showing a common touch with normal people; practicing reciprocity in relationships; working on their communications skills; and finally, showing political savvy within the organizations in which they worked. In closing, we'll focus on the context in which those social skills grew: within formal organizations and institutions, and informal clubs.

At their core, leaders typically held a fundamentally positive view of humanity. Cynical eye-rolling aside, these people believed in humankind's essential goodness. Their good cheer and enjoyment of relationships was genuine, not a disguise to mask secretly misanthropic feelings. Mickey Kantor, who served as President Bill Clinton's campaign chairman and drew across a wide and powerful network of friends to be one of his top fund-raisers in 1992 and 1996, was characteristically sunny when asked how he cultivated mentors during his career. "There are too many to count," Kantor said. "I mean, at every stage, people have just been very generous to me, starting with my parents, and going through teachers, different people I've worked with, and so on. I've been a very fortunate person."

Scientist Rich Roberts said something very similar. Reflecting on the potentially destructive competitiveness that can emerge among researchers striving for major breakthroughs, Roberts indicated his reliance on a version of the Golden Rule: "If you yourself are prepared to be cooperative and helpful, it brings out the best in other people . . . Some people try to take advantage of it, but for the most part, it brings out the best in other people."

These stories were not unusual. I heard similar things in a number of interviews I conducted with leaders of widely varying personalities. It provoked me to wonder whether these Somebodies' generous dispositions and positive energy were a cause or an effect of good treatment from others. In other words: What came first? Did they develop a positive outlook because others treated them well, or did they treat others well because of a positive outlook? My conclusion after finishing this book's research is that the answer lies somewhere in the middle: Leaders often have friendly, even magnetic, personalities, which increases the number of positive interactions they have with others, and those experiences reinforce their sociable natures in an ever-repeating virtuous cycle.

When I commented on this dynamic to Staples CEO Ron Sargent, and mentioned how impressively accessible many of my interviewees had been, Sargent replied, "I think you'll find that they're just normal folks, and in most cases, they're kind of like everyone else. There's probably a connection between the common touch and how they've been so successful." Certainly, leaders' likability and empathy came out in my interviews with people like Sargent, Mickey Kantor, or John Lithgow, each of whom had an unusually avuncular personality and an ability to put me immediately at ease. We'll delve further into this quality later in the chapter.

Beyond helping grease the wheels of social interaction, though, the ability to make positive connections with peers had tangible career benefits for these leaders. At the most basic level, Bill Mitchell of Arrow Electronics cited two separate instances in his career when personal contacts in his network introduced him to job opportunities about which he otherwise wouldn't have known. Robert Peiser, today the CEO of Imperial Sugar, took his first job with airline company TWA and commented on the value of networking from that point forward. In a very deliberate strategy, Peiser used his peer relationships at other companies as a hedge against the risk of job turnover. As he explained, "I have spent a significant amount of time networking, building relationships all over the country with people in many different fields and industries. This stems from my being in very high-risk industries where career shifts were likely. I have advised many young people that contacts in life are extremely important both for one's particular job performance and one's career management."

Leaders also understood early in their careers that social activity goes beyond individual relationships with specific people. Broader reputation is particularly important early in a career, when you're trying to win assignments and get the chance to demonstrate your potential. Paul Norris, CEO of WR Grace and Company, explained, "[E]arly on, I think it's about learning, and growing, and developing, and having people developing confidence in your fundamental capabilities."

Once you gain others' confidence, good things follow. In place of the traditional notion of an "old boys' network," former Cabinet Secretary Donna Shalala, now the President of the University of Miami, postulated a rough "overlap theory" to explain her and others' ability to get confirmed to high-level government appointments. If I know someone who knows you, the theory goes, I'm more likely to feel reassured of your trustworthiness, your quality, and your approachability.

Shalala described her experiences with Presidents Carter and Clinton: "I mean, when Presidents of the United States were calling around [to learn] who could fill out their administrations, you know, it's the overlap theory. Lots of people that they knew knew us . . . If you look at where people come from, there are probably four members of the Clinton Cabinet who were on the same boards [of different companies, charities, and other organizations] together. I mean, I knew 90 percent of the Clinton Cabinet. The only people I didn't know were Carol Browner and Janet Reno. Everybody else, I had met at some other point in my career."

Many of the leaders I interviewed had similar stories of friendship with other Somebodies—experiences shared, difficult times commiserated over, contacts introduced, jobs offered, and so on. Just to illustrate a few:

- Carol Bellamy and Donna Shalala met at a party in New York in 1972. Both were former Peace Corps volunteers but didn't know each other previously. Bellamy has gone on to head the Peace Corps and UNICEF, while Shalala served in two Presidential administrations and now is President of the University of Miami. Throughout their long and varied careers, the two women have maintained a strong friendship, sharing both good times and bad.
- Morris Dees's college business partner, Millard Fuller, with whom Dees started the direct-mail business that they later sold for millions, went on to found Habitat for Humanity, which stands alongside the Southern Poverty Law Center as one of the nation's leading progressive nonprofits. Put another way: Of all the Southern boys who met at the University of Alabama in the early 1960s and struck up friendships, it was these two who created a business together, became independently wealthy from it,

then moved on to their good works in the nonprofit sector. One has crippled the Ku Klux Klan, while the other has partnered with former President Jimmy Carter to fight the scourge of homelessness. As Dees put it with a chuckle, "How 'bout that?"

- Dan Evans and Slade Gorton met as young men and began rebuilding the Washington State Republican Party together in the 1950s. Evans, of course, went on to become Governor and Senator, and Gorton a Senator.

How much does the so-called overlap theory explain? How much success sprang from mutual familiarity, and how much from more extended interactions? Conducting the research for this book, it became apparent that certain webs of relationships are more successful than others. Was it merely coincidence that future leaders socialized together when they were young, anonymous Nobodies, or did they do specific things to boost each other? A number of interviews suggested that Somebodies' socializing with each other was far from coincidental.

Perhaps not surprisingly, I found that leaders often drew intellectual sustenance from their peers. Many cited specific instances in which others' intervention had aided their progress at a critical juncture in their early careers. Bill Phillips, for example, drew significant stimulation and support from his lab group at MIT, where he did his graduate studies. He remembered, "It was a fairly tight-knit group, and so when there were new research results, and things were going well or badly in the lab, everybody knew it, because everyone got together, ate lunch together, we were always talking about things." In fact, the fateful shift in research physics then occurring, from more old-fashioned atomic physics and a newer branch, based on research with tunable lasers, became apparent to Phillips through his interactions with his lab group. "[J]ust seeing what was going on . . . I thought this was something I wanted to do. Not that what I was doing wasn't interesting, but I could see that this was something new. And I thought it's better to go with the new than the old."

Similarly, in a different department at MIT, the Center for Cancer Research, Phillip Sharp benefited early in his career from having laboratory space near a core of other talented young researchers. The director of the Center, Salvador Luria, drew Sharp's retrospective appreciation in his Nobel Prize autobiography. "Salva was a visionary who protected his young faculty [including Sharp] from unnecessary interruptions, thus allowing their research programs to flourish in an ideal scientific environment. He was also a role model for how a scientist could shape and lead a community."

The intellectual fruits of good collaboration appeared in many Nobel Prize winners' narratives. Daniel Kahneman, today a professor of psychology at Princeton, described a rich partnership he built at Hebrew University with Amos Tversky, himself an accomplished scholar.

In his Nobel Prize autobiography, Kahneman wrote, "The experience was magical . . . Amos was often described by people who knew him as the smartest person they knew. He was also very funny . . . I have probably shared more than half of the laughs in my life with Amos. And we were not just having fun . . . With him, movement was always forward. Progress might be slow, but each of the myriad successive drafts that we produced was an improvement—this was not something I could take for granted when working on my own."

In summary, then, leaders drew a variety of benefits from peer relationships as their careers started. Whether it was intellectual stimulation, job referrals, competitive inspiration, or other social support, society's Somebodies often depended heavily on relationships. This dependence may explain why so many of the leaders understood the importance of a cooperative ethic and persuasion, as opposed to forced or demanded acquiescence from others. As has been well chronicled in other leadership studies, the command-and-control model of organizational behavior seemed largely outdated for the current generation of Somebodies.

WR Grace's Paul Norris explained one early epiphany that shaped his social skills. "One of the things I learned was how to manage all the relationships inside the business. One of the things I can remember is going out to a plant. I was a marketing manager, and in that company, you would be responsible for commercial development of new product opportunities, in your product line. I went to a pretty good-sized plant, I was talking to the plant manager, and I wanted them to make an experimental run of a new product. It became clear to me that I didn't have the authority to make him do this. I knew this, but that crystallized in my mind that you had to sell your ideas throughout the company regardless of how much authority you had. People gave you as much authority as they thought you deserved. The rest of my career, I felt that if somebody reported to me and I had the formal authority to get them to do something, if I had to use that authority, I failed. In other words, if I couldn't convince somebody on the logic of what I wanted to do, and the need to do what I wanted to do, and I had to resort to the order, then I failed. So I still feel that way today."

Naturally, the next question to arise was how leaders performed their relationship magic. What specific tactics or techniques did they use to get along with allies and enemies alike? The research did not uncover any revolutionary new ideas on this topic, but underscored the importance of four traditional social virtues: the common touch, reciprocity, communications skills, and political savvy.

The Common Touch, or Likability

The leaders whom I interviewed weren't mandarins, or idols on the proverbial mountaintop removed from common circulation. To the contrary, they typically came off as remarkably humble, approachable, and friendly. A good example was Daniel Burnham, the former CEO of Raytheon, who offered his philosophy: "The people you're working with may not have graduate degrees, but I look at them, and I see my mother, my cousins, my friends growing up. I think they're regular people. I treat them all the same. Not because I'm trying to manipulate them, but because that's the way to lead: you treat people right, treat them fairly, and most of them will respond and push toward goals."

Burnham continued: "Humor is a good way to relate to people, too. I want people with real personalities, and real lives, who can joke with me. I love it when people treat me with disrespect. I mean, you should've seen Larry [Bossidy, the legendary CEO of Allied Signal]. With Larry, *no one* ever doubted who the boss was, but we used to joke with each other all the time. And he'd tell us to go stuff it in the you-know-where [chuckles] . . . It all helped build a spirit of camaraderie."

Being able to relate to the rank-and-file translated directly into business value in some cases. As Paul Fireman shepherded Reebok's growth from a start-up to the Fortune 500, he never had to deal with organized labor, due to his personalized approach. Fireman said, "I've never had a union. People know I care about them. The one year [I spent] in the warehouse [at the beginning of my career] gave me some good experience. It showed people that I didn't hold myself above them, and it also helped me understand things from their perspective, a little bit. They could see that after I changed jobs, I still treated them well. That's really important."

For politicians like Dan Glickman, the ability to engage people and relate to them is even more essential. It drives one's ability to gain and hold political power. He explained, "People don't like hotshots around them. They won't vote for hotshots . . . They vote for people who they think are like them . . . [T]hey like people that are likeable. That's a big thing." Generalizing from politics, though, Glickman pointed out the way people give the proverbial benefit of the doubt to those they like. "[I]n any line of work, people have to like you. If they don't like you, you can't get past first base. This is the great trait that both Bill Clinton and George [W.] Bush had. They are both fundamentally fairly likable people . . . I'm just talking about—there are a million other examples . . . If people like you, they're willing to open their door to you, they're willing to forgive you, they're willing to be accessible to you."

One part of this likability is humility, which helped some leaders understand that they can learn lessons even from unexpected sources. AutoZone CEO Steve Odland said, "Our company has 50,000 people, and I'm the CEO, and I know I'm no smarter than many of the people in this company. We have wonderful people in this company at all levels, and they're at the level that they're at for different reasons. They're either at different points in their career, or they don't want the responsibility or they're not great people—they're great technicians, but they're not great people-people—whatever it is, there's a lot of reasons, but regardless of their level, we can learn from all of them. The other thing I learned is, these same people—you've got a low-level manager in the company [for example], but they're the leader of their church, or they're teaching Sunday school, or they're off coaching Little League ball—they are leaders! Even CEOs who have outsized egos and think they're the smartest and most brilliant people in the whole world—don't look to other CEOs to learn, look down in the organization. Look at real people doing real things, and that's where the real lessons are."

Significant amounts of management literature testify to the real value of engaging others in meaningful relationships to unlock their potential. CEO Kirk Thompson gave color to that idea as he explained his team-oriented approach in the early 1980s, as he helped build up JB Hunt. "[A]n organization that's growing and has aspirations is one that requires a team effort. I think that is probably one of the basic tenets that anybody has to know. I've seen companies, large companies, that are pretty autocratic, and when that autocratic CEO or founder leaves, in a lot of cases, they've surrounded themselves with people who . . . tend to be dependent on that autocratic style. When the kingpin's gone . . . it just kind of collapses. I know of a company right now that I think that's in that mold, and it's a large Fortune 100 company that just looks to me like, the guy that was there, the previous CEO, was very autocratic and crack-the-whip kind of guy, and they tend to surround themselves with weaker people, and that's just my own personal opinion, as opposed to a collaborative, participatory style of management.

"My favorite Yogi Berra saying—and of course, you know, he slaughters the English language—but he's got such great philosophy, and one of them's a saying I've used over the years: 'If you ain't got no animals, you ain't hardly got no circus.' It's so true. You can have the best game plan in the world, good products or services, but if you don't have people that can execute and carry it out, then you're just, you're lacking. You want—you may succeed, but you won't get to the pinnacle unless you involve lots of people, particularly in a large organization."

Oscar and Emmy winner David Frankel spoke in much the same way about his work as a film director. Whenever he entered a new set to work with actors, camera crew, and editors, Frankel focused on leveraging the full talents of his team. "I think I have what you'd call a highly collaborative working style," Frankel began. "I always go in assuming that the other people on the project know more about their parts of it than I do, just by default, just by nature of their focus. I don't think the dictatorial style—where one person, the director or whoever, thinks he knows what's right all the time—I don't think that works very well . . . If you look at the great directors, like Spielberg or Scorsese, they're always learning. They're always bringing in the best talent, the best ideas from all over the world, and looking to incorporate that into their work, to get better. It's a way of leading that I think works better."

Reciprocity

It seems basic, but another important point raised by the leaders in their discussion of peer relationships was the proverbial Golden Rule, treating others as you'd want to be treated. The principle of reciprocity underlies many of the comments I heard. "In the business world, it's all about negotiation," said Ron Sargent, CEO of Staples. "And you do things for people, you do favors for people, you help other people in some way or another, and that tends to come back to you in a kind of good karma sort of way. I think the hard-charging business person, kind of a shark, always on the offensive—'take, take, take'—I think does not speak well for his or her longevity."

Sargent sounded themes similar to the earlier ones on reputation. "To me, it's very important to develop and nurture the reputation of somebody that can be tough, but they're very fair, they're very genuine, they're not a politicker, they don't stab people in the back. People have long memories, and your reputation and your integrity are those key things in life that you want to protect." As I listened to these words from Sargent, I realized how deeply he holds reciprocity among his core values. I also wondered whether my generational peers maintain the same priorities in their impatient rush to achieve big things in small amounts of time.

There was no question where the Somebodies stood on the issue of reciprocity. Like Sargent, Spartan Stores CEO Craig Sturken viewed leadership through the prism of reciprocity. Both in following and leading others, he'd felt the dynamic in the play. "As I went through my own career, I saw how I'd always go the extra mile for people that I admired, for people that I respected, for people that treated me fair, for people that rewarded me financially. I'd go the extra mile for them. I came to the conclusion that if I would do that, then others would do that."

Communications Skills

A third key interpersonal skill cultivated and practiced by leaders, and one of the more obvious ones, is their ability to communicate fluidly. Whether in verbal or written form, society's Somebodies tended to express their thoughts effectively. In certain fields, like business or government, the need for strong communications skills stands out particularly clearly. Jim Middleton, CEO of USAA Insurance, has become increasingly aware of communications as he entered the ranks of senior management. "I speak, oh my God, four-five-six times a week to groups of ten to groups of three-four-five hundred, and it just makes a huge difference when you can connect with people, eye to eye."

Interestingly, though, public speaking didn't come naturally to Middleton and all other leaders. Leadership is not limited to gregarious extroverts, after all. Introverts learn to adapt, not always through their own will. Middleton remembered valuable experiences he'd had even before taking his first job. "I had a speech coach in high school. I had to take speech in high school—back then, it was required. I hated public speaking. It scared me and made me sick. He forced me to be on the debate team—and this speech team typically won State in Indiana. He had really good speech teams. I just thought, you know, I really hate this. We had Saturday things, and I wanted to go and play basketball, and he worked schedules around so I could play basketball and still be on the speech team. But when I look back, him making me do that is probably what has made the difference in my whole career." Middleton stated flatly, "If I had to walk away with any one thing that's made a difference in my whole career, both careers, it's probably communications." The most important quality he possessed as a leader, in other words, was a learned skill.

Former Congressman and Cabinet Secretary Dan Glickman also urged young people to work overtly on their communications skills for careers in politics. "If you don't have strengths in certain areas that you need to have, then you need to go out and get schooled on them. Like if you're fearful of public speaking, you can't be in politics without doing that," Glickman said. Fellow elected official Jeremy Harris, Mayor of Honolulu, stressed the importance in his job to "communicating complex ideas and issues simply and understandably."

The impact of clear communications goes beyond traditionally interactive work, as well. Scientist Bill Phillips felt that his undergraduate training at a small liberal arts college helped him as he entered the ranks of top-shelf physicists. "I was better prepared to communicate, both in writing and orally, than were a lot of my contemporaries, because I came from a liberal arts college where that was something that was highly valued." At first, Phillips's comments puzzled me. Though I realized the stereotype was not exact, my presumption was that science rests on objective truths; facts almost independent of the need for communication. Simply by uncovering the reality of the way our universe is organized, after all, these leaders in scientific fields do their jobs, don't they? Not really.

"Actually, you can have the best idea in the world, but if you don't get your idea out there, and help peers incorporate your idea into their own work, you're in a spot of trouble [as a scientist]," said Harold Kroto, himself a Nobel Prize–winning chemist who has strong personal interests in another communications-related field, graphic arts. Kroto's and Phillips's comments provoked further reflection. I realized that even in less obviously social fields like science, leaders don't escape the interpersonal functions common in other professions, such as the need to focus people's attentions on important priorities, to build acceptance for one's ideas, and generally to persuade.

Savvy with Organizational Behavior and Politics

As backdrop to this discussion of interpersonal skills, it's important to note that good communications, reciprocity, and personability did not occur in a vacuum. They were not raw qualities whose simple application led automatically to success on the scale these Somebodies achieved it. A fourth element of interpersonal relationships that many leaders grasped either consciously or instinctively was political savvy. This catchall phrase included a number of qualities in different contexts: sensitivity to others' feelings, awareness of which people held key sway over particular decisions; and intuition about which points would be most persuasive to different stakeholders in a given argument. Put simply, leaders understood how to move others. In addition to the fundamentals of communications, reciprocity, and personability, leaders had a good understanding of when each of these would be most helpful, and adjusted their approach accordingly.

Certainly, the skills needed to navigate and manage a large organization of people, in business, government, and nonprofits, at least, differed from those needed to create new ventures. Bill Ruckelshaus, formerly in the Presidential Cabinet and corporate boardrooms, and now involved with an early-stage venture capital firm in Seattle, offered perspective on how many of the entrepreneurs he now sees differ from the people who often ascend and manage large organizations.

"In their ability to access, or to take the idea of either a product or service that they're trying to sell, and turn that into a business—that skill is not necessarily the same skill at all of moving in laterally or just moving up through a big institution and make that function well. People find themselves in situations where they've been very successful in starting up a new company and developing an idea, and they find all of a sudden they've got all these people problems—all these things they don't want to—they may not be any good at dealing with, or they may not want to deal with. It's just not something that gets them excited."

What are those organizational skills? Some of it has to do with expectations and communications management across multiple layers of an organization. Reflecting on his experiences with his first job in the military, CEO Jim Middleton offered his view that "if you're in that chain-of-command routine, which you're going to be, regardless of where you are, you have to be pretty aware of how you handle the upstream and sideways-type communications, whatever you're working on. I used to work on an issue, and I'd say, 'If people are going to come out of the woodwork on this, what will concern them, and who will be concerned with it?' And in my mind, I used to answer those questions, and then I'd go to those people and say, 'Here's what I'm thinking about,' so that when it got all done, I knew what their response would be, when I went in to talk my piece of it. It kind of was mechanical, but on the other hand, it really was looking at each thing I did in relation to sidewards and upwards, where do I need to get this thing greased?"

Middleton went on to share how his savvy helped him navigate one particular situation early in his first job, when he was still in his twenties. A potentially volatile issue ended up giving him exposure to senior decision-makers, while also keeping him in good stead with his immediate superiors.

"I happened to be involved in the early '70s in base closures—and there's a really hard, hard thing to be involved. The guy I worked for, and the guy he worked for, they didn't want to be involved in it, because they knew that if something went wrong, they knew just enough to be dangerous, so they always gave me . . . straight-in [access] to the two-star [general], who was our boss, and then his boss, who was a three-star [general]. I worked directly with them as a captain, and really nobody else got involved, because they didn't want the responsibility of having to deal with the news agencies and all that other business.

"Well, they didn't want anything to do with it, but I had to make sure they knew about it, because you never want to get your boss totally cut out of the pattern on what's going on, from a lot of standpoints. So that tended to work pretty well for me. I would play it from the standpoint of, 'Here's what I'm going to talk to him about, here's how I see it, and if there's any pieces of that that you want input on, I'd be happy to take it,' kind of thing. They pretty much said, 'No, you've got it. Keep moving.' They really didn't want it on their plate, but they were appreciative of the fact that I kept them up to speed on what was going on."

Again, though, as with communications skills, not all of this came instinctively to the Somebodies whom I interviewed. April Saul, a Pulitzer Prize–winning photographer, said matter of factly, "[T]here is a lot of office politics. There always is. I think that was my rudest awakening in the work world, to be honest with you. It wasn't just about who has the best idea or who's working the hardest. I mean, things just weren't based on merit, you know? You had to schmooze the right person."

Strikingly, in a pattern that appeared with numerous leaders I interviewed, Saul adapted to this reality, uncomfortable though she was initially. She saw how her working environment was structured, came to understand how opportunities fell to some and not others, and changed her behavior accordingly. After working at her first job at the *Baltimore Sun* for a couple of years, she became interested in moving to the *Philadelphia Inquirer*. Initially rebuffed in her attempt to get a job there, she pushed forward aggressively. Saul remembered, "My philosophy was always if you called someone and they said they didn't have an opening, when you were looking around for jobs and for where you wanted to be, you would say, 'That's fine. But someday you may be [looking for someone], so let's get to know each other.' So I think actually I made a connection by just coming up [to Philadelphia] and visiting. And, you know, I went to a party that the photographers were at, and got to know the boss, and you know, when there was a job opening, he called me."

Relationship to Institutions

As I conducted the research for this book and learned about Somebodies' social tendencies, I became interested in the bottom-line effect: How did leaders relate to formal institutions and organizations, and to informal clubs? In an era of the so-called "free-agent nation"[3] after all,

---

3. Phrase originated by Daniel H. Pink, *Free Agent Nation*. Warner Books, 2001.

many twenty- and thirtysomethings are more suspicious of institutions than our generational predecessors. This isn't to overdramatize the situation—many young people still rely on companies, government bodies, nonprofits, universities, hospitals, and other institutions, for employment and otherwise. Still, the end of concepts like lifetime employment and the growth of job mobility have undeniably changed the texture of young Americans' interactions with institutions. What did this mean for the Somebodies I interviewed, many of whom invested themselves in institutions, grew up in them, and now guide them?

To begin, it should be noted that not all leaders embraced institutions wholeheartedly. Writers like Tom Hallman and Paul Salopek endured professional odysseys beyond their first jobs as they struggled to understand which institution in society would best fit their talents and career aims. They had social skills, in other words, but they didn't channel them toward climbing organizational ladders. Even a consummate business and government insider like Bill Ruckelshaus, who saw the workings of power at the highest levels as a Presidential Cabinet member and corporate director, avoided entering business early in his career precisely because he disliked certain aspects of organizational life. Ruckelshaus said, "[Large corporations] just struck me as places I really didn't want to work. I didn't want to get myself caught in that kind of cookie cutter." Asked further about what he disliked about such organizations, Ruckelshaus talked about how "you came in at the starting level and tried to beat your way up, and how many ways there were to sidetrack you on the way to the top." In short, he saw many of the same disadvantages to the professional rat race that today's young people do.

At the same time, however, Ruckelshaus never lost his respect for institutions generally. While he avoided business, he maintained a strong interest in government, and he noted matter-of-factly that in his first job after law school at the Indiana State Attorney General's office, 3 percent of his salary was automatically deducted as a quasi-voluntary contribution to his political party. This was standard practice at the time, a way in which political parties tied individuals more closely to their fortunes. Ruckelshaus was not resentful of this, but rather held a balanced view of institutions' role.

"I do respect institutions, and think that one of the big social problems we have today in this country is the erosion of respect for institutions, whether it's government, corporations, labor unions, churches—all kinds of institutions today are under fire, sometimes for justifiable reasons . . . [I]nstitutions are no better or worse than the people that run them. Just as in this country we have such low esteem of corporations today, a lot of people that are in those companies are very good people. They're trying to do the right things—it's a very complex world we live in, they've got to deal with all these governance issues that they never thought a lot about."

Shirley Tilghman, President of Princeton University, expressed an appreciation for the special kinds of skills needed to succeed in organizational life. She started her career as a researcher in molecular biology first, a teacher second, and a university administrator and cross-field scientific leader only third. She understood the trade-offs among these different kinds of work, yet gravitated toward leadership of institutions, like Princeton: "At the beginning of your career, if you're going to be successful in science, you have to be utterly, completely focused on science . . . As I became more successful and visible in the field, you begin to get asked to do these other things . . . Most people discover relatively quickly whether they enjoy doing those things and whether they're any good at doing those other things. As it turned out, I both enjoyed doing those things and was good at them. As a consequence, you get asked to do more and more and more."

Former Congressman and Cabinet Secretary Dan Glickman was more ambivalent about institutions, but clearly recognized the evolution in his own views as his tenure in the House of Representatives lengthened. "At the beginning, when I was in Congress, I was a very free and independent spirit. I would oppose the President when I felt like it, and if the party didn't like it, that was tough. But the longer I was there, the more I became part of the system." Like Ruckelshaus, Glickman displayed a fundamental pragmatism, which probably aided his growth as a government official. "[W]hen you're part of an institution for a very long period of time, to be effective, you have to go along periodically. So if you wanted to get things done, or bills passed, or things brought back to your district, you couldn't be totally iconoclastic and independent. You kind of had to work in the system."

As I talked with leaders in different fields, the influence of a couple kinds of institutions came up several times. (Keep in mind, of course, that my research was not strictly scientific, as the CEOs I interviewed weren't exactly representative of all Fortune 500 leaders, the Nobel Prize winners weren't precisely reflective of all scientists, and so on. With a different group of leaders, in short, a different set of institutional influences could easily emerge, but they might not be altogether different than this set of three, either.) A couple of institutional affiliations are worth examining briefly.

The first of the institutions that multiple leaders mentioned was the military. It's no coincidence that until as recently as 1992 every President of the United States had served in the military, and that a decent percentage of the MBAs awarded to business-school graduates every year go to former military officers. Service in the armed forces, whether cause or effect, correlates with leadership attributes. Even—or especially—in this age of an all-volunteer military, when an increasingly small percentage of young people join the military as part of their early professional experiences, it was striking to hear the degree to which the military had influenced different leaders' early development.

For Admiral James Watkins, who went on to serve as President Reagan's Energy Secretary, the navy was an early and important part of his development. He hadn't necessarily planned on it, but events kept him in the military for several decades after he first entered the Naval Academy in 1944. Watkins remembered about his initial entry into the service, "World War II was on . . . I didn't know how long it was going to last. Being somewhat naïve and young, I said, 'I want to go to the Naval Academy, as my brother had before me' . . . I didn't initially intend to go in for a career. I just wanted to serve my country."

Despite the War's end, Watkins stayed at the Academy, graduated, and entered active duty. When he went out on his first cruise, he was hooked. "In the first six months of my tour on that destroyer, an old 2,200-ton World War II [era] destroyer, I really learned to love the navy. It was my association with career people—the Old Mustangs, as they were called. These were sailors that made officer rank. These were dedicated senior officers that commanded the ship—[for example] an Executive Officer that had been through the war—in some cases had

had their ships torpedoed out from underneath them, and they'd survived. This was a very wonderful group of people . . . I really learned from them, and they were inspirational to me . . . and [I got] heavy responsibilities early. Driving that ship in the middle of the night, around an aircraft carrier . . . all of the kinds of things we did, and the ports we visited—it was a totally new world to me."

Watkins represented thoughts similar to those of Jim Hagedorn and Jim Middleton, two corporate leaders who both served in the Air Force, as well as Senator Slade Gorton, who also served in the Air Force, first on active duty and then in the Reserves for over two decades.

A second kind of institutional influence that became apparent through my research was looser, tied less to a specific organization or entity, but rather to geographic location. I found that geographic proximity around the key centers for thought leadership, which varied by field, drove a positive synergy for many leaders.

Boston, for example, was a key hub for many in the scientific community. In the early- to mid-1970s, while physicist Bill Phillips benefited from an intellectually fertile lab at MIT, cancer researcher Phillip Sharp and Rich Roberts were just down the hall at the same university doing highly productive research themselves. All three would win Nobel Prizes.

Former Cabinet Secretary Donna Shalala pointed to the importance of the East Coast corridor of power from the first step of her career onward. "Spending time in New York and Washington really gave my career an edge. There are very talented people all across the country that never got the opportunities because they weren't in New York or Washington. And the power structure is in New York and Washington . . . I think it's very true in government; I think it's a little true in academia. [In academia,] There's a power base in the Midwest and in the West, because of the California institutions. [Pauses] It just helps."

Sorting through these and other leaders' stories of institutional affiliation, several lessons emerge for young adults. First and most important, institutions help leaders by acting as talent magnets. Attracting wide spectrums of people and allowing them to interact, work together, and grow together, key institutions become talent farms, in addition to whatever their primary purpose. As Nobodies work to become Some-bodies, they often became part of mutually helpful groups of like-minded others, and institutions helped them find those groups.

When Slade Gorton moved to Seattle as a young lawyer, for exam-ple, he joined a budding nexus of local power when he met several other Young Republicans in the Washington State area. "I . . . almost imme-diately fell in with a small group of Republicans who met once a week or so to chat informally about politics, that included the Pritchard brothers—Frank Pritchard Jr. and Joel Pritchard, who was later my head man, and no more than six or eight others, all of whom were here . . . [T]he Republican Party had just been practically wiped out in 1956. We had no statewide offices, and only a handful of people in the Legislature. [T]hese friends . . . encouraged me [in my first race for elective office]."

Institutions also helped Somebodies in a couple of other ways: by offering them credentials, a kind of institutional pedigree that intro-duces them to future audiences; and by teaching certain philosophies or methods of work that the organization has developed successfully. WR Grace CEO Paul Norris, for example, cited management theory he learned under Larry Bossidy, himself a General Electric disciple, which Norris has brought to his present business. "We manage our company the same way . . . It's human resource, process review—which means making sure you have the right people in the right places, and you man-age that talent pool. A strategic-planning process focused on what are the opportunities? Where are the best places to invest in, where do we want to make those investments? And a very rigorous annual operating plan driven by very aggressive productivity goals. And using Six Sigma as the overall operating philosophy of the company."

Norris paused briefly to reflect on the heritage of his training. "I'm sure people here would tell you either this was a great thing or a horri-ble thing. I brought that approach . . . because I used it in a number of different businesses when I was [under Bossidy], and it was a successful formula."

The benefits of institutional pedigree and specific lessons like the ones Norris cited, however, came up in my interviews far less fre-quently than strong relationships developed within institutions, with

key allies and friends. The reason for the differences is open to speculation, but after conducting the research, I came to believe that the
other benefits of institutions—pedigree and specific ideologies, processes, and frameworks—are quite simply less important than interpersonal relationships. The versatility and depth of the relationships
leaders developed as part of larger organizations drove significant
value through the rest of their careers beyond the first job.

The relevant conclusion for young people, then, may be this: beyond
their enduring and important value to society as a whole, institutions
can help your career more than you realize. However, rather than fixate
on institutions per se, for the purposes of career development, consider
the specific benefits leaders have historically drawn from them: relationships, first and foremost, pedigree, and methods for doing work.

Joining Clubs

Leaders' social energy also translated into informal activities beyond
their first jobs or formal institutions. They joined clubs—often lots of
them. Most of the time, the clubs weren't related directly to their actual
jobs but did entail responsibilities of their own. After seeing the pattern
in conversation after conversation, I realized that leaders are joiners,
people who habitually meet friends and colleagues through clubs and
community involvement. For a number of the men and women I interviewed, membership in different clubs was part of their holistic (if not
necessarily self-conscious) approach to uncovering professional and
personal opportunity.

Not surprisingly, joining clubs was a tendency particularly common among political leaders. Carol Bellamy, now the head of
UNICEF, became involved, tentatively, in New York City politics after finishing her first job in the Peace Corps. "I joined a political club.
I'd never been political in my whole life—nobody in my life had been
political. Then I ran for political office because I think I was the person least disliked in my club, so I kind of backed into that." That early
involvement led to various relationships that helped Bellamy later in

her career as she continued forward in politics and then moved over to the nonprofit world.

Similarly, Senator Slade Gorton and two other Washington State leaders whom I interviewed, former Governor Dan Evans and Congressional Representative Rick White, all described how they found and developed friendships with small groups of other like-minded young people as they entered politics. Creating informal networks, Evans and Gorton—beginning in the 1950s—and White—later in the 1980s and 1990s—relied on helpful peers in the Washington area to build intellectual and organizational capital, which helped fuel later political campaigns.

Some leaders viewed activities with clubs or charities not so much in personally helpful terms, but as part of a larger commitment to civic leadership. Curt Culver, MGIC's CEO, described his work as chairman one year of the United Way drive in his city of Milwaukee. Bob Catell, CEO of utility company Keyspan, discussed explicitly how he saw contributions to local organizations as part of his professional role. "That's been a hallmark of [Keyspan], and something that I've embraced when I've gotten into a position where I can influence that. Particularly the kind of company that we are, essentially a utility company—we call ourselves an energy company, but we're very much dependent on the community that we serve, and I have always felt that it's important to be involved and to give something back both personally and financially to the community, to help people who are less fortunate than we are."

I wondered upon hearing comments like Catell's whether the commitment to civic involvement and volunteerism really had been lifelong, or if it had developed only well after the first job, when leaders had achieved a certain measure of comfort and more leisure time. To a certain extent, I believed, the time and energy for extracurricular activities come with age, and the increased ability to carve out time for activities beyond work. When I asked Catell if he had joined in charitable activities earlier in his career, though, around the time of his first job, he pointed to a highly consistent record. He said, "I got involved with organizations like Junior Achievement, and things like that even when I was in much lower positions in the company. I looked for opportunities to volunteer my services."

To summarize, then, whether naturally outgoing or not, leaders were highly social creatures who leveraged relationships in a variety of ways, in a variety of contexts. A specific kind of relationship, that with mentors or teachers, is our next topic. Mentors deserve special attention apart from this chapter due to their important—but surprising—roles within leaders' lives.

END GAME:
USING A LITTLE MAGIC

Keep Learning,
No Matter Who the Teacher Is

What about mentors? Did leaders benefit from special relationships with older teachers and guides? Were there usually single, lifelong mentors, or more situational ones? How did they find these mentors, and what kinds of things did they learn from them?

Leaders were equal-opportunity learners. They didn't discriminate against any source of information that might help them improve themselves or grow their capabilities. Their relationships with mentors were tricky, though. On one hand, the Somebodies I interviewed were unusually good at finding, cultivating, and learning from mentors—typically older, more experienced people in the same field who provided guidance as they navigated the pitfalls of early career growth. That successful achievers seek out the benevolent sponsorship of older guides didn't surprise me. What did draw notice were two other facts.

First, with a few notable exceptions, leaders did not maintain lifelong mentors who helped them consistently throughout their careers. Instead, they took counsel from numerous situational mentors at different points along the way. The notion of a single consistent guide throughout professional life may not fit these people's needs and habits. Second, leaders did not necessarily assume that mentoring required a two-way relationship. That is, in some cases, when future leaders worked in their first jobs, they learned from negative role models as much as positive ones—learning what *not* to do, as well as what to do.

To begin, it's certainly true that some leaders succeeded in establishing conventional mentor-mentee relationships with older contacts. Nadine Strossen, for example, spoke at length about the reverence with which she regarded Norman Dorsen, a fellow legal scholar and her predecessor as ACLU President. Dorsen has been a key figure in the latter part of her career, spanning a couple of decades. "I remember the first time he sent me a handwritten note. It amazed me, because here was this man I'd had so much respect for. Since then, we've gotten to be very close, and he's provided enormously valuable help."

Strossen pointed to specific ways Dorsen helped: "He appointed me to committees [within the ACLU], which gave me opportunities to present to the board. He consulted on any number of topics. He gave me ideas about trying to take a leadership role within the organization."

Likewise, journalist Alan Miller met a very influential figure in his first job as a cub reporter in Albany, New York. Harry Rosenfeld, who had worked previously at the *Washington Post*, gave Miller a variety of lessons, which he carries to the present day. Miller said, "The lesson was the enduring value of starting one's career with a boss who has such high standards, drive, and integrity." Miller and his mentor remain in touch even now. "On the day our Pulitzer Prize for national reporting was announced, Harry was among the first to call. He sounded as excited as if he himself had won. He then hired a driver so that he and his wife, Annie, could come down from Albany to attend a party at my home in Virginia that weekend. 'I would have walked,' he memorably told those assembled. He also said that hiring me was one of the best things he'd ever done in his long career in newspapers. And, once again, under the most auspicious circumstances imaginable, I had a chance to thank Harry for so very much."

To draw on a third example of conventional mentorship, Norm Axelrod, the CEO of Linens 'N Things, praised a lifelong mentor he met at his first job. "Working at Bloomingdale's in the '70s and '80s was a pretty easy place to work. It was as hot a retailer as could be in the country. The leadership was exceptionally strong. The interesting point is, I think if you looked and went back, there was a cadre of people who have gone on to be enormously successful in retail that all worked in the same place . . . I still talk to the [man] who was the chairman of the board, Marvin Traub, at that time, and I think he felt that he was responsible for creating an environment that fostered that."

Apart from these relatively few stories, though, I found that steady, decades-long relationships like the ones described by Axelrod and Miller were exceptions rather than the rule. Most of the Somebodies spoke more of situational mentors than consistent ones. Aside from his parents, who've been lifelong influences, Nucor CEO Dan DiMicco did not restrict his comments to just a single individual in his professional life. That's not to imply he lacked gratitude for several key people who helped him, but rather that the identity of those people changed as his career evolved from his first job to beyond. "[E]very step along the way, there's always somebody that you develop a relationship with, where you can consider them to be a mentor, somebody who supported your efforts. I never really felt like I had anybody that you'd put in that classic mold as a mentor—they wrap their arms around me, you know . . . But I constantly received support from the professors, and the people I worked with in all the organizations I've been with, which haven't been all that many, but through all different jobs, and what have you."

Physicist Bill Phillips's approach was similarly to learn from whomever he could, both in terms of specific domain expertise and personal comportment, but that wasn't restricted to a specific individual or two. "I'm not sure I was conscious of cultivating people as mentors. Basically, if somebody had something interesting to teach me, then I was happy to learn from them. I mean, there's two aspects to mentoring that I think are important. One is that somebody can teach you some important things about the subject that you're studying or doing research on. The other thing is somebody can teach you about style. Ways of thinking about problems, ways of ordering your life, and these things are done both by direct instruction and also by example."

Wendy Kopp, the founder and CEO of Teach for America, summarized similarly. "I have trouble identifying a single mentor, though I have learned so much from so many people."

In some cases, leaders were careful about tying themselves too closely to a single mentor for specific reasons. For example, Steve Odland of AutoZone wondered if an overly close relationship with a single person would limit his independent development. "I've never really had a mentor. It's something that people told me in school—this is what you need to do, you need to get somewhere and you need to find a mentor. In order to get a great job, you got to find a mentor who can be your sponsor . . . I'm not saying it's wrong, but I never had one, and I never found it really worked. I watched people who had mentors get so tied up in one way of thinking, from that mentor, that it limited their possibilities. As long as the mentor was hot, and that way of thinking was hot, it worked, but things change so rapidly. So what I did was I got the advice and counsel from as many people as humanly possible. I just asked everybody."

In other cases, tying too closely to one mentor promoted office politics, which leaders sought to avoid. USAA CEO Jim Middleton, when he was in his first job with the Air Force, learned about this kind of danger from a man, ironically, whom Middleton considers to have been a strong situational mentor. Middleton's mentor had himself been burned. "His boss was lined up to be Chief of the Air Force, and [my mentor] was coming over with him and was going to make a star with him, and then . . . the boss died . . . unexpectedly. He was slated to be the Chief and died. That—once that happens, boy, that creates a whole different environment at the top level . . . That's a good example of when you're tied to somebody and something happens. All of your fate goes away, because he held it. One of the things [my mentor] told me—he told me that story when I first started working with him—don't ever get tied that closely."

The other interesting aspect of leaders' use of role models and mentors was the way in which they learned from negative role models as much as positive ones. Former Raytheon CEO Daniel Burnham said, "I had a couple of mentors, but they didn't know it. Nobody has to know they're a mentor. I know the traditional assumption is that you go and ask someone, and they do specific things for you. That's bullshit. He or she could be good or bad, but as long as you learn [that's what a role model is]. One guy I followed was a skillful businessman, and I tried to watch him, and I tried to mimic him. The other guy was a complete asshole. It was like the Berenstain Bears—just be the opposite! But in his own way, that guy was a role model."

Sometimes conflict with negative role models erupts in a more direct way. Many twenty- and thirtysomethings can sympathize with a situation thrust on many people, including future Somebodies: the difficult boss. Many a young person has agonized over the roadblocks that a hostile or even uncooperative manager can throw up in a budding career. For the leaders I interviewed, the "anti-mentor," or negative role model, represented yet another chance for adaptation and growth. For example, award–winning photographer William Snyder moved early in his career from a newspaper in Miami to the *Dallas Morning News,* where he still works today, more than two decades later. Very early in his tenure in Dallas, he encountered an editor who didn't like his work.

According to Snyder, the editor "was not a guy who really cared about anybody's career, per se, besides his own. And don't get me wrong, the guy knew an awful lot about this business and an awful lot about photojournalism. I actually learned an awful lot from him. But we just had a personality clash . . . I said to myself, after I realized what was going on, and I said, 'Fine, you can try to ignore me, but I'm not going to let you. I'm going to do such good work that you have no choice.'"

I chuckled at the apparent display of stubbornness and asked Snyder how long the stalemate lasted, expecting him to offer an answer on the order of several months. I was wrong: Snyder had a running feud with the editor for *seventeen years.*

He went on: "I see lots of people encountering this, and I've talked to lots of friends who come up against a boss that [doesn't] like them, or they don't like them. You've got basically two choices: You either say, okay fine, and you curl up in a ball, and everything gets worse and worse and worse; or you say, 'I'm going to do everything I can,' and it's not even a matter of running away, per se, because I don't think that's a good thing, either. I think what you have to do is just buckle [down], and you be as good as you can possibly be. And then one of two things will happen: You will be rewarded where you are no matter what, because they can't ignore you, or other people will take notice, and they will come knocking at your door and offer you things that are better.

"I had opportunities to leave, but they would've been lateral moves or you know, backwards moves, but they weren't backwards or lateral moves for the right reason, you know what I mean? Sometimes you have to take jobs and do things in order to get experience and take [a] step back in order to move forward. But this wouldn't have been—most of those wouldn't have been steps back to move forward. They would've just been an escape route, and I wasn't going to do that.

"So, there was about a three- or four-year track of just working very hard. [The editor] came in about '85, and I won my first Pulitzer in '89, for a project that started in '87 and was ultimately published in '88. You know, I just worked very, very hard to garner local and national attention with my photography. And it worked. The interesting thing is, this clash thing just went on and on and on. The last two Pulitzers I won, he and I weren't on speaking terms when they were announced."

Despite the bitter acrimony between Snyder and his titular boss, though, he remained aware of his need to display at least a veneer of civility to the rest of the staff. Snyder said, "Whenever we won Pulitzers, they take out full-page house ads, celebrating it besides the story they run on the front page. But what they have traditionally done is put the photograph of the winners on there, and then they'll generally put a photograph of the editor, whether it's the department editor or the section editor or whatever, the manager that was most directly responsible for it. The second Pulitzer that I won was something that I did entirely on my own, entirely on my own time, until I sort of shamed them into giving me back my vacation time, and that my boss didn't want me to do. So when I won, the managing editor came to me on the day of the announcement and said, 'Well, we know there's been some trouble between the two of you. We traditionally put these pictures on the ad. So I'm coming to you and asking you: What do you want to do? Do you want his picture on the ad?' I was like, 'That's not a very fair question.' Because if I say no, then I'm a jackass, I'm petty and this, that, and the other. But everybody knows that he had absolutely nothing to do with this, so from that standpoint, he also gets a lot of credit that he doesn't deserve. Ultimately, I said, go ahead and put it on."

The bottom-line takeaway regarding mentors and role models was the same as with peer relationships. From the beginnings of their careers, society's Somebodies were generally social people and tended to leverage personal relationships in a variety of ways, particularly for learning. They were not, however, bound by conventional stereotypes as to how relationships should be created, structured, or maintained, and in many cases did not have conventional mentor relationships that lasted from their first jobs onward.

Go Crazy in the Office, but Stay Sane at Home

Did leaders care about work–life balance early in their careers? How did they achieve it? Why was it important to them, if at all?

When Paul Fireman, the billionaire chairman and founder of Reebok, left his first job at an olive oil company to start his fledgling sports apparel and shoe company, he wondered what kind of impact the new business would have on his family life. He and his wife then had three children under the age of six, and his wife couldn't do everything alone, as she was pursuing her own entrepreneurial venture.

The potential for problems escalated in the business's first year, as typical early-stage business struggles, a tight cash-flow situation, and a nettlesome investor in the company raised Fireman's personal stress levels. Speaking about his investor-partner who had sunk capital into Reebok, Fireman recalled ruefully, "I was constantly being shown [by this gentleman] what I should've done, and there was some tension there."

Still, Fireman stubbornly clung to his family life. It even helped buoy his spirits in slow periods. He said, "I made sure I balanced it as well as I knew how. It was an interesting thing. The starting of a new business appeared to be filled with demands for your time. The truth was, in the early times, there was nothing to do! No one was calling us! That didn't mean that we weren't busy, but I had time for my kids as they were growing up."

Meanwhile, though Reebok would eventually anchor the Fireman family's fortunes, it was Fireman's wife's company that gave the young family some much-needed financial breathing room. Fireman said, "My wife was incredibly supportive. She started the business that financed our home . . . She had her own entrepreneurial business, the one that really helped for three or four years when I was still getting off the ground."

Like Fireman, the leaders profiled in this book are people with full lives. As they started their careers, besides their work, they had relationships with families and friends, hobbies, recreational pursuits, and of course, needed to rest sometimes. I was keen to know if they could balance it all. Today more than ever, the trade-offs between work and other pursuits loom as a central challenge to young adults entering frenetically paced, technology-enabled, seemingly overbusy lifestyles. What had the Somebodies done when they were Nobodies to address the seemingly intractable problem of Too Much to Do, Too Little Time? Did they address the problem at all?

What I found was a provocative mix of perspectives into which we'll delve through the rest of this chapter. Most, but not all, leaders professed to have little balance in their lives early in their careers. Typically, leaders did work extremely hard, sacrificing balance in favor of greater productivity and achievement. Some indicated that the lack of balance continued to the present day. Of that group, however, some leaders indicated that their lack of balance by other people's standards fit nicely with their own personal tastes and values. Others actually had maintained balance in their lives, and outlined specific ways in which they become more effective professionally when they devote time and attention to nonwork activities. In summary, leaders had a wide diversity of opinions on work-life balance, but the underlying commonality was a no-shortcuts adoption of hard work in their early jobs.

Many leaders spoke openly of their imbalance during their early jobs. Norm Axelrod started his career at Bloomingdale's corporate headquarters in New York before growing into his current position as CEO of Linens 'N Things, and he plunged into his first job with gusto. He spent many nights in the office, and the work grew to consume his weekends, too. Axelrod nearly experienced burnout. In his second or third year on the job, he suddenly realized that work had taken over more of his life than he wanted. "I lived near the office, and went in all the time, because there's always something you could do better. I realized at that point—I ended up buying a house, a weekend house, to get out of New York and get away from the business . . . I needed to find a refuge to get physically away."

The hard work in many cases took a toll on family life. Business founder Felix Zandman touched on the issue when reflecting on his work in the early days of Vishay, for which he left his first job. "I worked day and night, and my family suffered a little bit from that, but they got used to it."

CEO Gil Minor suffered through a divorce, which he attributed partly to his work-life imbalance. "[I]t wasn't balanced very well. I guess the first, oh, ten years of my life after school was about 80 percent work and 20 percent home, or personal, and maybe 75/25, but it was heavily weighted toward my career and work. I was traveling—I wasn't going all over the world, but I was getting in the car every week and traveling and being away from home. It ended in divorce. I'm not saying that was exactly the reason, but I think that had something to do with it. I have two wonderful children from that period of time, and I wasn't doing justice to them, as well."

The essential trade-off between work and family life came with warnings for some. Photographer April Saul recalled a jarring encounter with one of her role models in the industry. "I was a student at the Maine Photographic Workshops in the late '70s, and Mary Ellen Mark, who's . . . one of the most famous current woman photographers, at one point she said to me, 'April, are you thinking about getting married and having a family?' And I said, 'Well, someday.' And she said, 'Well, I couldn't have done what I've done if I'd gotten married.' So it was pretty clear to me early on that being a woman and trying to do this was going to be very different than it was for the guys."

As they jousted for positions at the pinnacles of their professions, women faced (and continue to face) special challenges with work-life balance, which surfaced in several interviews. While other research sheds more and better light on this topic, I was moved by the directness of former Texas Governor Ann Richards, for example. Richards started her career as a schoolteacher after graduating from Baylor University in 1950 and getting certified at the University of Texas. In our interview, Richards recalled the old-fashioned family and workplace norms that limited her initial professional choices: "The reality of it was, I never thought about anything other than marrying some guy, having a houseful of kids, and living happily ever after. That's what women in my generation did . . . My generation hoped desperately that they'd marry a man that'd take care of them, [and] they could live in a big house, they could have women over for tea, and they could have supper parties."

Later, of course, Richards became involved in politics. She started by helping other woman candidates (including Sarah Weddington, the lawyer who had argued *Roe v. Wade* before the U.S. Supreme Court) campaign in local races in Texas. Eventually, she edged into the arena herself, with her first race in 1976, for a seat on the Travis County Commissioner's Court. Sadly, she had a sense of the personal price as she embarked on her political career.

"I knew instinctively it was going to be the end of my marriage," Richards said. "I knew how much time it would take, and the kind of responsibility my husband would need to take with our children. Unless I was a halfway [involved] elected official, it wasn't going to work . . . It scared me to death. I cared very much for my husband, and he was very supportive. But I knew [government service would have a personal price]."

For a striking number of the leaders, it was clear that old habits died hard. Even now, years after their first jobs, in most cases, and well after each had established an impressive credibility based on success, they described continuing sacrifices. William Nuti, CEO of Symbol Technologies, tapped out one weekend e-mail to me that read, "I have only one speed, and although I have learned to take more breaks with my family during the year, I still work long and hard hours. For example, I am writing this response right now on a Sunday afternoon while my son awaits me downstairs to play. I have been at my desk (in the home office) since 6 am this morning—and do this almost every weekend. Beyond my own admitted 'workaholism' anyone who is successful in life knows that it takes an incredible amount of work and many sacrifices along the way. There is no free lunch in life. I do my best to balance."

Nuti was not alone. Carol Bellamy, the head of UNICEF, was happy with her lifestyle but recognized that it might not fit other people. "[Work-life balance] is one where probably I'm not a very good example. I haven't been married. I'm not trying to send some kind of message. That's just my own personal choice—but I don't think that I have a particular model I'm following. So in terms of family, and raising children and stuff like that, I actually haven't done that. So some of the choices I've made have been easier for me to make than somebody else. I'm fully aware of that. And again, this is a personal choice, not because this is the model that I think everyone should follow."

This was an interesting point to remember. Many of the leaders who led the most unbalanced lives by conventional standards did not necessarily feel that work occupied a larger place in their lives than they wanted. Rather, they believe that they were focused on the things in life that mattered most to them—things about which they cared perhaps more than other people did, but which felt comfortable *for them*. Norm Axelrod, the Linens 'N Things CEO who felt close to burnout in his first job at Bloomingdale's, said nonetheless, "I completely controlled that decision [about how much to work]. And my wife and I would probably tell you, we would make . . . very few changes about that . . . [W]e've been married twenty-eight years, also, so it was, it's been— career was so important early on that I probably sacrificed a lot of things. But I thought I was growing. I think my friends also at the time were also putting the time into their careers. I had a family a little later, and it just worked out great. But it was conscious—balance is a conscious decision. I would tell you I get back much more from working harder than anything else. I don't think I have any question that I feel comfortable with the balance. But it isn't what I think other people think is the normal balance."

CEO Craig Sturken remembered his first job as a very difficult time, but has no complaints about his current, even more rigorous lifestyle. Sturken began, "The first couple years I worked, when I got out of college, there was no such thing as balance. It was totally imbalanced. Imbalanced in [the employer's] favor—just totally. It was work until you drop. That was one of the motivating factors to leave them, the fact that I was killing myself and I wasn't financially happy."

Fast-forward to the present day, and a chuckling Sturken says, "I hate to tell you, here I am, fifty-nine years old, and the CEO of a Fortune 500 company, and I'm probably working harder than I have in the last thirty years . . . My wife and I are empty nesters, so we don't have children at home. I don't know. As opportunities—this opportunity is here, and I want to do a good job. I want to lead the organization properly, profitably, whatever. At the end of this task, it's a huge amount of money if I get it done . . . I have never gotten to the position where I am comfortable with the status quo financially.

"By the way, that's a very interesting phenomenon of what drives people. When a guy has a million dollars, why does he need more? Well, because now it's a different motivator—it's not having a million dollars, it's having two million, or— It's sort of remarkable. I'll be honest. My wife and I have a beautiful home. We have all of the toys, and stuff, cars, whatever you want—and it's not enough. It's like, give me more. I'm really amazed at that. I'm going to be sixty years old in October [2003]. By the way, her brother's the chief operating officer of a huge bank, and he makes a hell of a lot more than I do—a couple of million a year, he makes. He's the same way! He's the same way, and we laugh about it."

It would be misleading, though, to characterize all the leaders interviewed as this driven. Most acknowledged working unusually hard in their first jobs, and through much of their careers, even, but also told me about coping mechanisms they had developed to improve their life balance, or to preserve the important things from it that they needed. These coping methods generally fell into four categories.

Relying on Spouse

Leaders made time for love. A strikingly high number of my male interviewees, at least, mentioned their spouses in glowing terms, pointed to them as bedrocks of stability, and generally showed a heavy reliance on them. Though I didn't probe too deeply into the details of their early private lives, my sense from talking to the leaders was that a surprisingly high percentage—certainly higher than the average for the general population—had remained with their original partners, or at least had been in marriages stretching multiple decades. Many leaders told me touching stories of romance and of marrying their school-age sweethearts. I was amazed by the wholesomeness of these stories.

Millard Fuller, the Habitat for Humanity founder, talked at length about his wife and mentioned proudly on the day that we talked that the "night before last, we celebrated our forty-fifth wedding anniversary." Similarly, Alan Heeger eventually grew up to be a Nobel Prize–winning scientist, but his high school days stood out in his memory for nonacademic reasons. "My high school years were fun and frustrating, typical of the teen years. The most important accomplishment was meeting my wife, Ruth. I have loved her for nearly fifty years, and she remains my best friend."

For some leaders, besides critical emotional sustenance, spouses provided tangible support to their work, too. Congressman and Cabinet Secretary Dan Glickman's wife became a kind of professional partner as his career progressed. He said, "She was uncomfortable with the political life, but then later on, she became very comfortable with it, and became an active force in my political life . . . She was very active on Capitol Hill. She worked for something called the Congressional Arts Caucus. She was the executive director of it, which was kind of an ad hoc group of members of Congress interested in promoting the arts and humanities, and she was just, she was a very big force in my life, and my political life, too."

The clear message to aspiring young leaders: marry well, and develop sensitivity to your spouses' needs, too. Cabinet member Bill Ruckelshaus talked about balances that he and his wife negotiated over time. "My wife is a very intelligent woman, came through the same set of academic challenges that I did . . . [She was] really number one in everything she ever did. And then all of a sudden, she's supposed to become a mother and stay home with the children, and I go off and work and do whatever happens on the outside world.

"We went to Washington—when we first were married, she was going to law school at night. I had two children from—my [first] wife died, and so they were less than a year [old] when we were married. So she was taking care of those children in addition to the three other children we had between us. And she was going to law school because she needed this intellectual stimulation. She needed some stimulation outside of taking care of the children. I encouraged her very strongly to pursue those things, and when we went to Washington, she worked in the White House. She first worked for the Republican National Committee, then she went to work in the White House, and was one of the leaders of the early Women's Movement, back in the '70s. That was tremendous for her. I thought she balanced that very well, but boy, terrific strain, and it was that for both of us."

Ruckelshaus continued: "We now—we have ten grandchildren, and we see how our children cope with all that, and we've asked ourselves, 'God, how did we do that? Five children?!' First place, it takes an enormous amount of energy. I haven't got the energy now. But the balance is just something you work at all the time. Somehow we got through it. As long as you're thinking about it, and trying."

Preserving Family Rituals and Activities

A second important way in which leaders retained some semblance of work-life balance was to create and/or preserve family rituals. Regularity and structure in their personal lives provided a comforting anchor, a harbor amid the sometimes-rough seas of working life. When he was a bit beyond his first job, in his early thirties, CEO Bill Mitchell began doing a fair amount of international travel for his job. He found the work exciting and stimulating, but he distinctly remembered having a series of conversations with his wife on how to handle these travels.

Mitchell said, "I always went and talked to [my wife]. And where we got to [in this situation] was, 'Hey, this would be really good. [I] can support it, but we're going to need you to be home for the key events in the kids' lives, the birthdays, the holidays, the school plays, and all that stuff. And when you're home, you need to be home. You can't be on the phone all the time—there wasn't really e-mail at that time, but doing 'stuff'—and so while you're gone, work real hard and do those things, and when you're home, be home.' And we've always worked that out, and we made a deal, so that the last thing we did before I left and went and got on a plane is we'd have a sort of a family event, and the first thing we did when I got back was a family event. It was sort of to make sure there were rituals and ceremonies around the travel. That became very important."

In some cases, rituals did translate directly to less time at work and yet were kept. Sacrifices were made for a greater good. Physicist Bill Phillips acknowledged that his time with family and their weekly activities at church reduced his working hours, for example. "I made a conscious decision that I was not going to neglect my family or other aspects of my life, in favor of my career. But at the same time, I had the clear impression that this meant I wasn't going to get as much work done. And I was happy with that kind of trade-off, but I was well aware of what it meant. To spend more time with family, more time with church, meant that I was spending less time in the lab, and that means you get less done. But as far as I was concerned, it was a good trade-off. I was getting a lot done in the lab, and I was having a satisfying life outside of the lab."

A number of leaders mentioned the importance of maintaining active roles in their children's key activities. When USAA CEO Jim Middleton was doing his second tour of duty in the Pentagon as an Air Force officer who hadn't yet launched his business career, he coached his children's soccer teams despite a hectic work schedule. "[T]here was one fall when I was coaching my daughter's team and one of my sons' team. In northern Virginia, soccer is a big deal . . . They used to schedule Saturday games around me because they knew I had two teams to coach that day. Other than coaching and working, that's about all I did in that second tour up there." When his family returned to their native Texas, Middleton continued to make time for sports, which were a big part of his children's lives. The focus shifted to basketball. "All three of my kids, for instance, played basketball in high school, and I missed very few of their games in the three years they played. They had games all over South Texas, and my wife and I would take off. She'd go north, and I'd stay home, and vice versa . . . [O]ne of us would be at their games all the time."

Sacrificing Nonfamily Activities

There were no magic-bullet solutions as far as work-life balance. A third method leaders employed to preserve time for their families was quite simply to reduce nonfamily socializing and leisure. A number of leaders, such as Best Buy CEO Brad Anderson, JB Hunt CEO Kirk Thompson, and Cabinet member Bill Ruckelshaus, specifically mentioned avoiding golf, for example. Anderson and Thompson deliberately avoided taking up the sport, while for Ruckelshaus, it was something he sacrificed temporarily during a particularly busy period of travel.

"I'd come home here on the weekends, and I love to play golf, but I stopped playing golf. I couldn't go off playing golf on Saturday and Sunday when I'm home, then take off again on Monday. So weekends were really devoted to the family," Ruckelshaus said.

When Princeton University President Shirley Tilghman was starting her career as a molecular biologist, she balanced her work with the raising of her children by being extremely compartmentalized and efficient. She did it, she said, "by being extremely disciplined and by forcing myself to be guilt-free. [I was] consciously not beating up on myself, so that when I dropped my kids off at the baby-sitter, from that moment on, I was focused on work until it was time to pick them up. I didn't have long lunches. I didn't kibitz with people in the lab. I was all business, all the time . . . When I did pick up [the kids], I turned a switch in my brain, and I'd be totally focused on them again."

AutoZone CEO Steve Odland to this day avoids scheduling business meetings in the evening, and described other sacrifices he and his wife made to improve the quality of their lives with their children. "It's a constant effort. We delayed having children. We waited I think ten years after getting married before having our first child. My wife's a CPA, and we were both engaged, working, trying to put a little bit of money away, get started with a house and everything. It's a constant balance. It's something that is very important to me, and even today, you just have to go home at night and be with the kids. I try to keep things to day-trips, so that I can see them in the mornings and in the evening, even if I'm traveling during the day. I don't do business dinners very often. I turn down business dinners. I'll do lunches, I'll do meetings, I'll do breakfasts, but with dinner—I wouldn't get to see the kids . . . It's just something you have to make a priority. You've got to balance it all."

In terms of the tangible ways they balanced their schedule, in short, Somebodies had no special methods beyond those available to everyone else. To the extent they achieved balance, they did so by determining clear priorities for their time and then adhering to those priorities with discipline.

Recognizing the Benefits of Balance

One other approach to work-life balance deserves mention. It was more of a mind-set than an action: a number of leaders maintained work-life balance by reminding themselves of its value. This may sound like a Zen koan, and in some ways, it is. I found that a number of leaders focused on why they were making sacrifices to maintain their discipline in doing so. Work-life balance, in their telling, offered psychological comfort, essential grounding to their lives, and in some cases, an empathy to human experiences and feelings that was essential to productive work.

For Arrow Electronics' Bill Mitchell, the family rituals mentioned earlier provided a tremendous centering influence, which helped him remain productive at work. "Very early on, I figured out that wasn't so much for the family. That was for me. That was the way I could stay centered, and stay on focus, was to have the family there. That's always been a very, very important piece of my life—really the centerpiece of my life. That became terribly important . . . International travel takes a huge toll out of you. You get jet-lagged, you're tired a lot. If you weren't coming back to . . . something that was *very* stable, and very calming to you, you . . . very quickly saw that you lost your rudder. You were moving faster and faster and making less and less progress, and it just—it just wasn't a life. It got to be absolutely critical—again, it wasn't this flash of light. It was a sort of dawning that said, 'This is really important to you. You've got to make sure you do this, and do this right.' "

Mitchell thus came to his realizations about balance gradually; by contrast, journalist Tom Hallman actually had a flash epiphany about his work-life priorities. He had just won a journalism award early in his career and been offered a job at the *New York Times,* which he accepted during his visit there. Returning to the West Coast, though, as his wife entered the final stages of a pregnancy, Hallman had misgivings. "I flew back, the plane landed in Chicago, and as I was transferring planes to come back to Portland, I thought, 'Wait a minute. My wife is giving birth to this little baby girl. What do I want out of my life?' I thought, 'I want to have that work-life balance you talked about.' So I turned it down. I came back to the *Oregonian* and was the police reporter. I wasn't on any kind of glamorous beat, working Sunday through Thursday."

Still, Hallman made the most of his situation. He saw work-life balance as critical to his effectiveness as a writer. Without the ability to understand other people, their feelings and thinking, he felt he compromised his abilities to convey their stories accurately. "So I always tried to keep that balance between work and home life, because that's what gives you, that's what nurtures your soul. If you don't have the right kind of soul, you can't do the work that I do. Maybe if you're a computer whiz or something like that, but you deal with people in my job, so I've always tried to maintain that balance."

Photographer William Snyder sounded very similar notes to Hallman. He believed having a vibrant personal life promoted the empathy necessary for his job. He also tried to keep perspective on what lack of balance would produce, even in the event of professional success. Work, according to Snyder, "always has to be tempered by personal time, and playtime, and private time. [Without it,] you do burn out, I think, and in my business, especially where a large part of what we have to do as photographers, or even editors, is deal with other human beings, and empathize with them and understand where they are and where their heads are at—and get that, and send it back out in story form, whether it's written words or photographs—if you don't have your own life, if you don't have something away from work, you're not going to be able to do your work as well. You're not going to be able to be successful.

"I think after a while, too, no matter how successful you are, the successes start becoming hollow, shall we say, when there's nobody there to share it with you! Whether it's a friend or a spouse, or whatever, it's children—if you don't have a firm grounding, you kind of lose it. I've seen enough people that don't balance it very well, and they burn out pretty quickly, especially in this business. I think to be successful, you need a support system to keep you somewhat sane—at least I do."

Not all leaders defined the "support system" as Snyder or other people might. Some, as we saw, were satisfied with perpetually busy, intense lifestyles, and made trade-offs against their free time or personal relationships without blinking. Many leaders, though, did manage to create some semblance of balance in their lives, especially once they passed the initial stage of their careers. They relied on a variety of techniques for maintaining balance, and stuck to them with impressive discipline. An offshoot of discipline, willpower, receives our attention next.

If There's Magic in Success, It Lies in Willpower and Passion

So what was it? What was the magic ingredient in the recipe for success? Aside from hard work, good social skills, and the rest, how do leaders stand out from the legions of other eager-beaver young achievers?

Mike Luckovich's appearance can be deceiving. A casually dressed, medium-sized man with brown hair, he can walk down a downtown street on a warm summer night in Atlanta, where he lives with his wife and four children, and be recognized by almost no one. He blends easily into a crowd. He is Everyman.

Yet beneath his apparently normal exterior lies a highly unconventional, satiric way of looking at the world, and a wickedly sharp sense of humor to match. The official photo of Luckovich accepting his Pulitzer Prize from the President of Columbia University in 1995, captures this impish side—while most award recipients shake hands and smile earnestly for the camera, Luckovich let loose with a wide, intentionally goofy smirk, a kind of anarchist's grin.

Luckovich's ability to see current events with unique perspective, and then to provoke people's thoughts with his cartoons about them, are highly prized. Today he's one of the country's leading editorial cartoonists, and his work is syndicated in hundreds of newspapers and magazines. What's interesting is that Luckovich started his career as an unhappy life insurance salesman.

Graduating in 1982 from the University of Washington, he knew even then that he wanted to become a cartoonist, but found the field less than welcoming. Three hundred outbound résumés resulted in no offers back, and with no other immediate ways of making a living, Luckovich took a job with a friend's father's company. He was far from pleased.

"I'm not really a salesperson, but I had nothing else going on, and I was living in the State of Washington, so we'd travel to various little towns all across Washington State trying to sell union members life insurance, and it was, it was miserable. You didn't get paid anything—only if you sold a policy. It was all just on commission. But we were paying for the dumpy motels we were staying in, so it was a lot of pressure. Plus I was about to get married . . . It was really tough."

Luckovich refused to give up his dream, though, and continued to toil at cartooning outside of his job, sometimes putting in eight-hour shifts at his drawing board after his day job was finished. "I just knew that the thing that I love to do, editorial cartooning—that's all I wanted to do. So when I got the job as a life insurance salesman, I felt a little bit down about that . . . but on the weekends, when I wasn't selling insurance, I was drawing editorial cartoons and just giving them free to a suburban paper outside of Seattle, just so that I was still doing it and had a ready supply in case a job did open up. It was a little bit frustrating, because I wasn't doing what I wanted to be doing right away, but I just had this hope that something was going to happen. I didn't want to fail at that."

Asked how intensely he thought about his ambitions, and whether it was on his mind during the average day on his first job, Luckovich replied, "I was going through the daily grind with the insurance, but it was also a thing that was constantly on my mind. I would look at newspapers from around the country, or *Newsweek,* which was printing cartoons, and I'd think to myself, 'You know, I think I'm better than that person there, and that person has a job,' and so I'd think, 'Man, I just have to redouble my efforts and just keep, just keep doing cartoons on my own, and hopefully something's going to open up.'"

Eventually, an ad for a cartoonist's position, which later became the first paid job in the field that Luckovich ever held, came up in *Editor and Publisher,* the journalism industry's main trade publication. His interest in the job was so strong that he placed a literally constant reminder of its possibility in front of himself. "[A]s I was selling this life insurance, as I was driving from house to house, I would keep on the passenger seat of my Ford Pinto, I'd keep the page open in *Editor and Publisher* that had that ad for the cartoonist, just hoping I'd get it."

Luckovich was not alone in his burning intensity. Underlying each of the behaviors described in earlier chapters are the closest things I found to magic ingredients in the recipe for success. Interviewing Luckovich and other leaders, I found two such ingredients: first, sheer willpower, the ability to focus and translate determination to action, and second, a positive energy that appeared in many situations as passion, and other times as optimism. Willpower and passion were the secret sauces, what sportswriter George Plimpton might've called the X factors, the elements that destroy the equation between inputs and outputs and somehow produce something from nothing. In this chapter, we'll examine leaders' willpower and passion, and how they developed and manifested themselves.

Willpower and Drive

Time and again, the importance of persistence and mental focus amid difficulty appeared in my conversations with leaders. Senator Chuck Hagel captured the idea neatly: "The older I get, the more sure I am— of not many things [laughs]—but one thing I am sure of the older I get is that individuals can talk themselves into anything, and they can talk themselves out of anything. The human mind is a powerful, powerful dynamic . . ."

When businessman Felix Zandman started his company, Vishay, he wouldn't even consider its failure. Asked if there were any parameters beyond which he wouldn't have been willing to go, he protested vigorously. "No. No, no, no—there were no parameters. It was everything. Everything or nothing—no parameters . . . I gave everything for that, because I believed in that. And eventually . . . from this little invention, which is still working very well, the company was built all around, and it has sales today of $2.5 billion." Zandman certainly had his difficulties along the way. He recalled, "The first year was extremely difficult. I remember painting the walls of my own office. And my secretary working nights and so on, doing research together with me . . . I worked day and night." But he persevered.

Jim Hagedorn also displayed an almost maniacal commitment to success. As my interview with the Scotts Company CEO progressed, he became increasingly energetic and enthusiastic. First: "Most people don't take their jobs so seriously that they'll basically give up their lives for it . . . I think there's a special person who wants to do that, somebody who's just totally focused on it and—I'm a pretty aggressive person. I like to win. I like to get what I want." Then later in our conversation: "I don't view [these choices] as sacrifice . . . I'd go crazy if I was home every day. Okay? But I think to most people, they would view it as sacrifice." And summarizing a bit later: "I would say, 'Hagedorn is pretty focused. If he locks onto a target, he does not let it go easily.'"

Willpower and resulting personal drive also helped shape many leaders' ambitions. The straightforward desire to rise above the proverbial masses and take the reins of leadership animated many of the people whom I interviewed, particularly in the business world. This ambition didn't seem obnoxious or overreaching. If anything, many Somebodies embodied an interesting paradox: being quiet and unassuming on a personal level, but maintaining serious professional ambitions. Channeled toward productive ends, the combination produced fascinating studies in personal intensity.

Hunger for Big Challenges and Ambitions

Willpower outletted itself in other ways, as well. Not only were leaders unusually skilled in their abilities to innovate ways over, around, under, and through obstacles, but their desire to succeed helped them identify those obstacles, too. Rarely did leaders waste their attention and energies on trivial goals. Typically through instinct, they realized the importance of tackling larger problems and not settling for easy paths.

Matt Espe, today the CEO of IKON Office Solutions, began his career in the GE training program. From there he moved on to a sales position in an office in Los Angeles and promptly tripled sales in his first two years. At the age of twenty-four, he was then offered, and took, a branch management position in San Diego, which gave him the opportunity for leadership relatively early in his career. Based on his experience in that first job, he synthesized a key guiding principle: "Never be afraid to take the tough assignment. The greatest opportunities to learn and to make a substantial contribution are found in the most challenging jobs. Early on, I earned the reputation of being someone who enjoyed difficult assignments, and I believe that reality has helped me get to where I am today."

In the realm of science, Bill Phillips showed similar perspective in his postgraduate thesis work. He took the highly unusual step of pursuing two different theses. One would ensure that he could produce demonstrable progress right away, while the other allowed him to experiment with emerging theory in a new, ultimately important branch of his field.

"During the time I was a graduate student, I realized that there was this shift going on—between what you might call the old-style atomic physics and the new style of atomic physics. Tunable lasers were becoming readily available to people in research laboratories . . . I told my thesis adviser, 'Look, I'd like to do something that involves lasers, because it looks like this is the new thing. This is the coming technology, and I'd like to get a background.' So he said okay, suggested a project, and I did it. And so I ended up with two completely different kinds of things for my thesis. That was a very important decision I made as a graduate student, because my career would not have developed—could not have developed—in the way it did had I not done that."

In short, leaders took care of the fundamentals, working hard, excelling, and acting decisively, but they also positioned themselves in front of opportunity by focusing on the difficult problems and issues in their field or organization.

Resonance of, and Faith in, the "American Dream"

A bit unusually in this age of jaded expectations and irony, many leaders I interviewed unabashedly expressed their love of America and its value system. Several specifically mentioned the American Dream and their confidence in the overall system by which this country runs. In other cases, the appreciation was more subtle, but clear nonetheless, particularly in the embrace of the American Dream's basic tenets: materially humble starts in life, followed by self-improvement through education.

Dan Glickman, a former Congressman from Kansas and Secretary of Agriculture in the Clinton Cabinet, remembered early childhood influences, "My dad and mother were both major forces, particularly my dad. He was from the school that you could do anything. 'This is a great country. You can do anything.'"

Staples' Ron Sargent explained his outlook by referring to a similar influence from his parents. "I think it's a little bit of your hard-wiring, by the time you're, I don't know, fifteen years old . . . In my family, education was very important, and I took to that like a duck takes to water. At the same time, I lived two doors down from a motorcycle gang, in kind of an inner-city environment, in Covington, Kentucky, which is a very blue-collar, working-class kind of neighborhood. Somebody got killed two doors down, with this motorcycle gang, when I was growing up.

"I also knew, very early, that I wanted to move out of the neighborhood and have a better life than my parents were able to have. That kind of drive is built in fairly early, and obviously, my parents pointed me toward education as the way. That made all the difference."

In almost identical language, Bill Nuti, the CEO of Symbol Technologies, remembered, "I never needed any inspiration to drive ambition. Ambition has always been a part of who I am. I come from a generally poor family and lived in a relatively low-income area of the Bronx . . . I knew from a very early age that I wanted something different in life."

Steve Odland, AutoZone's CEO, also got very specific advice from his parents, premised on confidence in the American system of education and meritocratic rewards: "The great equalizer in our country, the great thing that allows us to get ahead, is education. I've never been much of an athlete, and my parents pointed that out to me. 'Son, you're never going to get an athletic scholarship anywhere. We really can't afford to send you to college, so you're going to have to start thinking about what you're going to do. Our advice to you is that you're going to have to get an academic scholarship. You better work your tail off in high school.' This was the beginning of high school. 'Your grades are pretty good, and you're pretty smart, but you better work your tail off, because if you get great grades, you'll earn scholarships, and if you get a good scholarship, you go to a good college. If you go to a good college, it'll open up doors later.'"

These kinds of stories from the leaders raised goose bumps for me. In one sense, this project was the search for confirmation of the American Dream—can basic fundamentals like honesty, fair play, hard work, and high ambition still produce greatness?—and these were people who had lived the Dream in their climb from Nobodies to Somebodies. Besides the inspiration, though, it was important to note that the Dream very often played a tangible role in these leaders' lives. They placed their faith in the basic system of cause-and-effect, effort-and-reward that runs our society. If they delivered results in their own work, they were consciously aware of the fruits they would taste.

Passion for Subject Matter

For many of the people I interviewed, a passion for their field provided the fundamental motivation they needed to build their careers. This kind of motivation appeared particularly often with artists, which is not surprising, given their typical need to take a first job with relatively low pay. Without love of the subject matter, after all, they would lack reason to work through drudgery, to tolerate problematic issues, annoying colleagues, and other difficulties.

For Paul Salopek, Pulitzer Prize–winning reporter for the *Chicago Tribune*, enjoyment of his craft pervaded his work from the time he entered journalism, though he didn't realize it as consciously in his younger days. "I firmly believe if you can't write every day, then—if you feel you mustn't write every day, you shouldn't be in the business. I'm that fanatical about it. It's like breathing. It's got to be essential to who you are and what you do . . . I've come to this understanding of my passion in a very roundabout way, but I'm delighted, because at least I've come about to it, and other people sometimes don't.

"So it's not acclaim, it's not money . . . [It's] just the act of moving through the world in the way a storyteller does, where the thing you're out there getting, what grabs you, what gets you, what grabs you in the gut, is saying, 'Aha, there's a story unfolding in front of me, and I can tell it.' It's almost a shamanistic sort of power. So that's what rings my bell. The accolades and everything else are great. I'm delighted, I'm honored, I'm humbled, I'm flattered, but I did not get into the business to win Pulitzers or be a global correspondent, or XYZ."

Though the intrinsic nature of the work was not his sole motivation, Senator Slade Gorton, too, passionately enjoyed his first job as a legislator. He very much enjoyed getting into the details of proposed laws, and rhapsodized about his experiences in the Washington State Legislature. "You worked well into the night, a whole lot of the time. They were extremely intense experiences, which meant that you got to know the other members down there extremely well. We had no staff. When I was . . . Majority Leader in my last term, I had a secretary and an intern. But before that, you had none at all. Most of the times, you didn't have an office! Your office was your desk on the floor. So you had to read all the bills, try to figure them out on your own the night before, debate on them. It was wonderful training, and of course, it was wonderful from the perspective of helping to set public policy."

On a more sensate level, Harold Kroto wrote in his Nobel Prize autobiography of his very elemental enjoyment of chemistry. "I, like almost all chemists I know, was also attracted by the smells and bangs that endowed chemistry with that slight but charismatic element of danger which is now banned from the classroom."

Grammy-winning songwriter Tia Sillers echoed, "Just give me a guitar and a pen, and I'm happy. Music gives me meaning in life." This kind of appreciation for the most fundamental elements of their craft colored many of the narratives leaders offered about their early careers.

Passion for Intense Experiences in Their Own Right

Related to but slightly different from topics discussed earlier in this chapter—like hunger for big challenges or passion for the subject matter—was passion for intense experiences. A number of leaders described intense feelings or experiences they had had in different contexts, and their thirst for the intensity itself. For those leaders, I came to see, finding drive and motivation rested on finding those experiences and episodes that called out their passions and consumed their energy and attention. In some cases, the passion stemmed from their enjoyment of the underlying field, but my sense was that these people also enjoyed something intrinsic about the personal interactions and inner reactions triggered by such activity.

Kathleen Ligocki, now CEO of Tower Automotive, settled into her first lengthy job at a General Motors plant when she was still in her twenties. Diving into the chaotic environment, which did not exactly welcome female college graduates with liberal arts degrees, may have daunted others, but it activated something inside Ligocki. "[I]t was such an exciting situation [at the factory]—five thousand people in a closed environment, responsible for producing over a million parts a year. It was just very intense, very exciting. I just saw this world, saw all of the things going on, and really dove in. To be honest, I fell in love with the work the first day I walked into the plant. The people there—it was just a very close group of people, everyone working together in close quarters. That produced some soap opera–like moments, too, but it also led to some very good things. When you have that kind of enthusiasm and excitement, it's just infectious."

Returning to Scotts Company CEO Jim Hagedorn, we see perhaps the clearest portrait of someone who enjoys intense experiences in life. Hagedorn's first job came at a print shop in his twenties. He had returned home as the proverbial prodigal son, after having run away and lived somewhat of a vagabond experience in the late 1960s, and the sudden immersion in a conservative, working-class environment turned him on. Hagedorn said, "I think what it did is give me a dose of reality that really helped put my energy in context. I think I was always—I'm sure that I would I be A-double-triple-whatever—the ADD stuff that they talk about. Because, you know, I'm sure people would have diagnosed me with something as a kid, because I was a bad kid. But, what kind of kid runs away from home for two years and lives like a homeless person at fifteen years old? Now, I'm not saying it was a good thing, so don't get me wrong. But I do think it's really the same sort of Jim that's here. [My current work]'s just a much more productive use of my energy than, sort of, being a delinquent. You know what I mean? I think that really, I've just found a legal way to use my delinquency. [Chuckles]"

Eventually, Hagedorn bottled the energy he saw in himself, and before beginning the more conventional white-collar work at his current company, served in the Air Force. The intensity of the military still stuck out in his mind. "Let me tell you—all the stuff you do in the military, the camaraderie and esprit-de-corps, hanging out with some really supersmart guys who think about the same stuff as you, and it's all about just severe work—and I mean hardcore work, fly hard, party hard, go weird places—if you could take that energy to the civilian world. Listen, guys in the military, guys who had good jobs in the military for more than two years, so I'm talking like five or more years, especially if they fought in conflict—they talk about this shit for the rest of their lives! You know what I mean? You know it's an intense experience because like [mimics old man's voice], 'Oh, those wacky old days . . . ' They're still talking about that when they're old men! If you could harness that—because that's the energy I love—if you could harness that energy in a work environment, holy mackerel! You'd be rich, and people would have a great time working for you." Leaders like Hagedorn often recognized the attraction of this intensity and tried to bottle it, both for motivating themselves and others.

Passion for Ideals

Finally, it's worth mentioning that a number of leaders cited passion for their ideals as a major motivator. Millard Fuller, who founded and remains President of Habitat for Humanity, displayed vibrant enthusiasm for his group's mission. Several times during our interview, he cited the homes for more than 180,000 people built by Habitat workers since the group's founding nearly three decades ago. What came out only after we talked for a while, though, was the story of just how zealously Fuller pursued his ideals to found the organization.

Initially, after graduating from law school at the University of Alabama at Tuscaloosa, where he had met business partner (and fellow interviewee for this book) Morris Dees, Fuller pursued a very different path. He was highly driven to achieve conventionally measured success and focused on building his profit-making business. "I spent all my waking hours for the next eight years devoted to making money, every day," Fuller said. "We were very successful at it. When I got out, we owned two thousand acres of land, and horses, and cattle, and speedboats. I drove a brand-new Lincoln Continental and had maids. We were very wealthy."

Though successful by normal measures, the deeply religious Fuller didn't feel that way. "I became estranged from God, and I became estranged from my wife . . . I was working so hard that I wouldn't even go home. I'd sleep on the sofa at the office. The inevitable happened—we drifted apart." Eventually, events came to a crisis point. Fuller's wife decided she needed a break, and she left Alabama for a trip to New York City, to clear her own mind and consider divorce. This spurred Fuller into decisive action.

"I pursued her, and we decided we had gotten off on the wrong road in life," Fuller remembered. "We felt that the only way to get back on the right road was to do radical surgery to our lives . . . The decision was made one night in a taxicab . . . I just had this . . . revelation to give our money away. I had never thought of that. For eight years, every waking minute was about how to make money. I used to keep a diary, where I would estimate how much I was making per minute. I still got that diary! All of a sudden, what I'd spent eight years accumulating, I decided to give away . . . It was as clear as something could possibly be."

From that moment on, Fuller's ideals guided his actions much more directly. He in fact gave away virtually all his money, donating to charity the proceeds from the sale of his share of the ownership of his old company. Fuller and his wife then journeyed through various adventures over the next few years, starting at a religious farm community in Georgia, then traveling as house-building missionaries to Africa. From this work in various places, the idea and initial work for Habitat for Humanity were seeded.

For Fuller, then, the ability to discern his ideals and higher calling unlocked a magical energy and life force within him and others who joined Habitat. He said, "I feel like I'm a very rich person. I don't have much of the world's goods. I'm not suffering . . . but the thing that makes my life rich is knowing that because of my work, combined with that of other people of goodwill, 180,000 people around the world have a better place to live. Their lives are positively impacted."

"I believe in such a thing as a calling in life," Fuller said. "I think some people do miss their calling! And as a consequence, they go through their lives like Thoreau said, 'leading lives of quiet desperation.' Because if you miss your calling in life, you're never really totally happy. But if you get your life in line . . . you can live a more harmonious life."

The kind of ideals that unlocked the energy of which Fuller spoke can come from many sources. Religion was clearly the motivator for Fuller and a few others, like JB Hunt CEO Kirk Thompson. The environment was key for Sierra Club President Larry Fahn, who worked as a young lawyer on numerous pro bono cases on behalf of environmental causes. "I had a strong environmental ethic from early days in high school, when I was backpacking and seeing destruction of forests," Fahn said. "When I was a kid, there were oil spills on Santa Barbara's coastline, so I had this idea that I was going to be getting involved in some way in conservation."

For some leaders, the surrounding culture made a difference. In particular, many in the current generation of Somebodies came of age in the 1960s and pointed to the idealism of that era as a key early-career influence. Mickey Kantor, the Commerce Secretary in President Clinton's

Cabinet, started his career as a civil-rights lawyer and was very much influenced by the social-justice movement of Martin Luther King and others. "It was such an exciting time, the '60s. I didn't have a lot of qualms, actually—I knew it was what I wanted to do, what I had to do."

Carol Bellamy laughed fondly as she remembered the decade with nostalgia. "The '60s were a time of enormous energy and activity in this country, a time when you really did believe every human being could make a little bit of difference. I don't want it to sound too dramatic—there were days in the Peace Corps where I'd say, 'Oy, God, what am I doing?' Anyway, it was a time of a lot of excitement and things happening."

It wasn't just leaders in the overtly social or political spheres who were influenced. The era touched some in other fields, like science, as well. Nobel laureate Paul Nurse remembered, "My time as an undergraduate at Birmingham [from 1967 to 1970] was extremely stimulating both as a biologist and also for my more general intellectual development. It was the heady times of the '60s when everything could be challenged and everything seemed possible. I met my wife, Anne, who was a sociology student, and her influence together with activities associated with the student movement of the time opened up my interests amongst other things in the theater, art, music, politics, and philosophy."

Positive Approach to Life

Ultimately, leaders' willpower and passions made them very positive people. They drove hard toward their goals, had high ambitions, and displayed passion for many things in their lives. For many of the interviewees, this fundamentally forward-leaning posture and outlook colored everything they did. At times, I found myself wondering if Somebodies could actually be as earnest and upbeat as they seemed, or if their good cheer was merely a façade, a cover for more skeptical, glinty-eyed approaches to life.

For example, I was wrapping up one of my interviews, with MGIC CEO Curt Culver, when a thought struck me. Culver is a congenial man who had just finished telling me the business story behind his ascendance to the top of the country's largest private mortgage insurer. It was a story that rested on old-fashioned values and hard work. Culver has never lost touch with his Midwest roots, maintains strong family ties to the present day, and also mentioned how he had taken on civic leadership in Milwaukee by co-chairing a United Way fund-raising drive during a recent holiday season. As his narrative wrapped up, I joked with him about how his tale sounded so positive and upbeat that it gave new meaning to the movie titled *It's a Wonderful Life.* Culver paused, then exclaimed with a chuckle, "Well, it has been. It is!"

Leaders displayed a positive, can-do spirit like Culver's with striking frequency. In most cases, it seemed that this trait was native to the Somebodies whom I interviewed. Staples CEO Ron Sargent explained, "I think as your career progresses and you have some successes, and you have some failures, that affects you and how you look at the world, but I was born an optimist, and still am."

In other situations, optimism and a positive outlook didn't always come easily, but leaders fought hard to maintain it. Scientist Paul Nurse admitted freely to some dark moments in his early twenties when he was mired in difficult lab work, but his core beliefs never wavered. In his Nobel Prize autobiography, he stated his strong belief that "I have an idealistic view of science as a liberalizing and progressive force for humanity."

The effect of a positive outlook was not to ignore reality and float through life in a heedlessly happy bubble, but rather to sustain strong self-confidence. The self-confidence has been described elsewhere already, but to close this section, I'll offer one last example, which came from the writer Michael Vitez. As Vitez left one of his first jobs in journalism, his essentially positive outlook shaped his choice at a critical fork in the road. "When the *Washington Star* folded, and I was twenty-three, the *National Enquirer* offered me a job, sight unseen, at double my pay. It was that, or go to the *Chicago Sun-Times* as a cop reporter, or to the *Hartford Courant.*" Vitez regarded the choice as a classic crossroads between immediate excitement and increased pay versus longer-term respectability, and opted for the latter but didn't paralyze himself with second-guessing. "I believe life would have been exciting and rewarding whichever path I had taken, because I was optimistic and enthusiastic and had a good attitude."

Things Don't Have to End Where They Begin

Is there any one lesson from leaders' stories that stands above the rest? What's the most important thing they have to teach us? What's common across gender, age, geography, and area of specialization? When we're talking about professional achievement, what is the Real Deal?

When I initially approached Kathleen Ligocki, the CEO of Tower Automotive, requesting an interview, her answer came via e-mail and was a brief one. It questioned whether she'd be the best model for my proposed book. Sure, Ligocki had the corporate bona fides—she'd worked her way up the auto industry over two and a half decades, starting at General Motors, moving over to Ford, where she eventually became Vice President of Canada, Mexico, and North American Strategy, and then to Tower, where she's one of the only women heading a Fortune 1000 company—but was she "normal" in her business experiences? In her brief message, Ligocki noted with tongue slightly in cheek that she'd been a Marxist in college who "read a lot of Che Guevara" and did a six-month archaeological dig in Mexico right after graduation. She'd also "bummed around" in Spain for a stretch. To put it mildly, she hadn't had a prototypical path to the executive suite. How would this fit with the rest of my book?

Actually, Ligocki's experience exemplifies the final and perhaps most important lesson shared by the leaders I interviewed: life is an organic, change-filled process, constantly dynamic, and things rarely end where they began. As former Texas Governor Ann Richards put it, "Because things change, the ones who rise to the top are the ones who're willing to change themselves. They don't stay in the same rut. They don't get glued to the same goals. They don't see themselves continuing in the same vein as when they got out of college or high school. What are you willing to risk when an opportunity comes along? Are you willing to throw away everything to go chase an idea? Are you willing to disavow what you told yourself you would do and be?" To Richards and other leaders, the answer was clear: for those people who have the vision, creativity, and perseverance to improve themselves, change is absolutely possible.

For leaders, change was in fact necessary. Personal and professional growth was a part of every single leader's story about his or her early career. Whether with their overt commitment to adaptation and self-improvement, their intellectual curiosity, or even their ability to rebound from failure—a topic on which we'll hear again from Kathleen Ligocki—leaders were highly dynamic people.

Adaptability and Self-Improvement

Following typically good starts to their careers in the first job, leaders continued to build their skills and reputations with specific steps for professional growth. As CEO Gil Minor put it, "in our business, you've got to grow or go. The status quo is just not acceptable. You can't continue to do business the same way for very long, because the market around you changes. Customers change. Circumstances change. So I learned that early on."

Minor was far from alone. Leaders adapted themselves and their skills in two different but related ways. First is leaders' ability to adapt to environmental change—their response to some element of their company, industry, or field that changes. Second is self-initiated change by leaders in themselves—expansion of skills or other personal growth.

In terms of adaptation to environmental change, I found leaders developed a strong sense of organizational behavior and an understanding of how to adapt to it very early in their careers. Paul Norris discussed the adjustments he had to make after leaving his first job at WR Grace for another company called Engelhard and then beyond that to Allied Signal: "[T]he most important thing I learned when I left Grace was: As you move to a different culture, you will learn different things, and it's important to be able to operate in different environments. The keys to being successful in the Grace Davidson environment were not the same as the keys to being successful in the Engelhard environment.

"So what you need to do as you learn is to change your style to be more compatible with the culture that you're in. It's not that you have to give up your ethics or your integrity. But if confrontation works in one organization, but collaboration works in another, if you recognize that, you'd be confrontational in one place and collaborative in another . . . [W]hen I was at Allied, Larry Bossidy joined the company after I had been there, and I realized that I now was changing and adopting as to how to work in two different cultures within Allied Signal. One which was the culture before Larry joined the company, and the other was the one after Larry joined the company. I think I was successful in both cultures, but my behavior was different. I suspect my behavior was more natural in the second than the first."

Ultimately, to optimize one's performance, Norris suggested that even the choice of employment be premised on your personality. "I think if you have the choice, you ought to try to find the place where your natural behavior or your natural tendencies are matched to the culture."

The second type of change leaders made centered on self-initiated improvements of the leader's own capabilities. To begin, the notion of self-improvement is premised on the idea that destiny is at least partly controllable, and that one's raw capabilities can in fact be honed. Compared to others who have a more deterministic view of personal development, who believe the cosmic die are cast from early in life, I found that leaders amply acknowledged their early influences—parents, friends, and experiences—but at the same time remained resolutely committed to the idea of self-driven growth.

Steve Odland, CEO of AutoZone, discussed his view that "leadership is so personal. It's interesting how two children from the same family, with the exact same parents, upbringing, households, sometimes sleeping in the same bedroom, can turn out so differently. Some of it, of course, is DNA, in the random mix, but some of it is different experiences where one has just developed into and learned how to do these things, and others haven't. So I believe . . . that DNA matters in leadership, but I think you can learn a lot."

Self-improvement for leaders came through three primary stimuli: reading, reflection, and, plainly put, further work. The mark of many achievers was their tenacity in sticking to one or all of these three.

Earlier we touched on journalist Tom Hallman's extensive reading of biographies, which helped humanize leaders in his mind and provided psychological comfort in his early to mid-twenties as he wondered how to work through his own difficulties. Hallman insisted that an openness to new inputs is critical for healthy development: "I think a lot of people don't ask for [such inputs], because they also don't want to hear what you need to do to improve. In my background, being a Nobody led me to be open to those kinds of—I didn't believe I was smart. I didn't believe I had much talent. My grades didn't reflect it, so I was open to criticism. That openness is what ultimately made me very sure about what I do. Not cocky, like I don't have any room for improvement, but I know when I'm on the path, and even now, at forty-eight, I'm still trying to grow . . . I'm sure you're going to find this with everybody who made Somebody, became Somebody—it's the burning desire to improve."

The reflective component of self-improvement was very important to Jay Gellert, CEO of Health Net, who had done his own reading and thinking about how to keep his energy and motivation high. Gellert said, "[M]ost of the people I know, by a certain age, are just hanging on. They've lost the joy, they've lost a lot of stuff. I think why do it if you're going to be miserable? You know that new Kennedy book [by Robert Dallek]? There's a quote early in there, which Bobby Kennedy used, 'Youth isn't a time of life; it's a state of mind. It's courage over timidity, it's a yearning for adventure over a sense of ease.' I think people lose their youth way too early in this business process."

Translating reading and reflection to action, many leaders attempted to improve themselves through continued effort, both in their first jobs and beyond. Describing the period just after college, before he had yet landed his first job in the cartooning industry, Mike Luckovich described the discipline in his campaign for self-betterment: "I would spend eight hours, sometimes drawing into the middle of the night, trying to get a drawing just the way I wanted it. Even though I wasn't getting paid for it, I just wanted to have it the best that I could . . . [T]he only way I could control [disappointment] was to keep drawing, and keep getting better, and I guess my thought was . . . 'No matter what I'm doing, as long as I'm selling this life insurance, or whatever other crummy job I'm doing, I'm going to keep drawing and get so good that I will be the very best, and someone will have to hire me.'"

For Robert Peiser, professional growth was a key part of his evolution from his first job at TWA as a finance specialist to his current position as CEO of Imperial Sugar: "I have transformed myself from being a pretty typical CFO type to one who is now much more interested in people development, communications, and leadership. I don't think I displayed many of those characteristics in my early years."

Peiser actually left his first job at TWA in part for more change and personal growth. "I was comfortable there but perhaps no longer challenged as much. Stepping out into another company was a big step out of my 'comfort zone' but one which was exhilarating and challenging—and ultimately the right decision. It is difficult to step outside of one's comfort zone, but sometimes critical for the right career progression."

Intellectual Curiosity

Another driver of leaders' dynamism, their capacity for self-improvement, was intellectual curiosity. Several people focused on the mental stimulation they get from their work, and the way it's attracted them at times even more than money. For example, Nobel Prize–winning scientist Rich Roberts highlighted the sometimes playful, exploratory nature of his research: "Puzzles and games [are] what I've always loved. Anytime anything seems to be a game, then you can count me in."

Gander Mountain CEO Mark Baker said, "I've always enjoyed solving problems." This attitude or curiosity was highly resilient in many leaders. After future Raytheon CEO Daniel Burnham was laid off from his first job at RCA, for example, he went to another large company called Carborundum. He actually turned down a previous offer to wait for this job, which involved cross-functional work across a large conglomerate. In his mind, "Going to Carborundum was an opportunity for intellectual curiosity. As I started to do those different things, across business units, I started to see the richness of business. I started to see the ability to link between many different things—it was that networking and assimilation of differences that I found interesting. It was interesting, as opposed to a power trip. I wasn't in it just for the ability to control things—it started out more as curiosity. As I began to get analytical assignments linking together manufacturing, finance, and marketing, I had the chance to do a lot of different things, and that really helped me grow."

Arrow Electronics CEO Bill Mitchell didn't see the opportunities for intellectual stimulation right away, but as his career progressed past his first job and he rose in seniority, he found increasing career motivation based on his interests in business, particularly abroad. "I really did like international business. I liked it, I liked doing it, I liked the challenges it provided. I liked the complexity of it, the people you met, the things that you were able to learn—there were just all those things that went along with it.

"And I said [to myself], 'There's something you can do here, and if you can do it for companies that have important international operations, then there's a chance you can take more responsibilities.' It turned out—I found out that I liked managing people, I liked managing organizations. As I grew and developed and had management responsibilities, I found out I liked it. I liked the strategic challenges—so a lot of the things that I began to be introduced to as I got higher in the organization, I really liked. The business challenges, the strategic challenges, I liked the people challenges, so I got more excited and said, 'Let's see if we can get a little further.'"

Though his perspective was not necessarily a common one, actually running counter to many sentiments I heard, Health Net CEO Jay Gellert raised an interesting thread of speculation: "As we've learned over the last fifteen years, commerce is more about ambition and drive and fo-cus than it is about deep thinking. The question you get to is in the fu-ture, with the complexity of the world and the fact that basic information is going to be readily available, it may get to refocus this where people will have to have a more curious, less intense state of mind to successfully lead organizations in the future, than they have in the past. Will the past model be the right model?" The possibility of a more cerebrally-based style of leadership deserves more investigation in future studies.

Failure

Failure and leaders' reactions to it merit special attention for a couple of reasons. Obviously, it's interesting to know how these top achievers, people now at the tops of their respective fields, failed early in their ca-reers. It's also interesting because failure demonstrates how leaders are forced to recognize needs for change and then to react accordingly. They don't necessarily make better short-term decisions than average people, and they don't make fewer mistakes. What leaders do is grow more from their mistakes than the average person, and repeat them less often.

To begin, it's important to note that leaders welcomed failure in a sense. They viewed it as part of the growth process. JB Hunt's Kirk Thompson articulated his belief that difficult conditions help lessons stand out more clearly. "One thing you learn a whole lot more by failure than you do by success. You don't learn a lot of stuff on the mountain-top. Where you learn it is in the valley . . . It may sound like a platitude, I guess it is a platitude, but it is so true. You learn so much more in the valley about yourself, about life, about where you went wrong, or what you need to do to get out of it. When you're on the peak, everything's hunks and chunks and life's wonderful. What's to learn? You just do—you learn more in the trenches than you do riding the horse."

For leaders accustomed to much success on their way to the top, failures helped keep matters in perspective. Matt Espe, CEO of IKON, remembered the successes from his first job—he tripled sales in his territory for GE over a two-year period—but also, notably, a key failure. "While the assignment was, overall, a great success, I can also think of one interesting lesson from this experience. In my first six months, I was actually 'fired' off of one of my accounts. The reason cited—the customer felt I was arrogant. This was definitely a wake-up call. I quickly learned that even when you are doing extremely well, it is important to solicit feedback from your peers, your supervisors and, most importantly, your customers."

Of course, all people, both high achievers and not, receive negative feedback from mistakes. What I found is that perhaps more clearly than others, leaders understood and responded to those signals. They learned from failure that they cannot rest on their laurels, that continuous self-improvement and change is important. CEO Gil Minor saw that with a major failure he experienced early in his first job after business school. He had been charged with building a new division of a larger conglomerate company. It involved promotions for independent retailers within a larger chain of pharmacies. "We had a voluntary cooperative plan that we put together. I mean, it was an enterprise that was going along very well, but I went a little too far. I added some services to this business that didn't work . . . I mean, I'm on a *roll*. Everything's going along, and I say, 'This looks good. Let's do this.' Well, it turned out to be a disaster. The guy I hired wasn't any good, and so we had to abandon part of that effort. Well, I had to go before the board and explain . . . Believe me. I was on my own. [Laughs] There wasn't any sympathy in the room. So I explained to them what was going on, and they said, 'Okay, we're going to close it down.' And I said, 'Well, give me a little more time.' And they said, 'No, you've had plenty of time. Let's close it down. We'll take our losses and move on.' Which of course was the absolute right decision to make. I was too close to it . . . But that was a wake-up call!" Nearly two and a half decades after the episode, Minor still remembered the lessons he had learned. "That I better listen to some people along the way . . . [Y]ou know, the humility part of it makes a lot of sense, especially if you're willing to learn from your mistakes."

Another lesson leaders take from failure is the importance of resilience. Referring to his disastrous experience with the business expansion, Minor remembered, "Fortunately, I was not taken down . . . I was more determined than ever to succeed. So, give me another chance. I got another chance, and believe me, I made plenty of mistakes along the way! . . . I was not discouraged with my overall ability to take something and run it and make it successful. I just needed to go about it a different way."

Returning to Kathleen Ligocki, the CEO of Tower Automotive, we get another perspective on how failures can help develop the mental toughness that defines resilience. In her view, "The business world is filled with lots of different rocky waters, and you have to have resilience, frankly, to get through it . . . [I]t's very competitive, both within your firm and in the marketplace. If you don't have that toughness and drive, I think it's very tough to succeed. It's challenging on a daily level, too, of course, just delivering results day in and day out. You've got to be tough to do that."

"The best people in business aren't those who don't make mistakes. The best are those who make mistakes, get up, and move on. I tend to be a risk-taker, and risk-takers make mistakes. The important thing is being able to learn from your mistakes, fix the important ones, and keep moving forward. That's resilience. There certainly are maintenance-mode managers, people who set up stable systems and keep them running, and they have their place. But I'm the kind of person who goes into new places, makes big moves, turns things around. You need to have resilience to do that. You make ten decisions, and seven of them are right. The other three, you've got to be tough, figure out what went wrong, and fix them in a hurry."

What gives leaders this kind of resilience, this ability to accept less-than-ideal outcomes and continue forward with hopes for a better tomorrow? For Staples CEO Ron Sargent, the answer lay again in the interplay between innate personality and instructive experiences. He felt that one of his biggest mistakes, committed shortly after he had left his first job to join the young company at Staples, helped develop his core trait of tenacity. Asked about watershed moments in his career, Sargent began, "We had started our existing delivery business, and it became a mail-order business, but we weren't servicing the large-company segment, because you really need a sales force, and it's called a contract stationer business. We did the build versus buy [study], and we decided we'd rather buy, so we acquired seven companies, and my job was to run those companies, but also to integrate them. Turn them into one whole—and a key part of that is you've got to get everyone on the same information systems.

"On April 22, 1996, we converted the first and largest of those companies onto a new systems platform. We did that, and we weren't ready to do it. We were so time-pressed, and so time- and date-driven . . . We said we're going to do this . . . I think it really clouded my judgment. [My mind-set was] 'I told you I was going to get this done by April 22, 1996—yeah, we've got a few minor bugs to fix, but we'll work them out, and we'll do that on the fly.' I think from my perspective, I walked off a cliff that day.

"A week later—obviously, we had a contingency plan, and we debated about whether you go back to the old system, or you just keep struggling with the new system. Then I made my second mistake in a week, which was continue on. It took us a *year* to recover from those two decisions, and that's why April 22, 1996, stands out in my mind.

"That was a good time of learning. One, to know what I'm doing, and make it event-driven, rather than date-driven, in terms of decisions. But, to me, the biggest learning, the guy who helped me walk off the cliff was the guy who was heading our I/S function at the time. He decided it was a mess, and he was going to leave the company and leave the business, and I had to make a decision myself: is my career over or not, and I decided even if my career was over, I wasn't going to leave a mess. I was going to slog through this, day by day, over the next year, to get this thing fixed. A year later, we got it fixed. I'm sure my career took a hit, but it wasn't over, and from that moment on, things continued to get better, and this part of the business is not only 30 percent of our sales, but I guess it's about 40 percent of our profit, and it's the fastest-growing part of our business [today]."

Sargent's distinction about learning is critical. Any person can and does absorb the blow of mistakes, but only a wise few consistently take the feedback implied in the fallout to improve their skills and approaches in later experiences.

Sargent summarized: "That year was a real career watershed year for me. I made mistakes, I learned from those mistakes, but I'm tenacious. I'll stick with something to right it. That was probably my—after [the decision on] leaving Kroger to join Staples—that was probably the thing that jumped out at me. And it wasn't one of my big successes, it was one of my biggest failures."

Pulitzer Prize winner Paul Salopek was perhaps most eloquent in summarizing the risks and rewards inherent in embracing potential failure. Strands of his thoughts appeared in the narratives of many different leaders I interviewed. Reflecting on his own experiences with his first job in journalism, Salopek declared that opening oneself to failure is a necessary condition to success. Without openness to life's opportunities, and corresponding vulnerability, the possibilities for success become much more limited.

"I had to make myself available to the possibilities that would move me along toward an honorable goal, whatever that is. Whether it's going to be your career, whether it's going to be your relationship or whatever, and the way that I did it was by, I tried to make myself vulnerable, intentionally vulnerable. Physically, and as much as possible, emotionally—because that leaves you open to the delight and the magic of possibility. If you fear not, if you're too comfortable, if you've made yourself invulnerable, you've built sort of, you know, a comfortable blockade or palisade around you, I think you're going to miss out on some of these possibilities that float by, that other people may attribute to serendipity, but may or may not be serendipitous. If you miss that, then I think that just constricts your horizons one notch further.

"So my parting advice would be, make yourself vulnerable to change, to discomfort, to the unexpected. And in fact, embrace it. You'll find that you may not always get what you're looking for, but in the end, you'll look back and see that everything eventually adds up to something, at least, if nothing else, in telling you what you don't want to do. So that's why I was only half joking when I told you in the e-mail, go ahead and get your college degree. You need it today, absolutely, but also don't dismiss the option of going out and doing some tests and doing some manual work somewhere, and then something that's completely, completely different than what you normally do. And that way, you bump into mentors, unexpectedly. Ones that you would never—you know, we think of mentors as people in the business, people in academia. Nonsense. My crucial mentors were a barely literate ninety-year-old farmer in northern Mexico, a foul-mouthed seaman on the Indian Ocean, whatever—a woman who rides a motorcycle alone across Australia. These are people who, unless you're open to meeting them and you're willing to meet them on their terms, you don't know what they'll do for you."

The simplest conclusion came from novelist Tom Clancy. When I asked him what he learned in his first job, he replied bluntly, "All life is a learning experience, and there is no such thing as an unimportant fact."

Reasons for Pulling Back

Before finishing this chapter on change, and leaders' ability to adapt themselves over time, it's also worth examining those situations in which leaders pulled back—in which they adjusted previously grand ambitions to something a bit more modest or controlled. Not all movement in a career is forward, after all. Sometimes, the path not taken, or sidestepped, can be as valuable as the one actually followed. At a few junctures in their working lives, leaders showed the ability to alter their ambitious plans, to refrain from certain opportunities and possibilities. This trait seemed particularly impressive, because it ran counter to the basic personality type and usual behavior of many leaders. It was in a way the ultimate demonstration of flexibility and openness to change.

For a few people, changing plans and holding back from opportunities stemmed from the most basic issue of physical safety. Photographer April Saul won two Pulitzer Prizes but was candid in discussing a crossroads decision at which she pulled back. "I went to Bosnia . . . I was so affected by hearing about the women who were raped, and all of the things that were happening to women in the war . . . It wasn't just raped women. I [spoke with] women who were affected by the war, and refugees . . . Just as I was about to leave there, I got an offer to go into . . . a place where there was a lot of carnage going on . . . with some really famous war photographers, the best and the brightest of them, to go with them on this expedition to do this.

"I called back to my boss, and he said, 'Boy, that would be great. It's up to you, but that would be great.' And after I hung up with him, I thought, 'You know, this isn't what I do. I don't know how to dodge bullets.' I had some really crappy secondhand police bulletproof vest with me [laughs]. It was one of those times when you have to define what it is you do, and what I do is—I don't do the bang-bang stuff."

Former Congressman Dan Glickman relied on a similar mix of personal knowledge and risk-reward calculations when he considered a run for the U.S. Senate. Eventually, Glickman said, analysis of his own circumstances was more persuasive to him than conventional wisdom on political career paths. "I thought that we needed a Democrat as well as a Republican in the Senate. Kansas hadn't sent a Democrat to the Senate since 1932, and I think it was just, frankly, a lot of ambition, too. You know, this is not that unusual. Over half of the members of the U.S. Senate today are former members of the House. It's just kind of a career path that a lot of people take. But I never took it.

"I think what I thought about intuitively was I probably couldn't win. If I could've won, I might've decided to do it. Maybe it was just my internal compass saying, 'You know, Glickman, it's great, being a Senator is great, but you'd rather have what you've got than lose in a statewide race.' It turned out I probably couldn't have beat Dole all those times. And so I think that was a real personal crisis for me, because you know, after thinking you could do about anything, I wrestled with that very, very strongly, several times over my Congressional life."

In the case of music critic Lloyd Schwartz, a clear-eyed assessment of professional prospects lay at the root of his caution, as well. He had passed an opportunity straight out of graduate school to join the faculty of Fairleigh Dickinson, in part because he wanted to continue pursuing his own acting and poetry careers. A few years later, though, as he neared his thirties, the calculus changed. A job offer to teach at Boston State College, which would get Schwartz's academic career back on track, entailed serious sacrifice—sacrifice Schwartz made this time.

The Boston job "meant having to give up acting on the stage," he said. "It was very hard, and I was seeing people—my colleagues, my acting, theater colleagues, whom I had really admired . . . go on to leave Boston and either start real careers, like Stockard Channing and John Lithgow and James Woods and Tommy Lee Jones. But there were also people who were equally good who left Boston for New York or Hollywood and couldn't get anywhere. And were not getting cast."

So with the hard trade-offs of adulthood upon him, Schwartz swallowed hard, gave up his own acting ambitions, and began down the path that would help him become an award-winning critic. "I really—I thought that this was a turning point," he remembered. "Could I devote myself completely and obsessively and give up everything to have an acting career? I wasn't sure I could live that way . . . I was trained to be an academic. It was something that was also deeply important to me . . . I thought I was a good actor, but I thought you had to be really lucky . . . I thought, 'I don't—it's not my nature to trust that much to my luck.'"

Former Cabinet member Bill Ruckelshaus provided perhaps the best case study of self-knowledge and adaptability leading to choices that might surprise others. Ruckelshaus gained brief national celebrity in the early 1970s as one of the members of the Attorney General's office in the Nixon Administration, fired in the infamous "Saturday Night Massacre" by the President. In that case, Ruckelshaus's sense of personal ethics and integrity outweighed his desire to maintain his job in the Nixon administration. He was someone who also made careful choices at other junctures, though. Earlier on, Ruckelshaus had passed on chances to enter the business world due to his dislike of the stiflingly bureaucratic culture he saw in large private enterprises. Later, Ruckelshaus joined a Seattle law firm at the partner level, but with a surprising arrangement that he suggested to the firm himself, based on his personal interests. "I [took the job] on the assumption that I wasn't going to practice law. They told me what they were going to pay me, and I said, 'Cut it in half.' I told them, 'I don't want you depending on me to bring in a bunch of clients, justifying my salary. So I only want half of what you're offering.' Which was fine with them!"

Ruckelshaus exemplified what I saw in many leaders: a surprising flexibility and willingness to take unconventional paths. These people who ascended to their positions of esteem at the top rungs of various establishment ladders were, ironically, those who also remained open to their own unconventional notions and ideas. They didn't assume that certain starting points in life implied certain ending points. They didn't follow preprogrammed career tracks. They didn't accept others' assumptions. Above all, they understood and embodied constant growth and personal reinvention. For a book on Nobodies who became Somebodies, this was the most important and perhaps the most fitting lesson of all.

Closing Thoughts

This book started with a conviction and a question. The conviction was that young people today remain as much defined and driven by aspiration as generations past. We want to understand ourselves and to make a mark on the world, to find what it is we are meant to do, and to do it well. The question was whether older people could help guide us on this journey through an increasingly complex, fast-moving world.

I waded in knowing that the question wasn't necessarily an easy one. The defining idea of America, what we've taken to calling the American Dream, is that a person can start with no money in her pocket, no connections or benefits from her name, and pull herself up by the bootstraps to achieve significant things. But how Nobodies become Somebodies has remained largely mysterious to most of us. The process seems at once short and long. We've all witnessed it happen within a single lifetime—but it does in fact take years if not decades of intelligent, hard work, integrity, and perhaps a bit of luck. Would some of those leaders who've scaled the proverbial mountain have wisdom to share? I was delighted to find that the answer was yes.

Looking back now on the fifteen months of research that went into this book, the conversations I had with society's Somebodies by e-mail, over the phone, and in their offices, I'm gratified by what they shared. I didn't expect to learn a magic formula for success, because much as my bank account would enjoy it, my guess was that becoming a Fortune

500 CEO, a Presidential Cabinet member, a senator or governor, or a Nobel or Pulitzer prize winner takes a bit more than that which can be crammed onto a six-disc DVD set for easy infomercial consumption.

What I hoped for, and got, was a set of stories about leaders and the early jobs they took when they, too, were Nobodies. By focusing on the first job, I believed I'd get more trenchant insights for young people. Frankly, it's hard for most of us to relate except at a theoretical level to concerns about multibillion-dollar mergers, or diplomatic delicacies with foreign heads of state, or which esteemed journal should publish our latest experiment's results. We can relate very easily, though, to issues like those tackled through this book's research: how leaders identified their vocations; what went through their minds as they began their careers; what motivated them; what daily habits and practices characterized their routines; which moves they made from one job or organization to the next; why they made decisions; how they handled failures, both big and small; and how they balanced (or didn't balance) relationships with peers, followers, mentors, institutions, and families.

By looking at the detail around their first jobs, I found the insight I was seeking. After getting past the predictable traits of hard work, upbeat spirits, and friendly, social personalities, the key differentiator of leaders was their deep self-knowledge and the resulting openness to change and improvement. These people often did the so-called Right Things in managing their careers—attending good schools, working toward responsibility, and persevering through difficulties with an outstanding intensity and forward-looking perspective—but they sometimes did Wrong Things, too. At various times, they chose odd jobs, they drifted for brief periods, and they made poor choices of organizations or issues with which to work. The factor that separated them from others, and that propelled their rise from Nobodies to Somebodies, was the constant emphasis on understanding themselves, taking in environmental feedback and conditions, and working toward the rich new possibilities available in each given situation.

This focus on self-knowledge and embrace of change is worth dwelling on. For perspective, consider a list of five other, common explanations for career success I tested in my interviews with leaders, and that may be true in certain circumstances, but weren't robust enough to stretch across the experiences of the 100 people in different fields and circumstances:

CONVENTIONAL HYPOTHESIS	REJECTED BECAUSE . . .
"They inherited their success. Someone gave them a free ride directly, or they were deterministically pointed toward success after being brought up with means."	Many if not most of the leaders grew up in families with modest means and spoke openly of their economic difficulties.
"They were just smarter than everyone else."	Even putting aside the modesty voiced by many leaders (to the effect that they possessed similar talents or intelligence as others who had not succeeded in the same way), it was interesting to note that a fair number were not necessarily huge scholastic successes in early childhood. Also, the decision-making processes they described for key crossroads around their first jobs were not particularly sophisticated or different from what the average person might say.
"They politicked their way to success. They simply knew the right people and made the right connections."	While leaders were often highly social people, almost all went through periods of professional loneliness and anonymity, and many professed not to have single, lifelong mentors.
"They just worked insanely hard, stayed on the conventional path, and were straight arrows all the way through."	While many did admit to workaholic-type tendencies, others pointed to work-life balance as a key source of strength. A number also took offbeat paths to discovering their eventual destinies. Finally, of course, many people who work hard don't get to where these people did.

CONVENTIONAL HYPOTHESIS	REJECTED BECAUSE . . .
"They just got lucky."	Proving this negative—that they did not get lucky—is virtually impossible. The cop-out explanation of random chance is theoretically applicable to almost all outcomes. However, it was interesting to hear many leaders discuss very specific things they did to position themselves for luck, to increase their chances for it, and to be ready when it arrived. Many people conceivably have lucky breaks, but why do only some capitalize? Why is it, as former Texas Governor Ann Richards said, that "The luckiest people I know are the hardest working"?

The importance of self-knowledge explains why some readers of this book may find rote application of its concepts useless, and why others may argue about the apparent contradiction among certain of those concepts. For example, critics may complain that a leader cannot be confident and at the same time use insecurities as personal fuel, as suggested in Lesson 3. Or they may wonder how to reconcile the circumstances of personal expedience that motivated many leaders in their first jobs ("I just needed to make a living!") with the greater ambitions and hunger for big challenges discussed in Lesson 13. They may argue that leaders could be risk-tolerant and open to serendipitous chance in their careers, or carefully conscious of their career moves, but not both.

I would respond to those people by urging a more nuanced reading of the concepts outlined in this book. Various qualities demonstrated by Somebodies may seem paradoxical when considered next to each other, but remember that each trait, habit, or practice works differently for different leaders—or for the same leader at different points in her career. To assume that rote application of some kind of Manual for

Success will automatically produce results is silly. The leaders profiled in this book built highly respectable bodies of life work, often over decades, by possessing the human intangibles of timing and wisdom: understanding when something made sense for them and when it didn't. More than raw intelligence, their savvy in knowing themselves and in remaining flexible to necessary changes is what propelled their careers from their first job onward. While perhaps not sexy, these qualities were the closest thing to a secret sauce in leaders' recipes for success.

Obviously, I have a healthy admiration and respect for the people profiled in these pages. If I didn't believe they have valuable perspectives to pass on to young people, I wouldn't have gone through the work of soliciting and synthesizing their thoughts. But separate from that respect for their professional accomplishments and perspectives, I want to emphasize my deep appreciation for the leaders' generosity in sharing their stories. I have a separate section for other acknowledgments, but certainly, the 100 men and women who gave me their time, their memories, and their wisdom deserve huge credit. When I originally approached most of them with my interview requests, I closed with the promise that "young people in the twenty- and thirtysomething generation will much appreciate the sharing of your insights and experiences!" It's a pledge I'm sure will be kept over a long time.

Also, it will be interesting to see how the story, both generally and for these specific 100 leaders, continues forward. The essentially human capacity for organic growth and self-improvement, which these leaders have displayed in the decades from their first job to today, will continue to manifest itself in their continuing work, I believe. Only a few had retired when I interviewed them. Most have years ahead of further contributions to society. I'll remain eager to see what the future yields as the engines of their imagination continue to crank away.

Aside from the other interests already mentioned, I wrote this book because I was curious about dreams and the romance of aspiration. I wondered how dreams translated into concrete achievement, because I felt that most of the time I saw two distinct populations, the dreamers versus the successful people, without too much crossover from one to the other. In my mind, I and other glinty-eyed peers tended to discount dreamers as soft-minded underachievers—nice people, but soft-minded nonetheless. Sure, I would read profiles of crazy dreams come true, people like Michael Dell starting the world's largest computer manufacturer out of a bathtub in his college dorm room with $1,000, or Jeff Bezos quitting a job on Wall Street and packing his car to drive cross-country in a quest to launch Amazon.com and the e-commerce era. But I've personally encountered a hundred other similarly bold dreams that ended in significantly worse circumstances. Also, looking at the career trajectories of people closer to my own life, those who do best in their early jobs, at least by superficial glance, appeared to be the serious, the focused, and the persistent, not necessarily the speculative, the footloose, and the flexible. I wanted to dream, but my suspicion, essentially, was that pursuing dreams is for dopes, and that if I wanted to succeed by conventional measures of money, influence, respectability, and so on, I should take conventional paths.

Let me pause and say that after finishing the research, I haven't suddenly decided that seriousness, focus, and persistence are bad and that dreams are singularly good. What I have come to understand is the sterility of this earlier thinking. Looking at the examples of society's Somebodies, I see that the first job should be pursued with all the type-A characteristics you can muster—if those things fit your personality and goals. And dreams are good—but only if they're really yours and if they adjust to the changing circumstances of your very dynamic life. What's most important is learning to hear the voice inherent in all our minds, our gut instincts, to be consistent about following that voice, and at the same time responding realistically to what's happening in the world around us, what people are telling us, and how the environment in a given situation is changing.

And let me say that I'm far from smug as I finish this book. I learned a tremendous amount by sitting at the feet (sometimes literally!) of the masters and hearing the rich diversity of perspectives of people who have done very well for themselves. My gratitude did not erase the sensation I felt as I began to know how much I don't know. Also, I recognize very clearly that there isn't a rote formula for success. Only time will tell how well I and others incorporate these lessons into our own lives.

Happily, though, since that winter day on which this project hatched almost a year and a half ago, there have been some encouraging signs. I've taken a respite from start-up life to return to the corporate environment, doing work that I enjoy with colleagues I respect. The friend and former colleague with whom I was having lunch that first day remains at the software company that licensed our technology. He has great hopes for its contribution to a growing niche of the Internet industry. Recently, he even lured another friend of ours away from a comfortable but overly safe job into the same startup company and its wild winds of entrepreneurial work. And it's not just them. All around, like blooming signs of spring after the long winter of the last few years' economic recession, I see people my age working hard, devoting themselves to their goals, searching for their big breaks, and enjoying the ride all the way. I see a whole lot of Nobodies looking to become Somebodies. It excites me.

Afterword: The Ending to the Story (for Now)

Both in the text of *Nobodies to Somebodies* and in the many tour appearances and media interviews since the book's release, I mentioned that the book was a labor of love. I wanted to draw a roadmap of life lessons and professional progress that might help me and my peers as we embark on our own journeys. Hence throughout the process—from the book's initial conception to its first drafting to its post-release reception—I've been keenly interested in how my twenty- and thirtysomething peers react to the material. What do they like? What do they not like? What do they wonder more about?

Here's what I can tell you: since the book hit the market earlier this year, the most common question from friends and acquaintances has been, "Was it worth it?" Lots of other questions were asked, ranging from vaguely academic inquiries into my research methodology to questions about the 100 interviewees and what's become of them—but the most common question inevitably centered on my own personal gains from this project. "Was it worth it?" After puzzling over exactly what this question might mean, or more precisely, what people hoped to learn from it, I settled on a seemingly simple interpretation: how much did I gain from all the effort of researching and writing the book, and then putting myself in the public eye with an implicit declaration that I have Ideas Worth People's Attention? Having gone through the whole process—the uncertainty and the hard work and the excitement and then finally the public reception—would I do it again? Did I learn? Did I have fun? Did my work on the book *pay off*, financially and otherwise?

My immediate answer to those questions was almost a defensive one: "Well, of course! Let me tell you about all of the interesting people I met while touring, or the business opportunities presented to me, or the cash that hit my bank account!" Whether spoken aloud or not, thoughts like these would often squirm too quickly into my head.

But after mulling over my friends' repeated queries, with a few months' perspective, I realize now that many of them were actually testing the central thesis of this book, the core assumption underpinning the entire venture. While they're wonderfully supportive of the book as an entrepreneurial venture, and they enjoy the idea of their friend having put his name on a small corner of the publishing universe, these friends still find themselves wondering . . . *if the system actually works*. To varying degrees, they feel and are confessing nagging doubt. Do the kind of old-fashioned inputs described in *Nobodies to Somebodies*—strong self-awareness, hard work, a sociable personality, and openness to new experiences and to change—actually produce the kind of outputs enjoyed by the book's 100 subjects? Will the formulae that worked for generations past still apply in this newer, faster, more complicated age? By using me as a proxy for the very topic about which I write—a striving young person attempting to make himself from Nobody into Somebody—these friends gain another datapoint, another bit of validation for nascent theories of life optimism or cynicism. After all, they can check in on me personally, hear about progress with the book, my own fortunes, and how they've changed or not changed, and then take their own mental measures: "Hmmm, he worked awfully hard to get those interviews, and the publishing contract, and he hustled all over the country on planes, trains, and automobiles to promote the sucker. Is all that effort worthwhile?"

I wish I had a simple answer for these people. Often a reductionist, bottom-line thinker myself, I can sympathize with the desire to find an ending to the story, a neat moral which summarizes that which has happened since this book came into the world, and I continued my own personal version of the quest described in this book. One storyline could be something like: Young man generates idea for book. Busts hump doing research and writing, and then goes on *Oprah* and the *Today Show* to hawk product. Runaway sales bolster book to top of *New York Times* bestseller list, after which young man becomes fabulously wealthy and quits day job.

But that's not the actual ending to this story.

Another storyline could run instead: Young man generates idea for book. Busts hump doing research and writing, then releases book . . . to empty air. No good reviews, no sales, no acclaim. Eighteen months of hard labor, spent without any tangible return.

But that's not the true ending to the story, either.

The best I can offer readers is the truth. And, as is often the case in these situations, the truth isn't so sexy or glamorous as to offer certain conclusions. It offers only glimpses, hints, nuance.

And for those curious and patient enough to desire those things, and who still want to know if this book was worth the effort it took to produce: I think so. I worked really hard on it, conducting the research and writing at nights and on weekends, while I kept my day job at Microsoft. The extremely long hours and stress of meeting a book deadline while juggling a full-time job contributed in part to a feeling of burnout that made late 2004 and early 2005 a little rough. My career at Microsoft might've been delayed a half-step or two, as my attention was distracted, superiors noticed, and I stepped away from the madding crowd to cut my own career path, not entirely direct. Still, I made a decent amount of money from the book, and from follow-up speaking engagements that arose due to the book. I met an interesting (and sometimes humorous) range of new people, readers attracted by the book and what I guess they saw as a young, accessible author. (I asked myself several times, "Do all authors hear these heartfelt personal stories and requests for counsel?") I saw a number of favorable articles and blog posts about *Nobodies to Somebodies*, and chuckled as we sold foreign-translation rights for Chinese, Korean, Russian, and Brazilian editions of the book. The book'll also come out in an audio format, and as you hold in your hands now, a paperback version. Not a bad set of outcomes. (If you're not aware, full updates at www.NobodiesToSome bodies.com.) And as far as the day job goes, I've stuck with it, seeing

the good parts of the position and continuing to build my career in corporate America.

That's not to say that everything has been great, though. I mentioned burnout, which started in part from the intense schedule
spawned by the book. I shouldn't say it lightly, because as those who've
experienced it know, burnout ain't fun. It's hard, grinding, and at times
dispiriting when you're facing another Monday morning with a to-do
list longer than your patience for dealing with it. The book started that
feeling of burnout. And what the book started, a movie finished. Perhaps addicted to the pace and the thrill of working on the book, in late
2004 I hatched a documentary movie project before the hardcover edition of *Nobodies to Somebodies* was even in print. For the movie, we
raised investor money, signed a deal to follow four elite triathletes
around for a year, and, as with the book, aimed to deliver to audiences a
portrait of excellence—people at the top of their fields, pushing themselves to extremes to achieve things about which the rest of us only
dream idly. (You can see more at www.WITmovie.com.) The movie's
not done, but it's already done something that the book alone could
not—it convinced me that two simultaneous jobs do not a good life
make. By the time this paperback edition of the book comes out, I
should be done with the writing, done with the moviemaking, and settled back into a more normal routine. I intend to stay there for a while!

Aside from the schedule demands, the movie also left a few open
questions in my mind. Like those friends whose restless minds continue to tug at the ball of string called Success, and who wonder what it
takes to be at the top of life's games, I can't say that I have complete,
rock-solid confidence that things will work out, that good kids who
keep their noses clean will all be rewarded amply. The book and the
movie demonstrate my curiosity and restlessness on this point, of
course, but the movie reinforced it, in a way. During the filming of our
documentary, I became close to one of the four triathletes we were following, a three-time world champion named Peter Reid. This is a man
who's been to the top of his sport not just once, but thrice, and who has
triumphed over rivals in one of the most difficult physical and mental
challenges we've invented as a society: the 2.4-mile swim, 112-mile cycle, and 26.2-mile run known as an Ironman Triathlon. If anyone fits

the platitude about "tough as nails," it's Pete. During the year that we filmed him, he went through an extraordinary personal journey, as he suffered a nasty staph infection, found out that his former wife would have a baby with a new partner, and endured growing doubts about his ability to maintain the highest standards of competitive excellence as he aged. I grew to respect and care for Pete tremendously as I saw him battle these demons, and by the time the culminating world championship race occurred in Kona, Hawaii, on October 15, 2005, I was intensely curious if he would be able to overcome all the obstacles to win again and to stand atop the sport of Ironman Triathlon.

Unfortunately, as with my own story about the hardback edition of *Nobodies to Somebodies*, there was no simple ending. Pete did not win the world championship, but he didn't embarrass himself, either. He fought gallantly for most of the race, leading a large pack through a grueling cycling course, and went into the final marathon leg down just a few minutes in the standings. He worked himself to a moment of truth, a showdown on the shimmering lava fields just outside Kona, with the eventual victor and of course with his own body's ability to summon a final push, and he wasn't quite able to get over the hump. Eventually, he finished the race third. Should he have done something differently? Could he have done anything to finish first instead of third? I truly admire Pete, and look up to him as I did the CEOs and Nobel Prize winners and senators from *Nobodies to Somebodies*, but of course I keep wondering.

There are times when this curiosity seems silly, other times when it troubles me, and still others when it makes me laugh with delight. Ultimately, whether with Pete in his future Ironman racing, or me with my creative endeavors, or my oh-so-talented-but-uncertain friends who wonder if they'll win all the prizes for which they compete, I just don't have complete answers. But I do have thoughts, and like everyone else, I have hopes. As far as Ironman Triathlons go, I'm sure I'll be on the courses next season cheering for Pete, Heather, Luke, and Lori. I hope they and my other friends find their hardest and most noble endeavors worth it.

Peter Han
Seattle, Washington
November, 2005

Appendix A
Capsule Biographies of the 100 Leaders

Business: Fortune 1000 CEOs

Brad Anderson is the CEO of Best Buy, one of the nation's leading electronics retailers, with nearly $20 billion in annual sales. He joined the Minneapolis company as a salesperson in 1973 and has ascended through its management ranks for the last three decades, joining the Board of Directors and becoming Executive Vice President in 1986, and then earning the title of CEO in 2002. Anderson received an associate of arts degree from Waldorf College in 1969 and then followed that with a BA from the University of Denver.

Norm Axelrod is the Chairman and CEO of New Jersey–based Linens 'N Things. He joined the company in 1988, after starting his career at Bloomingdale's in 1976. Axelrod has worked in a wide variety of functions across retail, acting as a buyer, merchandising manager, and divisional general manager. He earned a BS from Lehigh University and an MBA from New York University.

Mark R. Baker has served as CEO of Gander Mountain since September 2002, and was recently appointed as President. With eighty-two stores across fourteen states, Gander Mountain is a leading outdoor specialty retailer, focusing on hunting, fishing, and camping. Earlier in his career, Baker held various senior management positions with other retailers such as Home Depot and HomeBase. An avid outdoorsman, Baker is also a director of the Scotts Company, a company that manufactures and markets lawn and garden products.

Daniel Burnham is the former Chairman and CEO of Massachusetts-based Raytheon Company. After a brief tenure at RCA to start his career, Burnham moved on to The Carborundum Company, where he worked from 1971 to 1982, and then to AlliedSignal, where he became Vice President and Controller in 1982. He moved up through the plastics, fibers, and aerospace groups at AlliedSignal, eventually serving for five years as president of AlliedSignal Aerospace, the company's largest division. He moved over to Raytheon in 1998 and was at the company until 2004. Burnham is a director of FleetBoston Financial, First Data, and the Congressional Medal of Honor Foundation, among others. He received his BA from Xavier University in 1968 and his MBA from the University of New Hampshire in 1970.

Bob Catell is the Chairman and CEO of New York–based Keyspan Corporation. He joined Brooklyn Union, the pre-merger forerunner to Keyspan, in 1958 after a brief stint at the start of his career at AT&T. Catell worked as an engineer and rose through the ranks over a number of years, becoming CEO in 1991. He serves as an officer or director of numerous national industry groups, like the U.S. Energy Association, and local civic groups and charities. He received both his BS and MS in mechanical engineering from the City College of New York.

Curt Culver is Chairman and CEO of MGIC, the Milwaukee-based mortgage insurance company. He has been at the company for more than two decades, after a first job with a smaller company in the same industry.

James DeGraffenreidt is Chairman and CEO of Washington Gas, the utility company for the D.C. area. He started his career as a lawyer in private practice, and worked in public-practice law before shifting over into the business world. Before law school, DeGraffenreidt received his BA from Yale University. He sits on the boards of numerous local charities and civic groups, and is married with four children.

Dan DiMicco is Vice Chairman, President, and CEO of Nucor, one of the nation's leading steel makers. He has been with the company since 1982, when he joined Nucor's operation in Utah as a Plant Metallurgist and Manager of Quality Control. Prior to that, he was with Republic Steel as a Research Metallurgist and Project leader for seven years, from 1975 to 1982. DiMicco graduated from Brown University with a BS in 1972 and an MS from the University of Pennsylvania in 1975.

Matt Espe is President and CEO of IKON Office Solutions, the business communications solutions company based in Pennsylvania. Espe took his first job as a field sales representative with General Electric, beginning in 1980, and he rose through the company's ranks until 2002, eventually becoming President and CEO of GE Lighting. Espe graduated from the University of Idaho and earned his MBA from Whittier College in California while working for GE. He is married and has four children.

Paul Fireman is the founder and now Chairman of Massachusetts-based Reebok. One of the Forbes 400 richest people in America, he began his career with a small family-run company and worked there nearly two decades before finding the products that became Reebok's first offerings at a small trade show. He started Reebok in 1979 and has overseen its explosive growth to become one of the world's leading providers of athletic apparel and footwear. He is married and has three grown children.

Jay Gellert is President and CEO of Health Net, one of the largest managed health-care companies in the United States. He started his career with a small management consulting firm specializing in health care before working at a series of managed-care companies from 1985 to 1996. Gellert holds a BA from Stanford University and serves on several boards, including the American Association of Health Plans, Mivita, and Ventas.

Gerald Grinstein is CEO of Delta Airlines. He started his career as a lawyer, with stints as a U.S. Senate counsel and assistant to Senator Warren Magnuson prior to partnership with the law firm of Preston, Thorgrimson, Ellis and Holman in Seattle. Subsequent to that work and before taking his current position with Delta, he served as CEO of Western Airlines and Burlington Northern, and as nonexecutive chairman of Agilent Technologies. Grinstein serves on the boards of directors of Delta, Paccar, The Brink's Co., and Vans Inc. Born in Seattle, he graduated from Yale in 1954 and Harvard Law School in 1957. He and his wife, Lyn, have four grown children.

James Hagedorn is Chairman and CEO of Scotts Company, the country's top lawn-care products company. He began his career with seven years as a fighter pilot in the Air Force before joining his family's business, Miracle-Gro. At Miracle-Gro, Hagedorn drove international growth and helped engineer the company's merger with Ohio-based Scotts. He holds a BS from Embry-Riddle Aeronautical University. He serves on the boards of a variety of charities.

Dennis Highby is the President and CEO of Cabela's, one of the nation's largest direct marketers and specialty retailers of outdoor sporting equipment. After starting his career with outdoor retailer Herter's, Highby joined Cabela's in 1976 and has been with the company ever since.

Thomas Johnson is Chairman and CEO of Greenpoint Financial, a bank in New York. He has held the posts since 1993, before which he was President and Director of Chemical Bank. He is a director or trustee of numerous civic organizations. Johnson received his BA from Trinity College and his MBA from Harvard University.

Bruce Karatz is Chairman and CEO of KB Homes. He started his career as a lawyer in private practice and then joined KB Homes in 1972. He climbed the company's management ladder until 1985, when he was named CEO. Mr. Karatz is involved with a number of Los Angeles–area civic and charitable organizations and is a director of Honeywell, the Kroger Company, National Golf Properties, and his own company. He graduated from Boston University and received his JD from USC.

Parker Kennedy is Chairman and CEO of First American Corporation. He has worked at the company since 1977, becoming Vice President in 1979 and President in 1989. He began his career as a lawyer.

Lowry Kline is Vice Chairman and CEO of Coca-Cola Enterprises, the bottling arm of the world's largest beverage company. He started his career at a law firm in Chattanooga, Tennessee, and took on Coca-Cola Enterprises as a client in 1981. In 1991, he was named the company's general counsel and was promoted through a series of executive positions before being named CEO in April 2001.

Kathleen Ligocki is the President and CEO of Tower Automotive, a designer and producer of automobile components and assemblies used by every leading car manufacturer. She is one of the highest-ranking women in the automotive industry. Prior to joining Tower Automotive in 1993, Ligocki was an executive with the Ford Motor Company. Ligocki started her career as a factory foreman at a General Motors plant in Kokomo, Indiana. She holds a bachelor's degree from Indiana University and an MBA from Wharton.

Jim Middleton was President and CEO of USAA Insurance, the financial services company based in San Antonio, Texas. Before stepping down in 2004, Middelton was responsible for helping drive the company's growth to five million members and assets of $73 billion. After graduating with an MS from Purdue University, Middleton started his career in the Air Force, in which he served for twenty-one years. He also earned an MBA from the University of Texas during his service. He is married with three children.

Gil Minor is the Chairman and CEO of Owens-Minor, the medical and surgical supplies company based in Virginia. He joined the company in 1963 and left briefly to earn his MBA at the University of Virginia, in 1966. He has served as CEO since 1984.

Bill Mitchell has been the President and CEO of Arrow Electronics, located in New York, since February 2003. Soon after his career started, he moved to Raychem International and worked there from 1973 to 1993, where he headed various divisions of the company. In 1993, he moved to Nashua Corporation, which he led for two years before moving to Sequel, a privately held company. He then joined Solectron and helped build its global services division to more than $1 billion in annual revenue. Mitchell earned a BS in engineering from Princeton University and an MS in engineering from the University of Michigan. He is a director of Rogers. He has a wife and children.

Paul Norris is Chairman and CEO of WR Grace and Company. He worked for the Maryland company at three different junctures of his career, including his first job after business school. He joined most recently from AlliedSignal, where he was a Senior Vice President. Prior to AlliedSignal, Norris also worked for most of the 1980s at Engelhard Corporation. He graduated from Mt. St. Mary's College in Maryland and then received his MBA from the University of Maryland.

William Nuti is President and CEO of Symbol. He began his career with IBM and then spent more than a decade at Cisco, eventually becoming Senior Vice President of U.S. Theater Operations and Worldwide Service Provider Operations. He joined New York–based Symbol in August 2002. Nuti holds a degree in finance and economics from Long Island University and lives on Long Island with his wife and son. He belongs to several outside boards, both in the private and public sector.

Steve Odland is Chairman, President, and CEO of Memphis-based AutoZone, the nation's largest auto parts and accessories retailer, with more than $5.5 billion in annual revenue. Odland has been at the company since 2001, when he came from Ahold, a global supermarket operator. He also served at Sara Lee Bakery as President of the foodservice division, after starting his career at Quaker Oats Company, where he stayed sixteen years. In his time at Quaker Oats, Odland worked up from an initial position in brand management to serve in a variety of vice president roles. Odland is active as a director or contributor to numerous industry organizations and other public companies. He received his BA from Notre Dame and his masters in management from Kellogg.

Robert Peiser is President and CEO of Imperial Sugar. Prior to joining the Houston company in 2002, he worked at privately owned Vitality Beverages, and earlier for a variety of companies in different industries. Peiser began his career at Trans World Airlines. He holds an MBA from Harvard.

Ron Sargent is CEO of Staples, the leading office-supply retailer in the world. He came to the Massachusetts company in 1989 when it was a small regional player, and rose through a string of jobs until his promotion to CEO in February 2002. Sargent started his career at the Kroger Company after getting his MBA from Harvard. He also holds an AB from Harvard.

Craig Sturken is President and CEO of Spartan Stores. He has worked in the grocery industry through a career stretching more than four decades, including stints at Hannaford Brothers, Grand Union, and Great Atlantic & Pacific Tea Company (A&P). He joined Michigan-based Spartan in March 2003.

Kirk Thompson is President and CEO of JB Hunt, one of the country's largest trucking and logistics companies. He started his career at Arkansas-based JB Hunt and after a brief interlude at the accounting firm of Peat Marwick, returned to the company in 1979. He started as CFO and helped oversee the company's explosive growth to more than $2 billion in annual revenue today. Thompson has a degree from the University of Arkansas.

Roy Vallee is Chairman and CEO of Arizona-based Avnet. His first job was with Radio Products in 1971, in Los Angeles. He started as a warehouse worker and moved up through a variety of positions. After six years, he moved over to Hamilton/Avnet and ascended in responsibilities until becoming President and COO of Avnet in 1992. He is a director of Teradyne and Synopsys, and is active in a variety of charities. Vallee holds an associate of science from Don Bosco Technical Insititute.

Lars Westerberg is President and CEO of Autoliv, a $5 billion auto and truck parts company. It is a position he has held since 1999. Previously he was a President and CEO of Granges AB, a Swedish-based aluminum and plastics company. Westerberg holds a master's in electrical engineering from the Royal Institute of Technology in Stockholm and an MBA from the University of Stockholm.

Felix Zandman is Chairman and CEO of Vishay Intertechnology, a Pennsylvania-based company that he founded himself in 1962. Zandman was a Holocaust survivor who earned his Ph.D. in physics from the University of Paris, Sorbonne, and moved to the United States thereafter. He has published three textbooks and an autobiography, and holds thirty-nine patents.

Science and Academia: Nobel Prize Winners

Peter Agre is a professor of biological chemistry and medicine at Johns Hopkins. He won the 2003 Nobel Prize for chemistry. He lives with his wife and four children in Baltimore. Agre did his undergraduate studies at Augsburg College and received an M.D. from Johns Hopkins in 1974.

Aaron Ciechanover was awarded the Nobel Prize for Chemistry in 2004 for his research on the breakdown of proteins. Ciechanover was born in Haifa, Israel, and earned his doctoral degree in medicine in 1982 at the Technion (Israel Institute of Technology). He is currently a professor at the Rappaport Family Institute for Research in Medical Sciences at the Technion, in Haifa, Israel.

James Heckman won the Nobel Prize in economics in 2000 for his work on the theory and analysis of statistical samples. Heckman spent his high school years in Colorado, where he studied physics under Frank Oppenheimer, brother of famed physicist J. Robert Oppenheimer (the "father" of the atomic bomb). While Heckman later left physics for economics, Heckman's enthusiasm for "scientific empirical work guided by theory" was born in Oppenheimer's classroom. Heckman received his Ph.D. in economics from Princeton and went on to teach at the University of Chicago, where he remains a professor today. Heckman's research has focused on such topics as the economic status of African Americans, the role of regulation in affecting productivity and employment, and the causes and consequences of income inequalities. He is the author of several books and is married with a son and a daughter.

Alan Heeger won the Nobel Prize for chemistry in 2000. He spent his undergraduate years in Nebraska, then moved onto the University of California-Berkeley for his doctorate in physics. While a graduate student, he worked part-time for the Lockheed Space and Missile Division, then took his first full-time job as a faculty member at the University of Pennsylvania, where he remained for the next twenty years. Since the mid-1980s, Heeger has worked at the University of California-Santa Barbara. He has a wife, two sons who are both academics, and four grandchildren.

Daniel Kahneman received the Nobel Prize in economics in 2002. Kahneman's groundbreaking work integrated psychology with economics and challenged the assumption that economic behavior is motivated solely by rational self-interest. A dual citizen of the United States and Israel, Kahneman has been a Professor of Psychology and Public Affairs at Princeton University since 1993. He is married to Anne Treisman, a fellow Professor of Psychology at Princeton.

Harold Kroto received the Nobel Prize for chemistry in 1996. He received both his bachelor's degree and Ph.D. from the University of Sheffield in the United Kingdom, where he grew up, and has spent time at a variety of institutions both in Europe and America since then, though his longest tenure has been with the University of Sussex.

Anthony Leggett was the co-recipient of the Nobel Prize for physics in 2003. A world leader in the field of low-temperature physics, Leggett has been a faculty member at the University of Illinois since 1983. Leggett did both his undergraduate and graduate work at Oxford University and was a professor of physics at the University of Sussex prior to joining the faculty at Illinois.

Paul Nurse won the Nobel Prize for physiology or medicine in 2001. He was born and raised in the United Kingdom. After receiving his undergraduate degree in biology from the University of Birmingham, he had graduate studies, a postdoctoral fellowship, and a series of academic positions at different universities. He has a wife and two daughters.

Douglas Osheroff won the Nobel Prize for physics in 1996. After growing up in a rural area of Washington State, he attended the California Institute of Technology for his undergraduate degree and then Cornell for graduate studies. After finishing his doctorate, he started his career at Bell Labs, working there for fifteen years. In 1987, he moved to Stanford, where he has worked since. He was chair of the school's physics department from 1993 to 1996, and served recently on the appointed panel to investigate the *Columbia* shuttle disaster.

Bill Phillips was the recipient of the Nobel Prize for physics in 1997. He grew up in Pennsylvania and attended Juniata College, a small liberal arts school in the state. He moved to MIT for graduate and postdoctoral studies, alternating between research there and at the National Bureau of Standards for the next few years. Phillips has a wife and two children.

Richard Roberts shared the Nobel Prize in physiology or medicine in 1993 with Phillip Sharp (below). He was born and raised in the United Kingdom, where he attended Sheffield University. After receiving his bachelor's degree, he came to the United States in 1969 for postdoctoral studies at Harvard University. After a number of years of productive research, Roberts joined New England Biolabs, a small private company, in 1992. Roberts has a wife and four children.

Phillip Sharp shared the Nobel Prize in physiology or medicine in 1993 with Richard Roberts (above). After growing up in Kentucky, he attended Union College, then did his graduate studies at the University of Illinois. His postdoctoral studies led him to the California Institute of Technology, where he arrived in 1969. After a productive five years there, Sharp moved onto MIT in 1974, where he remains today. Sharp holds a wide array of awards, honorary degrees, and membership in scientific associations. He is a cofounder and Chairman of the Scientific Board of Biogen, where he is a director, and is a member of the editorial board of Cell. He has a wife and three daughters.

William Sharpe received the Nobel Prize for economics in 1990. He attended the University of California-Berkeley and then graduated with a BA and MA in economics from UCLA. After brief service in the Army, Sharpe joined the RAND Corporation in 1956, while also working toward a Ph.D. at UCLA. He received his Ph.D. in 1961, then moved to Seattle for a faculty position at the University of Washington. In 1968, Sharpe moved to the University of California-Irvine, and then in 1970 to Stanford University, where he has remained ever since. Sharpe has maintained active private interests beyond his academic work, founding a consulting firm and consulting to numerous organizations. He has a wife and two children.

A. Michael Spence was the co-recipient of the Nobel Prize in economics in 2001. For part of his childhood, he lived on a farm outside of Toronto and attended school in a two-room schoolhouse. Spence did his undergraduate work at

Princeton and was a recipient of a Canadian Rhodes Scholarship. Following studies in mathematics at Oxford, Spence earned a Ph.D. in economics at Harvard. Later he returned to Harvard as a professor, where his pupils included Steve Ballmer and Bill Gates. From 1984 to 1990 Spence served as Harvard's Dean of the Faculty of Arts and Sciences, and he later served as Dean of the Stanford Business School.

John Sulston received the Nobel Prize in physiology or medicine in 2002. He attended Cambridge University and then later continued his studies in biology and genetics in the United States and Britain. With a team from Washington University, Sulston worked to sequence the genome of a particular species of worm. Sulston was honored with British knighthood for his services to genome research in 2001. He has a wife and two children.

Government: Cabinet Members, Congressional Representatives, Governors, Mayors, and Senators

Chris Bell was a Congressional Representative from Texas. He was born in Dallas and graduated from the University of Texas with a degree in journalism in 1982. He started his career as an award-winning television and radio reporter and then received his JD from South Texas College of Law in 1992. A decade later, he was elected to represent a Houston district in Congress. Bell is married with two children, and he has held leadership roles with a variety of civic and charitable organizations.

Bill Bradley graduated with honors from Princeton University in 1965, a three-time basketball all-American and the winner of the Sullivan Award as the country's outstanding amateur athlete. He captained the gold-medal-winning U.S. basketball team at the 1964 Olympics in Tokyo and then attended Oxford University as a Rhodes Scholar, earning a graduate degree. He then played professional basketball for the New York Knicks for ten years, helping contribute to two world titles, and then represented New Jersey in the United States Senate for three terms, from 1978 to 1996. He ran for the Democratic nomination for President in 2000. Bradley is a native of Crystal City, Missouri.

Jennifer Dunn was a six-term representative to Congress from Washington State. Born in Seattle, she graduated with a BA in English literature from Stanford University, then worked for five years at IBM. She moved into Washington politics thereafter, becoming the chair of the state Republican Party from 1981 to 1992, while also serving as a delegate to various UN conferences on behalf of the Reagan and G.H.W. Bush Administrations. She has two sons.

Dan Evans was a three-term governor of Washington State and a Senator on behalf of the state to the U.S. Senate. He was born and raised in Seattle, attended the

University of Washington, and started his career in the U.S. Navy in World War II. He also worked as a civil engineer and contractor before being elected to the Washington State Legislature in 1956 and beginning his rise in politics.

Dan Glickman was a nine-term representative to the U.S. House of Representatives from Kansas, and then Secretary of Agriculture in the Clinton Administration. He grew up in Wichita, received a BA from the University of Michigan and a JD from George Washington University, and worked briefly as a Congressional aide before moving back to his home state in 1970. Glickman worked in his family business and as a school board member until he was elected to Congress in 1976. He is now Director of the Institute of Politics at Harvard University.

Slade Gorton was Senator from Washington State from 1981 to 1987 and then again from 1989 to 2001. After being born and raised in Illinois, he graduated from Dartmouth College and received his JD from Columbia University. He served in the Army and later in the Air Force Reserve while working as a private-practice lawyer and state legislator in Washington. As his political involvement grew, Gorton became Washington State Attorney General and was appointed to various state and national government commissions. Most recently, Gorton served on the 9-11 Commission investigating the terrorist attacks of 2001.

Chuck Hagel has been Senator from Nebraska since 1996. He was born and raised in the state, then volunteered to fight in the Army infantry in 1967 to 1968, serving in Vietnam in 1968. He returned home to graduate from the University of Nebraska in 1971. He moved to Washington, D.C., and held a variety of jobs in government and private life, then went back to Nebraska, working as an entrepreneur prior to his election to the Senate.

Jeremy Harris is Mayor of Honolulu. After being born in Delaware, he earned two undergraduate degrees at the University of Hawaii, and a master's degree at the University of California-Irvine. He began his career as an instructor at Kauai Community College in Hawaii, then ventured into politics as a delegate to the 1978 Hawaii Constitutional Convention. After several years in local politics, Harris became the mayor in 1994, and lives with his wife in the Kalihi Valley section of the city.

Mickey Kantor was Secretary of Commerce in the Clinton administration He was a national chair of the Clinton/Gore campaign in 1992 and a top fund-raiser. Prior to that, the Tennessee-born Kantor received a bachelor's degree from Vanderbilt University, and after four years in the Navy, a JD from Georgetown University. Kantor began his career as a civil rights lawyer, eventually working in private practice for nearly two decades. Kantor is a former director of Pharmacia and Monsanto and remains active with a number of private and public organizations. He is married and has three children and three grandchildren.

Greg Laughlin was a Congressional representative from Texas who served from 1989 to 1997 in Washington. He was born and grew up in Texas, graduating from Texas A&M University in 1964 and then the University of Texas law school in 1967. He then served in the Army for several years until returning to his legal career, beginning with a stint as Assistant District Attorney of Harris County from 1970 to 1974.

Linda Lingle is Governor of Hawaii and the first woman to lead the state. She was born in Missouri, graduated from California State University-Northridge in 1975, then moved to Hawaii that year, after which she founded a small publishing house. She entered politics as a member of the Maui County Council in 1980, serving for a decade before being elected Mayor of Maui County in 1990. She lost her first bid for Governor in 1998 by 1 percent of the vote, but won in her second attempt, in 2002.

Gary Locke served two terms as Governor of Washington State from 1996 to 2004, making him the first Chinese American governor in U.S. history. Born into an immigrant family, Locke was raised in Seattle and went on to earn a bachelor's degree from Yale University and a law degree from Boston University. Prior to becoming governor, Locke worked as a deputy prosecutor, was elected to the Washington State House of Representatives, and served as chief executive of King County. Locke's wife is a former reporter for the NBC television affiliate in Seattle. Together they have two children.

Tom Petri is a Congressional Representative from Wisconsin who started his career after law school as a clerk to a judge in Wisconsin, then volunteered in the Peace Corps and worked as a private-practice lawyer. He served as a member of the Wisconsin state senate from 1973 to 1979, then entered the U.S. Congress in 1979, where he has served ever since. Petri received both his AB and JD degrees from Harvard University.

Ann Richards served as Governor of Texas from 1990 to 1994. That job capped an electoral career that began in 1976, when she was elected to the Travis County Commissioners Court, and that included a stint as Texas's State Treasurer and gave the keynote address at the 1988 Democratic National Convention. Richards also worked previously on behalf of other political candidates and as a teacher. She received her undergraduate degree from Baylor University and her teaching certificate at the University of Texas in Austin. Richards today serves of the board of directors of JC Penney, TIG Holdings, and the Aspen Institute.

Mike Rounds was sworn in as Governor of South Dakota in 2003. Rounds is a lifelong resident of Pierre, South Dakota, and attended college at South Dakota State University. Prior to his current post, Rounds was elected to serve for five terms in the South Dakota State Senate, and served as State Senate Majority Leader for six years. He is married with four children and is also a licensed pilot.

Bill Ruckelshaus served in two different Cabinet-level posts, heading the Environmental Protection Agency and the Federal Bureau of Investigation, and also serving as Deputy Attorney General of the U.S. Justice Department. He also held senior posts at Weyerhaeuser Company and Browning-Ferris Industries in the 1980s and 1990s. Ruckelshaus remains a director of several corporations, including Cummins Engine Company, Nordstrom, and Weyerhaeuser. He grew up in Indiana and holds a bachelor's degree from Princeton University and a JD from Harvard University.

Donna Shalala was Secretary for Health and Human Services in the Clinton Administration, as well as an Assistant Secretary of HUD in the Carter Administration. Her career has included a wide variety of posts in academia and government. After working as a Peace Corps volunteer after college, she spent periods working for the Municipal Assistance Corporation for the City of New York, and heading Hunter College of CUNY, the University of Wisconsin-Madison, and the University of Miami, of which she's currently President. Shalala is a director of Gannett Company, UnitedHealth Group, and the Lennar Corporation. She holds an AB from Western College for Women and her Ph.D. from Syracuse University.

James Watkins was Secretary of Energy in the first Bush Administration. That appointment followed a thirty-seven-year career in the Navy, in which he rotated through a large number of roles. Watkins worked with Admiral Hyman Rickover in the buildup of the country's nuclear submarine program, also commanded the Sixth Fleet, and became Vice Chief of Naval Operations. Watkins grew up in California and graduated from the Naval Academy in 1949.

Rick White was a Congressional Representative from Washington State and now heads TechNet, a top political group based in California, representing the interests of the high-technology industry both regionally and in the nation's capitol. White started his career with a string of private-sector jobs, including dock foreman, assembly line worker, and grill cook, and then worked as a private-practice lawyer prior to entering politics. White grew up in Indiana, received his BA from Dartmouth College, attended the University of Paris, Pantheon Sorbonne, and received his JD from Georgetown University. He now resides with his wife and children in California.

Arts and Entertainment: Winners of Emmy, Grammy, Oscar, Pulitzer, or Tony Awards, and Authors of *New York Times* Bestsellers

Russell Carollo won the Pulitzer Prize for national reporting in 1998. He has a journalism degree from Louisiana State University and a history degree from

Southeastern Louisiana University. He has worked for newspapers around the country, most recently for six years at the *Dayton Daily News*.

Tom Clancy is the mega-bestselling author of a string of fiction books, typically geopolitical thrillers centered on highly detailed portrayals of characters with military and spy backgrounds. Clancy earned a degree from Loyola College in Maryland and started his career as an insurance broker. He kept alive his dreams of writing a novel while shifting over to become an insurance agent, and his writing became immensely popular starting in the early 1980s.

Gordon Clapp is an Emmy Award–winning actor who appears on *NYPD Blue*. He has also worked in the past on films such as *Moonlight Mile, Rules of Engagement,* and *Eight Men Out,* and a wide variety of television shows. Clapp spent a portion of his early acting career in the early 1980s with a little-known theater company called Neptune Theatre, which is still operating today in Halifax, Nova Scotia.

Bill Dietrich received the Pulitzer Prize for national reporting in 1990, for his coverage of the Exxon *Valdez* oil spill. Today he continues to work as a staff writer for the *Seattle Times' Pacific Northwest Magazine*. He holds a degree in journalism from Western Washington University, is married, and has two daughters.

R. Bruce Dold received the Pulitzer Prize for editorial writing in 1994 for his writing on the Illinois child welfare system. Today Dold works as the editorial page editor for the *Chicago Tribune,* a post he has held since 2000. Dold holds undergraduate and graduate degrees in journalism from Northwestern University. He is married and has two daughters.

Julian Fellowes is the Oscar Award–winning actor, writer, and producer who penned the screenplay for *Gosford Park*. His wide-ranging career has included writing for *Vanity Fair,* acting in *Tomorrow Never Dies, Jane Eyre,* and *Shadowlands,* and work on a large number of different television shows. The British-born Fellowes has one child and a wife, to whom he proposed marriage twenty minutes after meeting.

David Frankel is an Oscar and Emmy Award–winning director, producer, and writer who's worked on films such as *Fidel, Dear Diary,* and *Miami Rhapsody*. He has also directed episodes of television shows such as HBO's *Band of Brothers* and *Sex and the City*. His original break in Hollywood came as a writer for *The Ellen Burstyn Show,* after he had worked at an entertainment company called TelePictures for approximately five years. Frankel is a graduate of Harvard University.

Eric Freedman received the Pulitzer Prize for beat reporting in 1994 and is currently a Professor of Journalism at Michigan State University. Freedman previously worked as a reporter for nineteen years, focusing on public affairs, state government, and legal affairs. Freedman spent a semester as a Fulbright Senior Scholar in Uzbekistan and is also the author or coauthor of six nonfiction books.

Tom Hallman received the Pulitzer Prize for feature writing in 2001. He received a journalism degree from Drake University in Iowa and started his career as a copy editor for Hearst Magazines. He moved through a variety of other jobs in journalism before settling at the *Oregonian* in Portland, where he's worked for the last nineteen years.

Maria Henson received the Pulitzer Prize for editorial writing in 1992, for her work about battered women in Kentucky. Her writing focused statewide attention on the problem and led to a number of reforms. Henson built a career in journalism working for the *Lexington (Ky.) Herald-Leader,* the *Austin American-Statesman,* and most recently as the deputy editorial page editor for the *Sacramento Bee.*

Blair Kamin received the Pulitzer Prize for criticism in 1999, for his work as an observer and writer on American architecture. He received his bachelor's degree from Amherst College and a master's degree from the Yale University School of Architecture. After finishing graduate school, he joined the *Des Moines Register,* and after three years there, he moved to the *Chicago Tribune,* where he's worked since 1987. He has won a number of awards in both the journalism and architecture industries. He lives with his wife and son in Chicago.

John Lithgow has won enormous critical acclaim over a long career in theater, movies, and television. Lithgow's work includes a starring role from 1996 to 2001 in the comedy series *3rd Rock from the Sun,* for which he earned two Emmy Awards, a Golden Globe Award, and a Screen Actors Guild Award. Prior to his career in television, he earned Academy Award nominations for his roles in *The World According to Garp* and *Terms of Endearment,* and won a Tony for his performance on Broadway. His additional film credits include *Kinsey* (2004), *Shrek* (2001), *The Pelican Brief* (1993), and *Footloose* (1984). Lithgow is a graduate of Harvard University and was a Fulbright scholar.

Mike Luckovich received the Pulitzer Prize for editorial cartooning in 1995. He cartoons for the *Atlanta-Journal Constitution,* where he's worked since 1989, and is syndicated through a large number of publications, including *Newsweek* and the *New York Times.* He graduated from the University of Washington in 1982, and after starting his career as a life-insurance salesman, entered the field of cartooning with positions in North Carolina and Louisiana prior to settling down in Atlanta. He has a wife and four children.

Bill McKibben is a *New York Times* bestselling author whose books include *Enough: Staying Human in an Engineered Age; The End of Nature, Long Distance: A*

Year of Living Strenuously; Hundred Dollar Holiday; and *Maybe One.* His works have examined a host of man-made ills, including global warming, overpopulation, materialism, and the potential havoc of genetic engineering. McKibben began his career as a writer at the *New Yorker* magazine. He lives with his wife, the writer Sue Halpern, and their daughter in the Adirondack Mountains.

Alan Miller won the Pulitzer Prize for national reporting in 2003, with Kevin Sack. He works at the *Los Angeles Times,* where he's made his professional home since 1989. He started his career in Albany, New York, after receiving a bachelor's degree from Wesleyan University in 1976 and a master's degree from the University of Hawaii in 1978.

Paula Newby-Fraser is the most successful Ironman triathlete in history. From 1986–2002, Newby-Fraser raced up twenty-three Ironman titles, eight world champion titles, and set the Ironman world record that still stands (8:50:24). Today Newby-Fraser continues to compete and is a partner of Multisports.com, an endurance sports coaching company. She is the author of *Peak Fitness for Women* and co-wrote *Cross-Training: The Complete Training Guide for All Sports.*

Paul Salopek received two Pulitzer Prizes, first in 1998 for explanatory journalism, and then in 2001 for international reporting. He was born in California and raised in Mexico, and had a series of colorful adventures before graduating from the University of California-Santa Barbara in 1984. He started as a journalist in 1985 when his motorcycle broke down in New Mexico and he took a police-reporting job at the local newspaper to earn money for his repairs.

April Saul won the Pulitzer Prize in 1997 for explanatory journalism, with Michael Vitez (see p. 214). She received her bachelor's degree from Tufts University and her master's degree in journalism from the University of Minnesota, after which she entered the field as a photographer. Saul started her career at the *Baltimore Sun,* then moved to the *Philadelphia Inquirer* in 1981, where she's been since. She has won a wide variety of awards in her field, and now lives in New Jersey with her two children.

Lloyd Schwartz won the Pulitzer Prize in 1994 for his classical music criticism. Schwartz holds an undergraduate degree from Queens College and a Ph.D. from Harvard. He is the author of multiple books of poetry and has taught at Boston State College, Queens College, and Harvard. He is currently an English professor at the University of Massachusetts, the Classical Music Editor of *The Boston Phoenix,* and a regular commentator on NPR's *Fresh Air.*

David Shaw won the Pulitzer Prize in 1991 for his criticism of media coverage of the Virginia McMartin preschool child molestation case. Shaw has been a media critic for the *Los Angeles Times* since 1974 and is the author of five books. He is also a contributor to several national publications, including *GQ, Esquire, Food & Wine,* and *Condé Nast Traveler.* Shaw holds a degree in English from UCLA and is married with a son.

David Shribman won the Pulitzer Prize in 1995 for beat reporting, when he was at the *Boston Globe.* Shribman is now at the *Pittsburgh Post-Gazette,* but has had a highly successful journalism career across a number of newspapers, including the *Boston Globe,* the *Wall Street Journal,* the *New York Times,* and *Fortune* magazine. Shribman is a summa cum laude graduate of Dartmouth College.

Tia Sillers won the 2000 Grammy Award for Best Country Song of the Year, for cowriting the mega-hit "I Hope You Dance," recorded by Lee Ann Womack. The song was also named the 2000 Country Music Association's (CMA) Song of the Year. Sillers's additional song credits include Pam Tillis's number one "Land of the Living" and the Dixie Chicks' "There's Your Trouble." Sillers is a native of Nashville, Tennessee, and earned her undergraduate and master's degrees from the University of North Carolina-Chapel Hill.

William Snyder is a three-time Pulitzer Prize winner, having won the 1989 award for Explanatory Journalism, the 1991 award for Feature Photography, and the 1993 award for Spot News Photography. Snyder has worked as a photographer for the *Dallas Morning News* since 1983, and prior to that he worked for the *Miami News.* Over the years, his subjects have included the first free elections in Haiti, the explosion of the *Challenger* space shuttle, orphans in Romania, and the Barcelona and Atlanta Olympic Games.

Michael Vitez won the Pulitzer Prize in 1997 for explanatory journalism, with April Saul (see p. 213). He was born and grew up in the D.C./northern Virginia area. After graduating from the University of Virginia in 1979, he worked at a variety of newspapers in the area and in the Northeast more generally before settling at the *Philadelphia Inquirer* in 1985.

Nonprofit Organizational Leaders

Carol Bellamy has been the Executive Director of the United Nations Children Fund (UNICEF) since 1995. Her last position prior to that was Director of the Peace Corps, where she became the first volunteer to return as the agency's head. In between her two stints with the Peace Corps, Bellamy enjoyed a varied career in government and the private sector. She began at a private law firm, then worked in various New York government agencies, followed by more than a decade as a lawyer and banker at Wall Street firms like Morgan Stanley and Bear Stearns. She holds a BA from Gettysburg College and a JD from New York University.

Morris Dees is Founder and Chief Trial Counsel of the Southern Poverty Law Center, one of the nation's leading advocacies for civil-rights law. After growing up the son of an Alabama farmer, Dees transferred early entrepreneurial energies into a publishing company, which he eventually sold to the Times Mirror Company. He founded SPLC in the late 1960s and has been there ever since. He has also been active in Democratic politics, acting as finance director for George McGovern in 1972, national finance director for Jimmy Carter in 1976, and national finance chairman for Ted Kennedy in 1980. Dees is the author of three books and holds bachelor's and law degrees from the University of Alabama.

Marsha Evans is President and CEO of the American Red Cross, a position she has held since 2002. Prior to joining the Red Cross, Evans held the top staff position at the Girl Scouts of the USA and had a distinguished twenty-nine-year career in the U.S. Navy. Evans retired from the Navy in 1998 as a rear admiral, one of very few women to reach this rank. Evans holds a BA in Law and Diplomacy from Occidental College and a master's degree from Tufts University's Fletcher School of Law and Diplomacy. She lives with her husband, a retired Navy jet pilot.

Larry Fahn is President of the Sierra Club, America's oldest and largest grassroots environmental organization. Fahn is also the Executive Director of As You Sow, a nonprofit organization dedicated to promoting corporate social responsibility, and has represented a wide array of individuals, small businesses, and nonprofit organizations through a solo law practice. Throughout his career, Fahn has tackled issues such as water policy, nuclear power, off-shore oil drilling, and enforcement of environmental toxics regulations. He holds a degree in environmental studies from UC Davis and a law degree from the UC Hastings Law School.

Millard Fuller is the Founder and President of Habitat for Humanity International. Since creating the organization in 1976 with his wife, Linda, he has led the group in creating homes for more than 180,000 families in 3,000 different communities around the globe. For this work, he received the Presidential Medal of Freedom in 1996. Fuller graduated from Auburn University and got his law degree at the University of Alabama in Tuscaloosa, and also successfully started and sold an entrepreneurial business before turning his life to Habitat and other religiously-focused work from the age of twenty-nine onward.

John Hennessy is the President of Stanford University. Hennessy joined the Stanford faculty in 1977 and previously served as Stanford's Chair of the computer science department, Dean of the School of Engineering, and University Provost. Hennessy is also the cofounder of MIPS Technologies, a multimillion-dollar company that designs microprocessors, and the coauthor of two textbooks on computer architecture design. He earned his bachelor's degree in electrical engineering from Villanova University and his master's and Ph.D. in computer science from the State University of New York at Stony Brook.

Wendy Kopp is the President and Founder of Teach for America. She created the organization in 1989, shortly after graduating from Princeton University. She has built the organization to more than 3,000 teachers and 7,500 alumni and is one of the country's top social entrepreneurs, recognized with a host of honorary doctorates from universities, awards from different organizations, and the Woodrow Wilson Award, the highest honor Princeton confers on its undergraduate alumni.

Chip Pitts is Chair of the USA Board of Amnesty International, an organization dedicated to the promotion of worldwide human rights. He is also a lecturer at the Stanford University Law School and a frequent writer, speaker, and commentator on the topics of globalization, human rights, and foreign affairs. Pitts worked in the 1980s to help end South African apartheid, has been a representative at the UN Commission on Human Rights, and has provided pro bono legal representation to hundreds of victims of human rights abuses. Pitts received his undergraduate degree at Tulane University, and his law degree at Stanford University.

Nadine Strossen has served as the President of the American Civil Liberties Union since 1991 and is also a professor of law at the New York Law School. She is a prolific legal scholar and writer, having authored numerous papers and a book, *Defending Pornography: Free Speech, Sex, and the Fight for Women's Rights,* which was named a "Notable Book of 1995" by the *New York Times.* Strossen sits on the boards of the ACLU, Feminists for Free Expression, and Human Rights Watch, and has received honorary degrees from a number of universities. She graduated Phi Beta Kappa from Harvard University and magna cum laude from Harvard Law School.

Shirley Tilghman has served as President of Princeton University since 2001, having joined the school's faculty as a professor of molecular biology in 1986. She is a renowned scholar and lecturer, with postdoctoral work on the cloning of the first mammalian gene. She helped start Princeton's multidisciplinary center for integrative genomics, helped the National Research Council on work related to the Human Genome Project, and is associated with a wide variety of academic and scientific organizations. Born in Canada, Tilghman earned her BS in chemistry from Queens University in Kingston, Ontario, and after two years of secondary school teaching in Africa, obtained a Ph.D. in biochemistry from Temple University.

Appendix B
Basic Question Guide for Interviews with Leaders

Below is the basic question guide used for the interviews with the 100 leaders. It offers a skeleton of the themes covered in the research, but does not fully reflect the discussions with different leaders. In many cases, I asked leaders additional follow-up questions specific to their field, organization, or personal experiences, and many conversations developed a life of their own, running off on tangents relevant to what the leader said. The most interesting of these extra thoughts are reflected in the text of the book, rather than this question guide.

- What was the first job you held after college? (If not applicable, perhaps because you didn't attend college, or because you went from college into graduate school, please feel free to describe a similar, relevant experience from that time in your life. Similarly, if you feel that the first few jobs, rather than the exact first job, per se, made a difference to your experience, please describe those instead.)

- What were your goals in taking the job? Did you have a specific financial or career milestone in mind?

- Did you strongly consider any alternatives to that job? Were alternative options primarily in the same field or widely different ones?

- Was there anything in particular about the position you took that made it more attractive than alternatives?

- How did your career progress shortly after you took this first job? Do any resounding successes or failures stand out in your mind?

- How long did you hold the job? How long did you work at the company where you started?

- Can you remember any "forks in the road," proverbial crossroads at which you had to make a difficult decision about your first job or career? (This could have been an ethical dilemma, a choice between two competing visions of your future, a significant distraction that almost derailed your career, or whatever. Again, this question is asked in an open-ended fashion, and any answer can be a correct one, as long as it's honest.)

- Did you have any early mentors, individuals who played an important role? Were these people you met on the first job, or earlier in life, or later?

- What kinds of outside activities and hobbies, if any, did you pursue when you were working in your first job? Did you cultivate a meaningful life outside of work?

- In terms of your leisure pursuits and relationships with family and friends, how did you achieve work-life balance? Did you consider yourself balanced?

- Can you cite any particular axioms/saws/epigrams that you followed in pursuing your first job and subsequent ones? This may have been something told to you by a friend or relative, or it may be something you read, or perhaps even something you created yourself.

- Looking back, do you feel you displayed any characteristics in your behavior or thoughts, in that first job, that pointed to your future success? (Please don't be afraid to be immodest; the question is motivated by a genuine curiosity, and speaking bluntly is appreciated. That said, if you feel extraordinary signs really weren't evident at this stage in your career, that would be interesting, too!)

- Do you consider the first job (lessons learned, contacts made, etc.) particularly important to your long-term development?

- In closing, do you have any final thoughts on what you gained from your first job, or lessons that others might learn from your experience in that position?

Appendix C
Further Reading

Below is a list of sources relevant to this book. In some cases, the ideas or information helped stimulate my own thinking, and in others, they touched on interestingly similar themes I thought worth noting. In any case, they provide further opportunities for those readers who wish to learn more about the personal work of leaders featured in this book. For further resources, visit www.NobodiesToSomebodies.com.

Books by or About the 100 Leaders

Barry, Douglas. *Wisdom for a Young CEO: Incredible Letters and Inspiring Advice from Today's Business Leaders.*

Bellamy, Carol. *The Story of the World's Children.* (annual series)

Breit, William, and Roger W. Spencer, editors. *Lives of the Laureates: Thirteen Nobel Economists.*

Bradley, Bill. *Life on the Run.*

———. *Time Past, Time Present.*

Catell, Bob, Kenny Moore, and Glenn Rifkin. *The CEO and the Monk: One Company's Journey to Profit and Purpose.*

Ciechanover, Aaron, and Alan Schwartz. *Cellular Proteolytic Systems.*

Ciechanover, Aaron, and Maria Masucci. *The Ubiquitin-Proteasome Proteolytic System: From Classical Biochemistry to Human Diseases.*

Clancy, Tom. *Battle Ready.*

———. *Call to Treason.*

———. *Carrier: A Guided Tour of an Aircraft Carrier.*

———. *Clear and Present Danger.*

————. *Debt of Honor.*

————. *Executive Orders.*

————. *Marine: A Guided Tour of a Marine Expeditionary Unit.*

————. *Patriot Games.*

————. *Rainbow Six.*

————. *Red Rabbit.*

————. *Red Storm Rising.*

————. *Shadow Warriors: Inside the Special Forces.*

————. *Special Forces: A Guide of the U.S. Army Special Forces.*

————. *The Bear and the Dragon.*

————. *The Cardinal of the Kremlin.*

————. *The Hunt for Red October.*

————. *The Sum of All Fears.*

————. *The Teeth of the Tiger.*

————. *Without Remorse.*

Dees, Morris. *A Season for Justice.*

————. *Gathering Storm: America's Militia Threat.*

————. *Hate on Trial: The Case Against America's Most Dangerous Neo-Nazi.*

Fellowes, Julian. *Snobs.*

Fireman, Paul, Samuel Kofi Woods, and Angel Martinez. *From the Pain Comes the Dream: The Recipients of the Reebok Human Rights Award.*

Frank, Thomas. *What's the Matter with Kansas? How Conservatives Won the Heart of America.*

Fuller, Millard. *A Simple, Decent Place to Live: The Building Realization of Habitat for Humanity.*

————. *Bokotola.*

————. *Building Materials for Life.*

————. *Love in the Mortar Joints: The Story of Habitat for Humanity.*

————. *More Than Houses.*

————. *The Theology of the Hammer.*

Fuller, Millard, and Diane Scott. *No More Shacks!: The Daring Vision of Habitat for Humanity.*

Fuller, Millard, and Linda Fuller. *The Excitement Is Building: How Habitat for Humanity Is Putting Roofs over Heads and Hope in Hearts.*

Gates, Henry Louis, Anthony P. Griffin, Donald E. Lively, Robert C. Post, William B. Rubenstein, Nadine Strossen, Ira Glasser. *Speaking of Sex: Hate Speech, Civil Rights, and Civil Liberties.*

Hallman, Tom. *Sam: The Boy Behind the Mask.*

Hargittai, Istvan. *The Road to Stockholm: Nobel Prizes, Science, and Scientists.*

Kahneman, Daniel, et al., editors. *Judgment Under Uncertainty: Heuristics and Biases.*

Kahneman, Daniel, and Amos Tversky, editors. *Choices, Values, and Frames.*

Kamin, Blair. *Why Architecture Matters: Lessons from Chicago.*

Kopp, Wendy. *One Day, All Children: The Unlikely Triumph of Teach for America and What I Learned Along the Way.*

Leggett, Anthony. *The Problems of Physics.*

Lithgow, John. *A Lithgow Palooza!: 101 Ways to Entertain and Inspire Your Kids.*

Luckovich, Mike. *Lotsa Luckovich.*

McKibben, Bill. *Enough: Staying Human in an Engineered Age.*

———. *Hope, Human and Wild: True Stories of Living Lightly on the Earth.*

———. *Hundred Dollar Holiday: The Case for a More Joyful Christmas.*

———. *Long Distance: Testing the Limits of Body and Spirit in a Year of Living Strenuously.*

———. *Maybe One: A Case for Smaller Families.*

———. *The End of Nature.*

McPhee, John. *A Sense of Where You Are: Bill Bradley at Princeton.*

Migdal, A.B., and Anthony Leggett. *Qualitative Methods in Quantum Theory.*

Newby-Fraser, Paula. *Paula Newby-Fraser's Peak Fitness for Women: High-Level Training for Women.*

Richards, Ann. *I'm Not Slowing Down: Winning My Battle with Osteoporosis.*

———. *Straight from the Heart: My Life in Politics and Other Places.*

Saloner, Garth, and A. Michael Spence. *Creating and Capturing Value Perspectives and Cases on Electronic Commerce.*

Sanders, Marc D., and Tia Sillers. *Climb: A Book of Hope, Strength, and Joy.*

Schwartz, Lloyd. *Elizabeth Bishop and Her Art.*

Sharpe, William, Gordon Alexander, and Jeffrey Bailey. *Investments.*

Shribman, David. *I Remember My Teacher.*

Stemberg, Thomas. *Staples for Success: From Business Plan to Billion-Dollar Business in Just a Decade.*

Strossen, Nadine. *Defending Pornography: Free Speech, Sex, and the Fight for Women's Rights.*

Sulston, John, and Georgina Ferry. *The Common Thread: A Story of Science, Politics, Ethics and the Human Genome.*

Tichy, Noel M. *The Cycle of Leadership: How Great Leaders Teach Their Companies to Win.*

Vitez, Michael, April Saul, and Ron Cortes. *Final Choices: Seeking the Good Death.*

Zandman, Felix. *Never the Last Journey.*

Helpful Career Management and Leadership Literature

Bronson, Po. *What Should I Do with My Life?*

Bennis, Warren. *Leaders: The Strategies for Taking Charge.*

Burns, James MacGregor. *Leadership.*

Farkas, Charles, and Phillippe DeBacker. *Maximum Leadership: The World's Leading CEOs Share Their Five Strategies for Success.*

Gardner, Howard. *Extraordinary Minds: Portraits of Four Exceptional Individuals and an Examination of Our Own Extraordinariness.*

Gardner, Howard. *Leading Minds: An Anatomy of Leadership.*

Gardner, John W. *On Leadership.*

Kotter, John P. *The New Rules: Eight Business Breakthroughs to Career Success in the 21st Century.*

Neff, Thomas, and James Citrin. *Lessons from the Top: The 50 Most Successful Business Leaders in America—and What You Can Learn from Them.*

Plimpton, George. *The X Factor.*

Rensin, David. *The Mailroom: Hollywood History from the Bottom Up.*

Rimm, Sylvia, and Sara Rimm-Kaufmann. *See Jane Win: The Rimm Report on How 1,000 Girls Became Successful Women.*

Shriver, Maria. *Ten Things I Wish I'd Known—Before I Went Out into the Real World.*

Websites

www.IMDBPro.com: Leading industry database for films and television.

www.Nobel.se: The official site cataloging resources on Nobel Prize winners.

www.PoliticalGraveyard.com: Excellent repository of basic biographical sketches on a huge range of government officials and politicians.

www.Pulitzer.org: The official site cataloging resources on Pulitzer Prize winners.

Acknowledgments

To start, I am sincerely grateful to the following people, good friends all, who used their time and connections to try to help me secure interviews for the book: Jason Costa, Danny David, Danielle Lipow, Jack Megan, Cile Montgomery, Rob Newcomb, Grant Ries, Reed and Brooke Sillers, Scott Svenson, Siri Tjernsen, and especially, Chris Bayley, who provided excellent guidance and encouragement during our monthly breakfasts at the Portage Bay Café.

Both in soliciting interviews and then collecting the volumes of information available on the leaders' backgrounds, I was assisted by the excellent work of a research assistant, Kelly Garrett. Her long and diligent hours, along with the understanding support of my longtime buddy Jim Pawlikowski were hugely helpful! Also, Andrew Ernst helped me with the technology needed to execute the work.

I extend my sincere thanks to the friends who read early drafts of my work and who gave me encouragement: Chris Nicholson, Guy Goldberg, Bob Mulroy, Shalini Sharp. Darrin and Shaula Massena were also excellent co-conspirators on our shared travels. I need to single out my sister, Hahrie Han Gehlbach, who along with her husband, Hunter, will become a university professor shortly after this book releases. True to her academic training, Hahrie was remarkable in her eye for detail, her aggressive demands for stronger arguments, and her overall sense of loving devotion to the project. While the faults of this work rest with me, I am extremely grateful to my sister for her help, both here and before on previous projects. I'm looking forward to returning the favors.

My editors at Penguin Putnam's Portfolio imprint, Stephanie Land and Sarah Mollo-Christensen, dealt very ably with my questions and gave me firm feedback in a gentle voice. My agent, Kim Goldstein of the Susan Golomb Literary Agency, was a big help in connecting me with Portfolio and walking me through the process.

Once I got to the contract review, Greg Gottesman gave me much appreciated help.

This is my first book, and one that grew directly out of a personal curiosity and numerous conversations with like-minded friends. I'd like to tip my cap to some of those not mentioned above, who helped push my thinking on these topics: Eli Aheto, Ben and Debbie Auspitz, Greg and Erica Babineaux, Elyssa Back, Lorraine Bardeen and Mary Rowe, Paul Bascobert, Alex Berzofsky, Phil Beukema, Alexis Borisy, Nick and Tammy Brady, Dave Buck, Sunny and Greg Charlebois, Karen Cho, Rob Cromwell, Carlos Cruz, Kurt Daniel, Chris and Paula Darkins, Nancy and Paul Davis, Michael Dees and Margaret Lee, Arthur Duffy, Yannis Dosios and Priscilla Glenwright, Katie Drucker and Ian Thompson, Hemant Dutta, David Eraker, Aaron Field, Jackson Gates, Paul Gautier, Courtney Graber, Carol and Soren Hagh, Drew Hansen and Julie Cooper, Will Hartmann, Brian Hayes and Cam Hoang, Shannon Holy, Chip and Vero Hellar, Ben Heller, Josh and Renee Herst, Anamarie Huerta and Ben Franc, Shilo Jones, Robert Jungerhans, Kevin and Cameron Khajavi, Tim Killian, Young Kim, Chris Kwak, Justin Label, Mike Lacey and Alechia Crown, Thong Le, Jeff Lehman, Duncan MacDonald, Angus Maclaurin, Doris Maillet, Siddharth and Ritika Mangharam, John and Sherry Lydik, Kristi Marchbanks, Carrie and David Marks, Chris and Christina Matarese, Richard McCarty and Kelly Quy, Michael and Catherine Minnig, Kirsten Morbeck, Elizabeth Morgan, Adam Moore, Dorothy Murphey, Megan and Ernest Notarte, MacLean Pancoast, Hyun-Kyung Park and Francis Tan, Dan and Josette Ramirez, Charlie Redding, Vasu Reddy, Sarah and Justin Richmond, Catherine Ries, Trace and Jennifer Roquemore, Conrad and Jennifer Saam, Abid Saifee, Herman Sanchez, Craig and Isa Shealy, Eunice Shin, Steve and Lizzi Silver, Christian Sinderman, Carl Sjogreen, Andrew Skoler, Jim Smith, Bhu Srinivasan, Jon Staenberg, Robert and Ann Steffler, Dave and Patti Steinberg, Lior Strahilevitz, Sulian Tay and Justin Baldauf, Ramin Toloui, Jeff Tomkins and Amy Clark, Travis and Kelley Twardowski, Ty Ueland, Niranjan Vasu, Jen Westhagen, Shae Wilkins, Pat Yankow, the Grupo de Ocho crew, and of course, my erstwhile and still-loved business partner, David Rickard, and his wife, Sarah Evans.

Also, as I continue my own long climb from being a Nobody to a Somebody, I've been inspired by several role models: Jim Kalustian, Eddie Pasatiempo, Rick Roquemore, Mark Sidran, Bob Tenczar, Alan Topfer, and again, Chris Bayley.

I've noticed that it's customary for writers often to close their acknowledgments with special thanks to their families. While many conventions of the craft eluded me, this one became clear immediately, because for me family is both the proverbial beginning and end—the source of my passion and eagerness for life's adventures, and the resting place at dusk, when energies have been spent and successes and failures come together. My in-laws, Jack, Deborah, and Allison FitzGerald and Joan and Dave Jackson, as well as their extended families, have been extremely kind to me in the years since I lurched into their living rooms as the gawky prospective son- and brother-in-law, and I am nostalgic already for the canoe trips, barbecues, Scrabble games by the fireplace, plentiful meals, and "Yankee Peddlers" that we've shared as a new family.

My own parents, Kye and Won Han, have always offered an incredibly supportive, protective, and unconditional love, while at the same time encouraging me to reach for high standards. In many ways, this book and its appreciation for achievement and aspiration grows directly from what Mom and Dad showed me. Their decency and hard work served as early examples to both my sister and me, and even now, I continue to understand lessons about life that I hadn't realized they were teaching me.

Last but first, I thank my wife, Meredith, who put up with many, many long nights and hardworking weekends as I researched and wrote this book. She appreciates sacrifice, purity, and excellence and allows me gently to reach for mine. As Meredith pursues her own ambitions throughout the next sixty years, I look forward to being her biggest fan. She draws out of me a love so strong it's breathtaking.

Seattle, Washington
January 2005

Index